# FORENSIC ANTHROPOLOGY

# FORENSIC
# ANTHROPOLOGY

*From*

## THE TO-BE-FORGOTTEN

T<small>HOMAS</small> H<small>ARDY</small>

These, our sped ancestry,
Lie here embraced by deeper death than we;
Nor shape nor thought of theirs can you descry
With keenest backward eye.

They count as quite forgot;
They are as men who have existed not;
Theirs is a loss past loss of fitful breath;
It is the second death.

We here, as yet, each day
Are blest with dear recall; as yet, can say
We hold in some soul loved continuance
Of shape and voice and glance.

But what has been will be—
First memory, then oblivion's swallowing sea;
Like men foregone, shall we merge into those
Whose story no one knows.

For which of us could hope
To show in life that world-awakening scope
Granted the few whose memory none lets die,
But all men magnify?

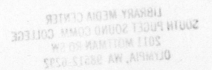

# FORENSIC
# ANTHROPOLOGY

## The Structure, Morphology, and Variation of Human Bone and Dentition

*By*

**MAHMOUD Y. EL-NAJJAR, Ph.D.**

*Department of Anthropology*
*Case Western Reserve University*
*Cleveland, Ohio*

*and*

**K. RICHARD McWILLIAMS, Ph.D., F.A.A.F.S.**

*Department of Anthropology*
*University of Nebraska*
*Lincoln, Nebraska*

CHARLES C THOMAS · PUBLISHER
*Springfield · Illinois · U.S.A.*

*Published and Distributed Throughout the World by*
## CHARLES C THOMAS • PUBLISHER
BANNERSTONE HOUSE
301-327 East Lawrence Avenue, Springfield, Illinois, U.S.A.

© *1978, by* CHARLES C THOMAS • PUBLISHER
ISBN 0-398-03648-9 (cloth) ISBN 0-398-06107-6 (paper)
Library of Congress Catalog Card Number: 76-53004

*Printed in the United States of America*
*N-1*

Library of Congress Cataloging in Publication Data

El-Najjar, Mahmoud Y
    Forensic anthropology.

    Bibliography: p.
    Includes index.
    1. Human skeleton.   2. Anthropometry.   3. Forensic osteology.   I.
McWilliams, Kenneth Richard, joint author.   II. Title. [DNLM: 1. An-
thropology, Physical.   2. Forensic medicine.   3. Forensic dentistry.   4.
Bone and bones. 5. Tooth.  GN70 E48f]
GN70.E43                        611'.71                        76-53004
ISBN 0-398-03648-9. — ISBN 0-398-06107-6 (pbk.)

## DEDICATION

### *To T. Dale Stewart*

*Whose contributions to forensic anthropology inspired the writing of this book.*

# PREFACE

SINCE PHYSICAL ANTHROPOLOGY emerged as a branch of science some 200 years ago, analysis of skeletal and dental morphology has been one of its primary avenues of investigations. It is not surprising that physical anthropologists emphasize the critical value of bone. They are completely dependent on the evidence provided by human osteological remains for any information regarding morphology, past biological relationships, adaption, and the direct traces of micro- and macro-evolutionary events.

In the past three decades there has been a rapid increase in the fundamental knowledge of human osteology. This book is written with the purpose of incorporating relevant information on human osteology into a single text. It is virtually impossible, however, to either review or cite all the published accounts dealing with the human skeleton. We have attempted to include all necessary data presenting new ideas and concepts and updating important literature. The authors realize that certain information may not be of interest to some students, but it has been included for the benefit of others engaged in various aspects of research in human osteology and forensic studies.

This text evolved from several years of teaching human osteology and recognizing the value of the human skeleton in forensic and anthropological studies. The primary objective of this text is to accommodate the needs of students in these disciplines. It is designed for students in physical anthropology, archeology, and forensic medicine to provide them with the necessary knowledge and understanding of the structure and variability of the human bone and dentition.

# INTRODUCTION

THE UTILITY OF THE HUMAN SKELETON is not restricted to physical anthropologists. Bone has always been a subject of great interest to students in many disciplines. Anatomists, surgeons, histologists, and biochemists, among other scholars, have focused on the analysis of the physical property and morphological variability for centuries. Interest in the anatomy and physiology of the human skeleton dates back to the fourth century BC when Herodotus (484-425 BC) described the natives of Asia Minor and commented on the thicker skulls of Egyptians compared to Persians. Herodotus attributed the differences to the fact that the shaven-headed style of the Egyptians exposed them to the rays of the sun. Hippocrates (460-377 BC) supported the theory of the influence of environment on human morphology and related the differences between various human groups to climate. Aristotle (384-322 BC) recognized that man's brain is larger than that of other animals in proportion to total body mass and noted that only man deliberates and meditates.

Erasistratus (320-357 BC) and Horophilus (335-280 BC) practiced human dissection at the university of Alexandria. Galen (131-200 AD), practicing exclusively on animals, wrote several monographs on muscle and fetus formation and underscored the similarity between apes and man. Following Galen, the infant scientific method fell into decadence and was replaced by the library methods of scholarship in Europe. Scientific style and inquiry continued, however, among the Arabs.

In 1240, Fredrick II of Germany decreed that all medical students must study anatomy and witness at least one dissection of a human cadaver. Partly as a result of this decree, Fredrick was excommunicated by the Pope. Against opposition, the investigation of human anatomy continued from that time to be part of medical education. In *De humani corporis fabrica*, published in Basel in 1543, Andreas Vesalius corrected the many errors of Galen's anatomical work and expanded it to create the modern subfield of anatomy. Comparative anatomy quickly arose with its importance for modern anthropology.

In the United States, physical anthropology began with Samuel G. Morton in 1830. Morton's interest was primarily in comparative human anatomy, phrenology, and in questions relating to the origin and biological affinity of the American Indians. In 1839 his truly monumental work, *Crania Americana,* was published "to give accurate delineations of the skulls representing different American Indian groups from all parts of the United States and to determine by the evidence of osteological facts whether the American Indians of all epochs have belonged to one race or to a plurality of races."

Joseph Leidy and J. Aitken Meigs continued Morton's work. Leidy published many scientific papers on various aspects of human skeletal biology. Meigs most important contributions were "The cranial characteristics of the races of men" and "The catalogue of human crania in the collection in the National Sciences in Philadelphia" (both in 1857) and "Observations on the occiput in various races" (in 1860).

Other nineteenth century osteologists in the United States include Jeffries Wyman (1814-1874), who gave us our first knowledge of the gorilla. In addition to his study of the skull, Wyman also examined the bones of the postcranial skeleton. George Peabody, Henry Bowitch, Frank Russel, Harrison Allen, Daniel Brinton, and Washington Matthews also made important contributions to human osteological research during the late nineteenth century.

Perhaps the father of North American physical anthropology is Aleš Hrdlička, long time curator at the Smithsonian Institution. Hrdlička's contributions included anthropometric and anthroposcopic observations, as well as medical studies, particularly of American Indian natives. Hrdlička founded the *American Journal of Physical Anthropology* in 1918. E.A. Hooton is another distinguished American physical anthropologist. Hooton's major contribution was the publication of his massive research of human skeletal remains, THE INDIANS OF PECOS PUEBLO, in 1930. For its time, and for many years to come, Hooton's work set the standard for studies of human skeletal remains.

This book is written with the intention of updating the work of earlier authors and providing the student with an easy to use handbook for recovering, analyzing, and reporting on human skeletal specimens. It is our hope that this text will give the necessary background for all interested students in the medical and biological sciences.

# ACKNOWLEDGMENTS

SEVERAL PEOPLE HAVE been very instrumental in making the final draft of this text possible. We would like to thank Mrs. Patricia Ann El-Najjar for the tedious work of making illustrations and assisting in the writing, rewriting, and editing. Mr. Joseph Katich, Lymen M. Jellema, and Miss Deborah Vaiksnoras assisted in photographing, drawing, and other technical help throughout. Mrs. Phyllis Ann McWilliams was most helpful in organizing, editing, and collecting original data.

M.Y.El-N.
K.R.M.

# CONTENTS

# FORENSIC
# ANTHROPOLOGY

# CHAPTER I

# RECOVERY AND TREATMENT OF BONE

THE RECOVERY OF BONE is usually the responsibility of an archeologist or a police officer. The care with which the recovery is performed varies greatly, but it is usually better if an archeologist performs the work, since his discipline includes knowledge of the careful excavation techniques needed. A police officer has many other duties and cannot devote the time that would be required to obtain the archeologist's skills. Ideally, a physical anthropologist should be called in to excavate bone found by either the archeologist or the police. In practice, this rarely happens. The cleaning, preservation, and storage is usually carried out by a qualified physical anthropologist. The police usually do nothing to bones to alter their original condition as found. An archeologist can usually be counted upon to clean, store, and preserve bone adequately, but not always perfectly in the opinion of most osteologists. The authors intend in this section to outline methods of excavation and treatment of bone which are satisfactory to the physical anthropologist.

## THE SITE

The foremost rule is: Allow no damage to occur to the bone beyond that which may already have been done. Without the bone no data exists for the physical anthropologist to work with; the bone or bone fragment which is missing is often the very part which would have answered some critical question such as age, sex, race, or cause of death. If bones are missing, returning to the discovery site may be beneficial in recovering the missing parts.

If recovery is your responsibility, map the site during the first visit. On that occasion you will notice things which you will become used to and miss in subsequent trips. The same caution goes for photographs. Photos help greatly to revisualize the site, but do not rely upon them to provide a map. Many things are distorted or obscured on photos which are made clear in a drawing. The map should include those features which are likely to be permanent in order to provide a way to reorient yourself if the site is visited again at a later date. Also include the grave (s) if visible, and any artifacts or weapons, clothing, etc. found on the surface. Keep notes as you dig. A portable cassette tape recorder is a convenient way to do this since you will say things you might not write down.

Methods for mapping a discovery site are presented by Brooks (1975) and Morse, Crusoe, and Smith (1976). The techniques are very simple to apply, and should prove adequate for most purposes. Furthermore, they are flexible enough to be readily modified if circumstances require it. Brooks recommends staking out contiguous five by five foot squares covering the area of most interest, such as the skeleton. In areas where the surface material is less densely concentrated, ten by ten foot squares may be used. The squares provide a visual aid in sketching the site and a framework for locating objects spatially in some detail. The squares may be designated in any of several ways. For instance; the ten by ten foot squares may be given letters of the alphabet and the five by five foot squares numbered 1 through 4 for each larger lettered square. In this way, only one small square would be numbered A-3, for instance.

Specific objects may be located within the drawing of the square by measuring their distance from any two adjacent edges. For instance, three feet one inch south of the north wall and two feet five inches east of the west wall. Some indication of magnetic north must be included in the map or sketches and in all photos.

A sketch of the skeleton should be made before any removal of the bone takes place. Note its position, direction, attitude, and preservation, and any bones missing or other disturbance. Photograph profusely since this is far better and cheaper than not getting the one picture that would have answered your question later. When removing the skeleton, clear all dirt away from the bones before attempting to pick them up. Bones often look more substantial than they are. Do not take chances. Never pick a bone up in the middle. Grip it at both ends and slowly rock it loose from the soil. Lift it only when it is free of the matrix. Try to empty the braincase of dirt since the weight of a ball of dried dirt in the skull will provide a battering ram which will demolish cranial joints. This can be done by using a small tool and removing dirt through the foramen magnum, or other opening if the skull is broken. Note that the attachment between the face and the braincase is very fragile and difficult, if not impossible, to restore. Do not pick the vault up without supporting the face. Teeth have often fallen out of the jaws even when the skull appears to be undisturbed. Count teeth and be sure that all are accounted for. Screen the fill for such small items.

Bag the bones in paper sacks or equivalent for removal to the lab. Label each sack with the site and burial number. Some advocate bagging each bone separately, but this is not necessary if enough padding is provided to keep the bones from rubbing together. Neither is it necessary to bag each hand and foot separately, although this is not a bad idea. Place the bags in a *roomy* box. Do not jam them in since this defeats all your efforts. Take a soil sample from the abdomen and another from the soil away from the bone, but still in the grave, for possible chemical analysis by soil chemists, toxicologists, etc.

Do not forget: *photograph, draw, and describe at the time.* No matter what you think, you will not remember!

## AT THE LAB

At the lab, unpack the bags of bones carefully. If the soil permits, brush the dirt from the dry bones. If this cannot be done, wash them under slowly running lukewarm water. Do this in a washtub, a sink with the stopper closed, or whatever appropriate means will prevent the loss of teeth, broken bone fragments, bullets, or other small objects. Allow the bones to air dry in the shade at room temperature to avoid cracking. After the bones are totally dry, usually twenty-four to forty-eight hours, restoration and preservation may be accomplished if needed. Any of a number of acrylic resins may be used for the purpose of preservation so long as they are soluble in a convenient vehicle like acetone. Mix the resin-acetone solution to a milklike consistency, or thinner, for maximum penetration. Be careful around acetone since it is very flammable.

### Preservation

To treat a bone with preservative, submerge it in the resin-acetone solution at least until bubbles cease to form on the surface of the solution. Pull the bone out of the solution with tongs and allow to drain until dripping stops, then set the bone on a mesh screen such as one-fourth inch hardware cloth to finish drying. Turn the bone often to prevent it from adhering to the puddles of resin which are bound to form. The bones should be completely dry in about eight to twenty-four hours and can be stored, or reconstructed if necessary, for study. Bones which are still wet from washing when immersed will become covered with a white film as they dry. If this happens, resubmerge the bones in acetone to drive off the water and wash away the film. When they are fully dry, repeat the preservation process.

### Restoration

Depending on how extensive the damage has been, restoration of the skeleton may or may not be a difficult and time-consuming project. If the breaks are the common ones, such as clean midshaft breaks of the long bones with no loss of fragments, restoration is simple. A badly crushed skull will tax patience, skill, and knowledge, in addition to being time-consuming.

If breakage has occurred, reconstruction should be undertaken.

Use a glue which is acetone soluble. This allows resetting of mistakes. Do not use a casein base cement since there is no solvent for it once it is dry. Masking tape about one-half inch wide will provide temporary patches and braces as needed. A sandbox is handy to stand bones in while glue dries. Toothpicks may be glued in as permanent braces where they are needed. A knowledge of osteoanatomy is invaluable in bone restoration since the process is much like solving a jigsaw puzzle: the picture to restore is in your memory, but the only time you have seen it in finished form is in a less than satisfactory two-dimensional picture in an anatomy atlas.

It is convenient to divide the available bone fragments at least into skull and not skull, but best to separate pelvis, femur, etc. Then, taking one group of bone at a time, attempt to fit fresh breaks together until reconstruction is complete. When the fresh breaks are patched, try the old, dirt-stained breaks. You will probably have some fragments remaining, but you are usually better off leaving them out than to damage your restoration trying to forcefully fit them. Never force a fragment to fit. If it does not fit: (1) the restoration will need to be taken apart and started again, this time allowing room for the piece you have just found; (2) warpage has occurred and the piece will no longer fit (typical of the skull vault); or (3) you are trying to glue the ischium to the frontal.

In storing the bones remember to avoid crushing or jamming the bones. Labels should be affixed to the bones using paint or waterproof ink, and to the box.

### FORENSIC STUDIES

When the skeleton to be examined is involved in a forensic problem, such as an apparent murder victim, special precautions must be observed and special methods used. Remember that this is a legal matter, and your opinion may be called for in court. You must observe certain formalities so that your evidence is admissible and credible, and you must be as thorough as possible since your opinion may help to convict or release a defendant.

Above all, keep records of everything you do involving the remains. You will need these in court to refresh your memory and to document what was and was not done. As an expert witness, you may take such records to trial with you to consult while you are on the witness stand. You must also preserve the chain of evidence, which means that anything which may be introduced into evidence in court will need documentable history since discovery, at least as far as who possessed the evidence at different times. The person who presents you with the remains should require a detailed receipt from you, and you should require the same any time the evidence is out of your custody, such as to an outside lab for x ray or when it is returned to the law officers or medical examiner.

Photograph the remains just as they are received by you. Also, during your examination, photograph any part of the skeleton which has a bearing on the identity of the deceased, as well as any evident trauma or pathology. Color slides are probably best for this since prints may be made from them if preferred, or the slides themselves may be projected for courtroom display or to jog your memory after the remains have been removed for burial.

Any skin which remains with the skeleton may have changed color due to decomposition. Caucasian skin may turn dark brown or black, and the skin of Negroes may turn ashy gray. Skin color is an especially poor method for race determination if decomposition has begun, and it almost surely has or your services would not be called for. Kerley (1973) suggests that skin color may be assessed from the amount of melanin granules and melanocytes in the subcutaneous layers in burned or partially decomposed skin. Hair form is also useful in race identification, if any remains. Scars and tatoos should be carefully noted and measured. In a case seen by one of us (McW), blackened skin appeared otherwise unaltered until it was placed in 10 percent formalin for preservation. The skin bleached out briefly, revealing a number of small scars and extensive tatooing. The skin soon turned black again, but the features were brought out quite clearly in ultraviolet photos and served to positively identify the deceased. Also, blood type flesh if possible.

After the above observations have been carefully made and documented, residual flesh should be removed from the bones. Be sure you have permission from the proper authority before accomplishing this step. The reasons for reducing the remains to bone are obvious. A physical anthropologist is impeded by flesh in this sort of examination since the majority of the criteria he seeks are in the bone rather than the decomposed soft tissue. Methods for removing soft tissue include: boiling, with or without the addition of detergent or other chemicals; pressure cooking or autoclaving; treatment with caustic chemicals; etc.

Snyder, Burdi, and Gual (1975) have presented a method for preparing skeletal material from fixed cadavers or incompletely decomposed remains. The method requires preparation of a mixture called antiformin, prepared as follows. Combine 150 grams of sodium carbonate ($NaCO_3$) and 100 grams of bleaching powder with 1 liter of water. The sodium carbonate should be added to 250 ml of water, while the bleaching powder is added to the remaining 750 ml, and then the two solutions combined and mixed. This solution should be stirred three to four hours, as necessary. Then add to this an equal quantity (1 liter) of a 15 percent solution of sodium hydroxide.

After cutting away the main mass of soft tissue surrounding the bone, place the specimen in a bath of antiformin sufficient to cover the specimen. For fresh tissue, use one part of the antiformin to eight to ten parts water. Heat the solution to just short of boiling and maintain this temperature for three to sixty minutes, depending on how fast the bone is being denuded. When only fragments of soft tissue remain, remove the specimen from the bath and brush the debris away. It may be necessary in some cases to repeat the boiling and scraping process several times. If the specimen is left in the bath overlong, the antiformin will begin to attack the bone itself. After the specimen has been removed, wash in running water and allow to dry. If desired, the bone may be degreased in benzol for twenty-four to forty-eight hours. It may then be bleached in either 3% hydrogen peroxide or in potassium hydroxide (KOH). The bleaching process is slow and may take more than twenty-four hours. Snyder et al. note that the antiformin can be filtered and reused several times, especially if a little fresh antiformin is added occassionally. The peroxide solution may be used repeatedly for bleaching, but works slowly when it is reused.

The following method is also offered by Snyder et al. for use when time is not critical. Soak the specimen in antiformin for up to four days at room temperature. This drastically reduces boiling time to as little as five minutes. Since repeated boiling and scraping may cause cracking and degradation of the specimen, this method is especially desirable for delicate bone such as skulls and scapulae.

To remove the tenacious intervertebral discs, soak the spine in a degreasing bath of trichloroethane for two or three days, rinse thoroughly in water, and soak in hydrogen peroxide for another two or three days. The discs should then be easily removable with no additional treatment. Also, the vertebrae will be bleached.

Any marks on or in the bones which bear on the history of the deceased should be sought carefully, documented, and recorded. These may include such things as evidence of old fractures or Harris Lines found on x ray, marks of such habits as tobacco chewing on the teeth, amputations or marks of old injuries (such as damage to the tables of the skull), and evidence of other surgical procedures.

As is well known, the dentition has often served to identify an individual. The aid of a forensic odontologist is invaluable in the examination of the teeth.

It will usually be necessary to put your findings into written form. Following the outline provided by this report will usually ensure completeness, but the form should be modified as circumstances require. No two cases are quite alike.

## Sample Report to Medical Examiner

### I. Introduction

On June 17, 1968, I was asked by Dr. _____, Oklahoma State Medical Examiner, to examine some skeletal remains purportedly found in a tributary stream of the Arkansas River in Tulsa, Oklahoma.

Preliminary examination by Dr. _____, in my presence, revealed a partial human skeleton clad in various articles of clothing. The latter was left with Dr. _____ and the bones were removed to my laboratory at 4:30 PM, June 17, 1968, for more detailed examination.

Following the initial examination at my office, the bones were cleaned of all soft tissue remains. Two sections of skin were removed and preserved. One of these, measuring approximately 13 × 30 cm, was from the posterior and medial aspect of the left calf and heel. The other piece, approximately the same size, was from the same area on the opposite side. The fragments are preserved in a 10 percent formalin solution.

### II. Bones Present

The partial skeleton consists of: twenty-four ribs, including two first and two floating ribs, the first cervical vertebra, ten thoracic vertebrae, one lumbar vertebra, the sacrum, both innominates, one coccygeal vertebra, the complete sternum, the bones of both legs with all the bones of the feet and ankles, the bones of the right arm and the left ulna.

Absent are the complete skull and mandible, the left humerus and radius, six cervical vertebrae, and one or two thoracic and four or five lumbar vertebrae, the hands and wrists, and the hyoid.

### III. Condition

Most of the skeleton not protected by pants or socks is entirely free of soft tissue. The knee joints are held together loosely by partially decayed ligaments and readily separate with a gentle pull. The same is true of the feet. The ankle and hip joints are disarticulated. No soft tissue remains on the pelvis and superior two thirds of the femora. All the bones is sound and uneroded by the depositional environment.

### IV. Pathological Conditions

No arthritis or other pathological changes are noted on any of the bones.

### V. Anomalies

None.

## VI. Trauma

None.

## VII. Age

All epiphyses are fused including those of the medial clavicle, suggesting an age greater than twenty-five years.

The aging criteria of McKern and Stewart (1957) are applied to the pubic symphysis. The results indicate an age of from twenty-three to thirty-nine years with a modal age of approximately thirty years.

Apparently this individual was between twenty-five and thirty-nine years of age, probably near thirty.

## VIII. Sex

The angles of the sciatic notches and the subpubic angle indicate that the skeleton is that of a male. The diameter of the heads of the humerus and femur (48 and 49 mm, respectively) supports this view as does the general robustness of the bones. There is no suggestion of femininity.

## IX. Race

In the absence of the skull, the best osteological area for race determination, it is necessary to rely on skin pigmentation. The most that can be said from this is that the individual was probably not recognizably (socially) Negro.

## X. Stature

Stature is estimated from femur plus fibula length using the multiple regression formula of Trotter and Gleser (1958). The results are:

Range:   $5'6\frac{1}{2}''$ to $5'9\frac{1}{2}''$

Most likely $5'8''$

## XI. Time of Death

Lacking knowledge of the circumstances of deposition of the body an estimate is doubly difficult. Assuming the body to have been in water the entire time prior to its discovery since its deposition, assuming that same water to contain a reasonable complement of fish and turtles, and considering the actual degree of decomposition of the soft tissues, then an estimated time elapsed since deposition would be from three to twelve weeks. Any variation in any of the above assumptions could greatly modify the estimate.

## XII. Death

The bones give no indication of the possible cause of death.

### XIII. *Individuation*

Not applicable at this time.

### XIV. *Summary*

The skeleton presented to me by Dr. ———— on June 17, 1968, purportedly discovered in Tulsa, Oklahoma, appears to be that of a Caucasoid or Mongoloid male, ranging in age from twenty-five to thirty-nine years. He stood between $5'6\frac{1}{2}''$ and $5'9\frac{1}{2}''$, centering around $5'8''$. He probably died between mid-February and late May of 1968. No evidence of cause of death was discovered in the skeleton.

# CHAPTER II

# THE HUMAN SKELETON

Bone is the major calcified tissue of all vertebrates. In its structure, bone is a dense material or matrix in which spidery cells, osteocytes, are embedded. The matrix is composed of collagen fibers, crystals of calcium phosphate complex, and a ground substance, or cement, containing muco-polysaccharides (Bourne, 1972). Bone is the hardest structure of the animal body with the exception of enamel and dentine. It is tough and slightly elastic and will withstand both tension and compression to a remarkable extent. Bone is composed of two kinds of osseous tissues: a dense, ivorylike structure making the outer portion of the bone; and bone composed of slender spicules, trabeculae, and lamellae joined into a spongy structure inside the bone (cancellous bone).

Living bone consists of approximately 50 percent water and 50 percent solids. The solids are composed of tissue hardened by impregnation with inorganic salts, e.g. carbonate and phosphate of lime. The proportion of lime increases in old age, so that the bone becomes brittle and easily broken.

Bone is a very specialized connective tissue which develops by a process known as ossification, osteogenesis, or simply, bone formation. During bone formation, certain connective tissue cells, called osteoblasts, secrete a material which is initially amorphous, but soon becomes densely fibrous, when it is known as osteoid, changing it to bone matrix (Bourne, 1972). Bone is a living tissue. Throughout life there is a two-way chemical traffic between bloodstream, cells, and matrix. As a result, the composition and structure is always changing. The bone-forming activity of the osteoblasts is matched with bone-removing activities of osteoclasts (Bourne, 1972).

Bone is filled with two types of bone marrow: (1) yellow marrow, found in the large cavities of the long bones, consists for the most part of fat and blood cells; and (2) red marrow, found in the flat and short bones, the articular ends of the long bones, the bodies of the vertebrae, the cranial diploe, and the sternum and ribs.

The human skeleton is the solid framework of the body. In addition, it serves to protect the vital organs and for the attachment of muscles. There are two main subdivisions of the skeleton: (1) the axial skeleton including the bones of the head, the neck, and the trunk; and (2) the appendicular skeleton which includes the upper and lower limbs. Below is a listing of the name and number present of each bone within the two subdivisions.  Included are the anatomical directions and descriptive terms.

*Axial Skeleton*

(a)  Skull
      frontal
      occipital
      sphenoid
      ethmoid
      vomer
      hyoid
      mandible
      parietal
      temporal
      maxilla
      nasal      2
      zygomatic (malar)      2
      lacrimal      2
      palate      2
      inferior nasal concha      2
      malleus      2
      incus      2
      stapes      2
              29

(b)  Vertebral column
      cervical      7
      thoracic      12-13
      lumbar      5
      sacrum      1 (5 in subadults)
      coccyx      1-3
              26

(c)  Sternum      1-3
(d)  Scapula      2
(e)  Clavicle      2
(f)  Innominate      2
      (pubis)      (2)
      (ilium)      (2)
      (ischium)      (2)
(g)  Ribs      24 (variable, but same in both sexes
              typically)
              31

### *Appendicular Skeleton*

|       |             |     |
|-------|-------------|-----|
| (a)   | Humerus     | 2   |
| (b)   | Radius      | 2   |
| (c)   | Ulna        | 2   |
| (d)   | Carpals     | 16  |
| (e)   | Metacarpals | 10  |
| (f)   | Phalanges   | 28  |
| (g)   | Femur       | 2   |
| (h)   | Patella     | 2   |
| (i)   | Tibia       | 2   |
| (j)   | Fibula      | 2   |
| (k)   | Tarsals     | 14  |
| (l)   | Metatarsals | 10  |
| (m)   | Phalanges   | 28  |
|       |             | 120 |
|       |             | 206 |

### *Anatomical Directions*

Front—ventral or anterior
Rear—dorsal or posterior
Upper—cranial or superior
Lower—caudal or inferior
Medial—toward the midline
Lateral—away from the midline
Proximal—toward the trunk or head
Distal—away from the trunk or head
Superficial—toward the surface
Deep—away from the surface
Palmar—toward the palm of the hand
Plantar—toward the sole of the foot

### *Anatomical Descriptive Terms*

Crest—a ridge, especially surmounting or bordering a bone
Spine—a sharp prominence or slender process of bone
Process—a slender point (thornlike)
Tubercle—a small tuberosity
Tuberosity—an elevation or blunt eminence
Trochanter—a marked tuberosity
Sulcus—a linear depression
Groove—same as sulcus
Meatus—a tubular opening
Foramen—an opening or hole

## THE SKULL

The skull is the bony structure of the head which includes the cranium, skeleton of the face, and the mandible or lower jaw. Skull bones vary in thickness, size, and shape in relation to each other and between different individuals. They may be flat (parietal and temporal), irregular (sphenoid), or curved (frontal). Skull bones are composed of two compact layers: the external table measuring about 1.5 mm in thickness and the inner table measuring about 0.5 cm in thickness. Separating the two tables is a layer of cancellous bone filled with red bone marrow, the diploe. The most thickened parts of the cranial bones are those at the junction of the coronal and lambdoid sutures with the sagittal suture, i.e. at bregma and lambda respectively. According to Pendergrass, Schaeffer, and Hodes (1956), thick bones are characteristic of Negroes, and are in general thicker in females than males. Examination by one of the authors (El-N) of several hundred Negroid and Caucasian skulls, both male and female, from the Hamann-Todd collection at the Cleveland Museum of Natural History, Cleveland, Ohio, confirms the above authors' suggestion. Pendergrass et al. (1956). further suggest that the thickness of the cranial bones is such a common characteristic in females it can be used as a diagnostic critera of the sex of an individual. In such cases, one must be extremely careful since several types of anemia, e.g. sicklemia, the thalassemias, iron deficiency anemia, rickets, and skull deformaties, will increase skull thickness.

There are several major sutures which join the carnial bones. The coronal suture joins the frontal and parietal bones; the sagittal suture joins the two parietal bones; the lambdoid suture joins the two parietal bones to the occipital; the basilar suture joins the occipital and sphenoid; and the squamosal joins the temporal and parietal bones. The sphenofrontal suture is located between the frontal and the great wing of the sphenoid. It extends forward from the lower end of the coronal suture and the anterior end of the sphenoparietal suture. The sphenoparietal suture separates the sphenoid and parietal bones. The occipitomastoid suture is located between the mastoid portion of the temporal bone and occipital bones.

### Frontal Bone

The frontal bone is a saucer-shaped bone which forms the forehead and the upper part of the orbital cavities. The metopic suture divides the frontal bone medially up to about two or three years of age, then is obliterated. In approximately 10 percent of cases the metopic suture persists into adulthood, usually with a higher incidence in females than in males (Pendergrass et al., 1956). A notch and/or foramen on the supraorbital margin, through which the supraorbital vessels exit posteriorly from the

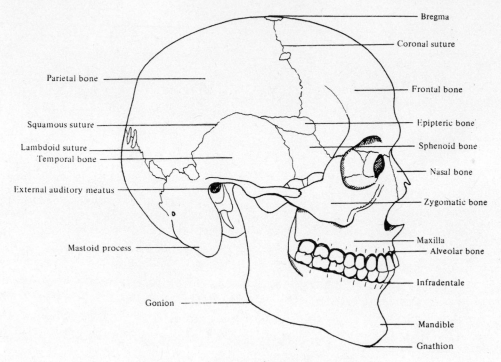

Figure 1a:  View of the right side of a skull.

internal orbit, is always present.  The frontal bone articulates with the two parietal bones at the coronal suture, laterally with the great wing of the sphenoid and the frontal process of the zygomatic bone, and below with the ethmoid, lacrimal, maxillary, and nasal bones posteroanteriorly.  Two large cavities, the frontal sinuses, are located above the orbits.

### The Parietal Bones

The external surfaces of the parietal bones are convex and normally smooth.  The two bones meet in the midline at the sagittal suture.  The parietal foramina may be present posteriorly along the sagittal suture.  Occasionally only one foramen is present and size varies.  The parietal bones articulate with the frontal bone at the coronal suture, the occipital bone at the lambdoid suture, and the temporal and upper portion of the sphenoid bones laterally at the squamosal suture.

### The Occipital Bone

The occipital bone makes the back (posterior) and a large portion of the base of the skull.  The external surface is thick, convex, irregular, and rough.  Two lines, the inferior and superior nuchal lines in the middle and

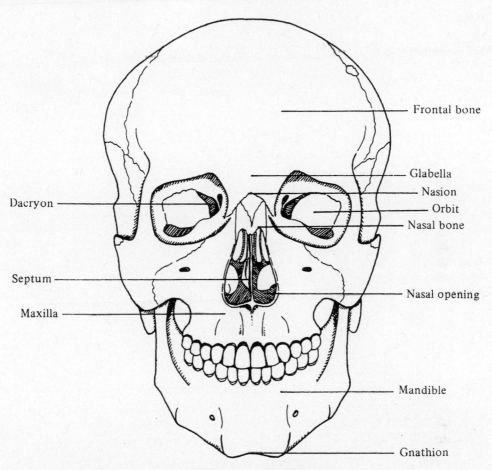

Figure 1b:  Front of the skull.

upper thirds of the occipital bone, and a well-marked projection, the external occipital protuberance, are present.  The basilar part of the occipital bone is a thick bone extending forward from the foramen magnum to the body of the sphenoid.  The extended plate posterior to the foramen magnum is the squama.  The occipital bone articulates with the parietal bones above, laterally with the temporal, and with the sphenoid in the front.  The internal surface is divided into two superior fossae that are triangular in shape and two inferior fossae that are quadrilateral in shape.

### The Temporal Bones

The temporal bone forms part of the lateral wall of the skull as well as part of the base.  The squama forms the anterior and superior part of the bone.  The large, winglike portion articulates with the parietal bones above.  The long, slender, bony projection medial to the mastoid process is the

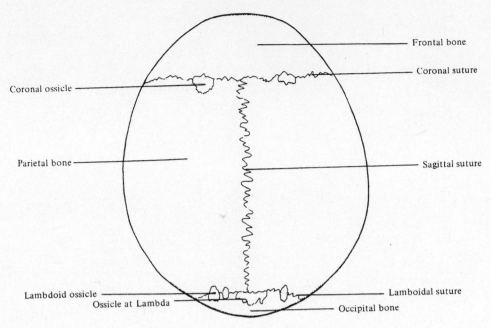

Figure 2a:  Skull vault.

styloid process.  Anterior to the styloid process is a round, smooth depression, the mandibular fossa, for the lodgment of the head of the mandible.  The zygomatic process forms the posterior portion of the zygomatic arch and articulates in front with the temporal process of the zygomatic bone.  The petrous portion is a dense, long, irregular projection between the great wing of the sphenoid and the lateral border of the basilar part of the occipital zone.  The cavities of the middle and inner ear are located in this process.

### The Sphenoid

The sphenoid bone is an irregular, butterfly-shaped bone located at the base of the skull anterior to the temporal and basilar part of the occipital bones.  It consists of four wings and a body.  The great wings are large plates or processes of bone projecting from both sides of the body.  The small wings are thin, triangular plates arising from the superior and anterior parts of the body which project laterally.  The body of the sphenoid approximates the basilar part of the occipital bone.  The depression in the upper surface of the sphenoid bone is the sella turcica, the seat for the pituitary gland.  The sphenoid articulates with the occipital, parietal, frontal, ethmoid, temporals, vomer, palatine, zygomatic, and occasionally the maxilla.

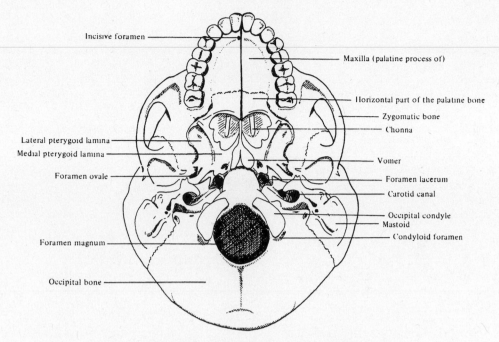

Figure 2b: Undersurface of the skull.

## The Ethmoid Bone

The ethmoid bone is thin, spongy, and irregular in shape. It lies in front of the sphenoid between the two orbits and forms part of the medial nasal wall.

### Facial Bones

## Nasal Bones

The nasal bones are two concavo-convex bones forming the bridge of the nose. They articulate with each other in the midline and with the frontal bone above. The lateral borders articulate with the frontal process of the maxilla and the internal surfaces with the ethmoid and the cartilagenous septum of the nose.

## Lacrimal Bones

Lacrimal bones are thin, scalelike bones the size of the fingernail, lying in the anteromedial wall of the orbit upon the ethmoid bones and forming part of the nasal cavity. They contain tear ducts and communicate with the nose.

*Forensic Anthropology*

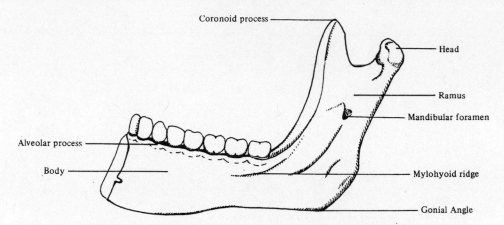

Figure 3a:   Medial surface of the right half of the mandible.

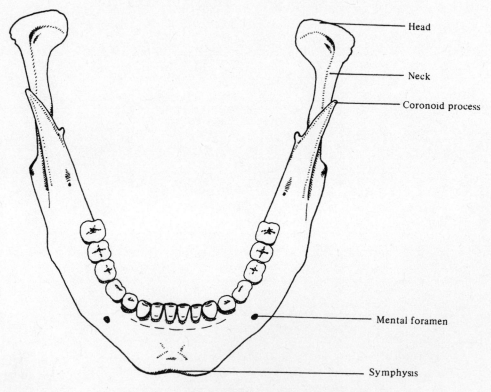

Figure 3b:  The mandible viewed from above.

### Maxillary Bones

The maxillary bones form the middle of the face and the upper jaw. Each maxillary bone consists of a large central mass, the body, and four processes. The body includes a large, irregular opening, the nasal aperture, and a large cavity, the maxillary sinus. The frontal (nasal) process is the upward projection which articulates above with the frontal and nasal bones and medially with the ethmoid and inferior concha. The zygomatic process is a triangular projection articulating with the zygomatic bone forming the anterior portion of the zygomatic arch. The alveolar process holds the upper teeth. The palatine process forms most of the floor of the nose and most of the hard palate. The two palatine processes meet in the midline and form the intermaxillary suture. The maxilla articulates with the frontal, ethmoid, nasal, lacrimal, zygomatic, inferior nasal conchae, palatine, vomer, and the maxilla on the opposite side.

### Zygomatic Bone

The zygomatic or malar bone supports the cheek. It articulates medially with the maxilla, above with the frontal bone, laterally with the temporal bone, and behind with the greater wing of the sphenoid. The posterior projection forms the anterior portion of the zygomatic arch, and the upward projection completes the outer wall of the orbit.

### The Mandible

The mandible is the bone of the lower jaw. It consists of a horseshoe-shaped body, the upper or alveolar portion which holds the teeth, and two perpendicular portions, the rami. Each ramus bears two processes, the coronoid and the condylar.

### The Hyoid Bone

The hyoid bone is a slender, horseshoe-shaped bone found below the mandible at the upper border of the voice box or larynx.

### Ear Bones

Within the middle ear cavity of the petrous portion of each temporal bone are three small bones called the malleus (hammer), incus (anvil), and stapes (stirrup).

## THE VERTEBRAL COLUMN

The vertebral column consists of seven cervical, twelve thoracic, and five lumbar vertebrae, the sacrum, with five fused vertebrae, and the coccyx in which three or five vertebrae are usually fused. Variation in the number of

**FIGURE 4a:  Atlas**

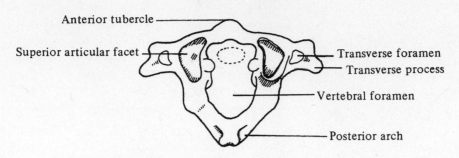

Anterior tubercle ———————

Superior articular facet ———

Transverse foramen

Transverse process

Vertebral foramen

Posterior arch

**FIGURE 4b:  Second cervical vertebra**

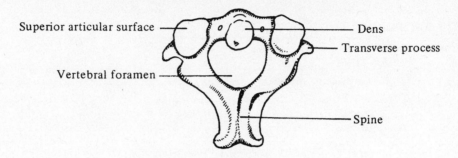

Superior articular surface ———

Vertebral foramen ———

Dens

Transverse process

Spine

**FIGURE 4c:  Sixth cervical vertebra**

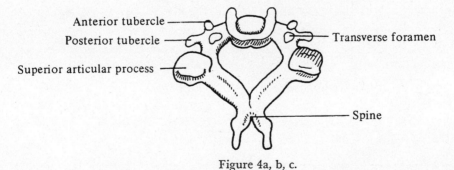

Anterior tubercle ———

Posterior tubercle ———

Superior articular process ———

Transverse foramen

Spine

Figure 4a, b, c.

vertebrae in all but the cervical segment is not uncommon.  The vertebrae, separated by discs made of fibrocartilage, are closely bound together by ligaments.

A typical vertebra consists of a central portion, the body which is cylindrical, and a rough superior and inferior surface with slightly elevated ridges.  Behind the body is a vertebral arch consisting of a laterally placed pair of pedicles and a pair of laminae making the vertebral foramen.  The pedicles are short, thick processes projecting posteriorly to connect the trans-

**FIGURE 4d: Sixth thoracic vertebra**

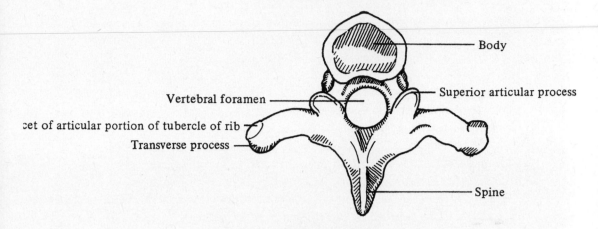

Body

Superior articular process

Vertebral foramen

cet of articular portion of tubercle of rib

Transverse process

Spine

**FIGURE 4e: Third lumbar vertebra**

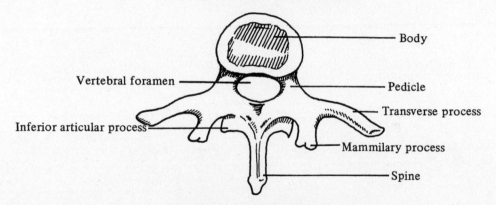

Body

Vertebral foramen

Pedicle

Transverse process

Inferior articular process

Mammilary process

Spine

**FIGURE 4f: Third lumbar vertebra**

Superior articular process

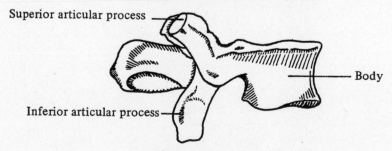

Body

Inferior articular process

Figure 4d, e, f.

verse process to the body. The laminae, broad and flat, are directed posteriorly and medially from the pedicles. Projecting backward from the laminae is the spinous process.

### Cervical Vertebrae

The cervical vertebrae are the smallest and are easily distinguished from the other vertebrae by the presence in each transverse process of a small foramen for the passage of the vertebral artery. The transverse processes are small and have no surfaces for articulation with the ribs. The spinous process is short and often is bifid at the end. The first cervical vertebra or atlas is a ringlike bone with no body and no spinous process, but with well-developed transverse processes. The superior articular surfaces on the transverse process are large, oval, and concave. They support the head by articulation with the occipital condyles on both sides of the foramen magnum. The second cervical vertebra is characterized by a thick process, the dens or odontoid process, which projects upward from the body. The dens is the displaced body of the first cervical vertebra. The seventh cervical vertebra resembles the first thoracic in its general morphology, particularly in the shape of the spinous process.

### Thoracic Vertebrae

The thoracic vertebrae are characterized by having facets for the articulation with ribs and no foramen for the vertebral artery. In size, they are intermediate between the cervical and lumbar vertebrae. The pedicles are short and the laminae are broad and thick. The spinous process is long and projects sharply downward in most of them. The transverse processes are thick, long, and strong. Minor variability in form and size may be present, but the general morphology is similar in all thoracic vertebrae.

### Lumbar Vertebrae

The lumbar vertebrae are the largest of all vertebrae. They are characterized by the absence of the transverse foramen and the articular facets for the ribs. On the posterior and lateral part of each superior articular process there is often a small bony projection, the mammillary processes. The spinous process is thick, short, and broad. The laminae are broad and short. The vertebral foramen is larger than the thoracic but smaller than the cervical.

### The Sacrum

The sacrum is a large, triangular bone. The first sacral vertebra is the largest, the succeeding ones diminish in size. The smooth, concave, anterior (or pelvic) surface forms the hollow of the sacrum. The posterior or dorsal surface is rough and uneven for the attachment of muscles and heavy ligaments of the back. The sacrum consists of cancellous bone surrounded by a thin layer of compact bone. On the anterior and posterior surface there

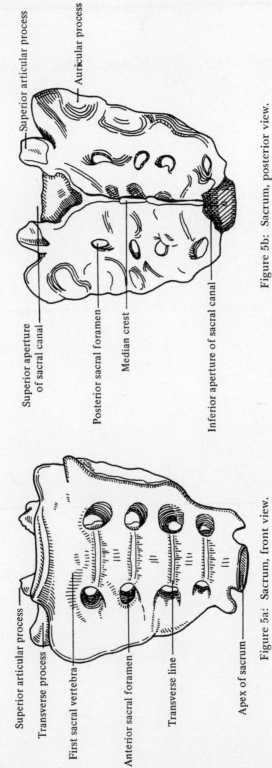

Superior articular process

Auricular process

Superior aperture
of sacral canal

Posterior sacral foramen

Median crest

Inferior aperture of sacral canal

Figure 5b: Sacrum, posterior view.

Superior articular process

Transverse process

First sacral vertebra

Anterior sacral foramen

Transverse line

Apex of sacrum

Figure 5a: Sacrum, front view.

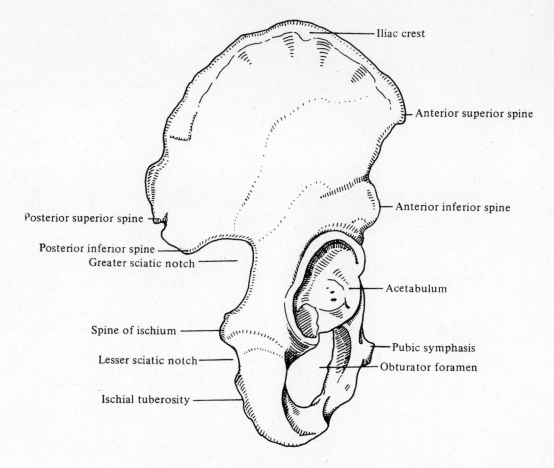

Figure 5c:   Right os coxa, lateral view.

are four pair of intervertebral foramina.  The sacrum articulates with four bones:  the fifth lumbar, the first coccygeal vertebra, and the innominates on each side.  (See Figure 5a, b)

### The Coccyx

The coccyx is a small bone forming the lower segment of the spinal column.  The coccyx usually consists of four coccygeal vertebrae, but may vary from three to five, which are normally fused in the adult.  The first is the largest and the last ones diminish in size.  All coccygeal vertebrae are lacking laminae, pedicles, and spinous processes.

## BONES OF THE THORAX

### Ribs

A typical rib is a long curved bone which articulates with two thoracic vertebrae, the one corresponding to it and the one above it. The eleventh and twelfth ribs possess only one articular surface for the corresponding vertebra. The first rib has but one articular surface. It is short, sharply curved and relatively broader than any other rib. Behind the neck, except in the lowest two ribs, is a small tubercle articulating with the transverse processes of the vertebra above it. The second rib is considerably longer than the first and more slender. The third to seventh ribs are increasingly longer, and the succeeding ones diminish regularly in size.

### The Sternum

The sternum (breast bone) consists of three parts: the upper portion (manubrium) is thick and broad and articulates on each side with the clavicle (collar bone) and the first rib; the middle portion (body or gladiolus) is thinner and narrower; and the lower part (xiphoid) is small and normally triangular in shape, but is highly variable. The xiphoid is cartilagenous in early life but often ossifies and fuses to the body of the sternum in adulthood. It may also fail to ossify. (See Figure 6.)

## BONES OF THE UPPER EXTREMITY

### Scapula

The scapula or shoulder blade is a flat, thin, triangular bone. The central surface is a broad, shallow concavity or depression. On the superio-lateral corner is a smooth oval surface, the glenoid cavity, into which the head of the humerus inserts. The dorsal surface is divided by a spine into the supraspinous portion above and the infraspinous fossa below. The scapula has three borders. The superior is concave and extends from the medial angle to the base of the coracoid process. At its lateral border is sometimes a semicircular notch, the scapular notch. The spine of the acromian forms the summit of the shoulders and articulates in front with the lateral end of the clavicle. The coracoid process is attached by a broad base at the superior border near the neck of the scapula. The auxiliary border begins at the margin of the glenoid cavity and inclines obliquely to the inferior angle. It is the thickest of the three borders. The vertebral border, the longest of the three, extends from the superior to the inferior angles. (See Figure 6a, b.)

**FIGURE 6a:** View of the dorsal surface of the left scapula

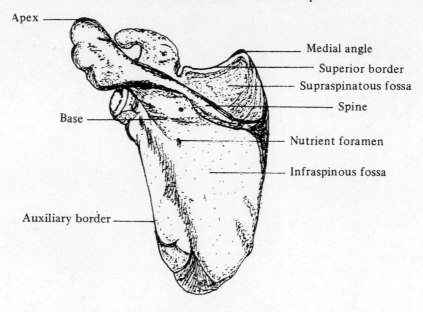

Apex

Medial angle

Superior border

Supraspinatous fossa

Spine

Base

Nutrient foramen

Infraspinous fossa

Auxiliary border

**FIGURE 6b:** View of the costal surface of the left scapula

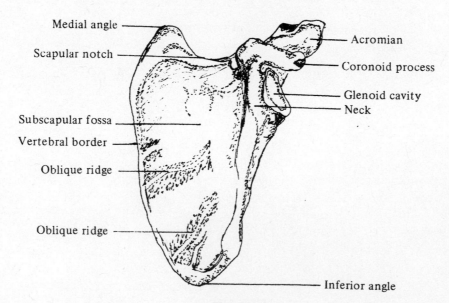

Medial angle

Scapular notch

Acromian

Coronoid process

Glenoid cavity

Neck

Subscapular fossa

Vertebral border

Oblique ridge

Oblique ridge

Inferior angle

Figure 6a, b.

Figures 6 through 9 are modified after Boots and associates. **Courtesy of Scientific Illustrations, 1954.**

'IGURE 6c: View of the ventral surface of a sternum     FIGURE 6d: View of the dorsal surface of a sternum

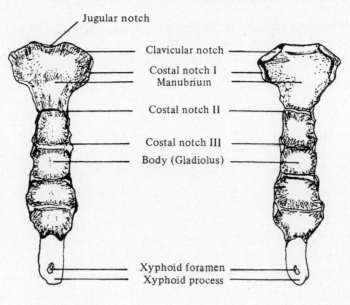

Jugular notch

Clavicular notch

Costal notch I
Manubrium

Costal notch II

Costal notch III
Body (Gladiolus)

Xyphoid foramen
Xyphoid process

FIGURE 6e: View of superior surface of a left clavicle

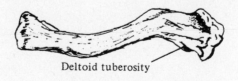

Deltoid tuberosity

FIGURE 6f: View of inferior surface of a left clavicle

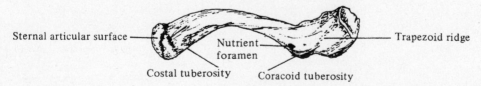

Sternal articular surface

Nutrient
foramen

Costal tuberosity

Coracoid tuberosity

Trapezoid ridge

Figure 6c, d, e, f.

### The Clavicle

The clavicle (see Figure 6) or collar bone is a long, slender bone which lies above the first rib. The medial end is rounded and articulates with the sternum. The lateral end is broad and articulates with the acromial process of the scapula.

### The Humerus

The humerus (see Figure 7b) is the largest bone of the upper extremity. At its upper (proximal) end is a large hemispheric knob, the head. The greater and lesser tubercles, or tuberosities, are two projections lateral to the head. The central portion of the shaft is round, but the bone becomes flattened laterally in the distal portion. The flattened distal portion forms two projections, the medial and lateral epicondyles. The distal articular surface is divided into two parts. The outer is a smooth, round process called the capitulum, which articulates with the upper end of the ulna. Proximal and anterior to the trochlea is a small depression, the coronoid fossa, in which the coronoid process of the ulna is inserted when the arm is flexed. The olecranon fossa is situated on the posterior surface of the trochlea. This fossa lodges the olecranon process of the ulna when the forearm is extended. Especially in females, the olecranon fossa is often perforated, allowing hyperextension of the arm.

### The Ulna

The ulna (see Figure 7a) is located on the medial side of the forearm. On the proximal end is a large, thick hooklike prominence, the olecranon process. The coronoid process projects anteriorly just inferior to the olecranon depression. The body or shaft of the ulna is convex laterally and dorsally. The lower end has a knobbed portion called the head beside which is a conical projection, the styloid process.

### The Radius

The radius (see Figure 7a) lies parallel to the ulna on the lateral, or thumb, side of the forearm. At the proximal end is a circular disc, the head, which articulates with the capitulum of the humerus and the ulna. On the medial side just below the head is the radial tuberosity. The body or shaft is narrower proximally and slightly curved and convex laterally. The distal end is larger than the proximal end and has a conical tip on the lateral side projecting distally, the styloid process. The articular surface for the ulna is called the ulnar notch of the radius. At its lower end, the radius articulates with two bones of the wrist, the scaphoid and lunate.

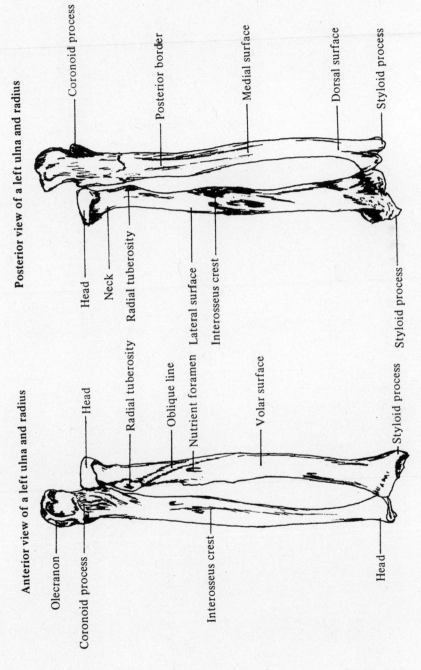

Posterior view of a left ulna and radius

Coronoid process

Posterior border

Medial surface

Dorsal surface

Styloid process

Head

Neck

Radial tuberosity

Lateral surface

Interosseus crest

Styloid process

Styloid process

Figure 7a.

Anterior view of a left ulna and radius

Head

Radial tuberosity

Oblique line

Nutrient foramen

Volar surface

Olecranon

Coronoid process

Interosseus crest

Styloid process

Head

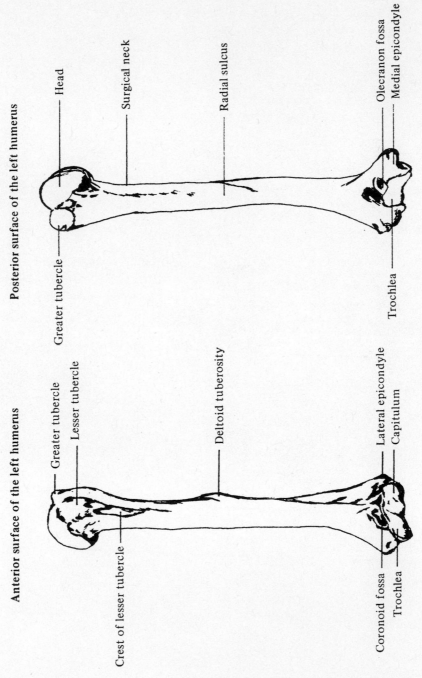

Posterior surface of the left humerus

Head

Surgical neck

Radial sulcus

Olecranon fossa
Medial epicondyle

Greater tubercle

Trochlea

Anterior surface of the left humerus

Greater tubercle
Lesser tubercle

Deltoid tuberosity

Lateral epicondyle
Capitulum

Crest of lesser tubercle

Coronoid fossa
Trochlea

Figure 7b.

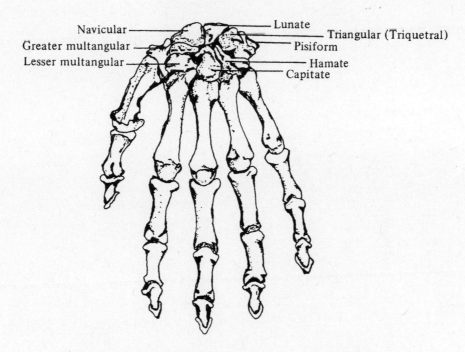

Navicular ——— Lunate

Triangular (Triquetral)

Greater multangular ——— Pisiform

Lesser multangular ——— Hamate

Capitate

Figure 8a: View of the dorsal surface of the left hand.

## The Bones of the Hand

The hand bones consist of five metacarpal bones, numbered from the radial or thumb side (see Figure 8a, b). The four medial bones articulate at their bases with each other and with the carpals. The first metacarpal (thumb) is the shortest and thickest. The metacarpal of the index finger (number one) is the longest, and its base is the largest of the remaining four. The third, fourth, and fifth diminish in size respectively. There are fourteen phalanges, three for each finger and two for the thumb. The phalanges of the finger present a flattened surface on the palmar side. The outer metacarpals articulate proximally with their carpal bones and the head of each metacarpal articulates distally with its proper finger bone.

## BONES OF THE LOWER EXTREMITY

### The Hip Bones (Os Innominati)

The hip bone (see Figure 5) is large, flat, and irregularly shaped. It consists of three fused bones: ilium, ischium, and pubis. At the junction of these three bones is a deep hemispheric or cup-shaped depression, the

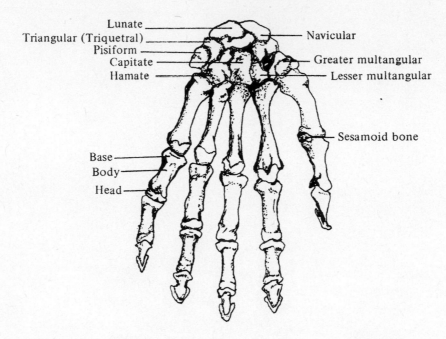

Lunate
Triangular (Triquetral)
Pisiform
Capitate
Hamate

Navicular
Greater multangular
Lesser multangular

Sesamoid bone

Base
Body
Head

Figure 8b: View of the volar surface of the left hand.

acetabulum, for insertion of the femoral head. The ilium, largest of the three, is concave and very broad. It consists of two major portions, the body which forms the upper portion of the acetabulum, and the ala, the expanded fan-shaped portion which bounds the greater pelvis laterally. The ischium forms the inferior and dorsal portion of the hip bone. It has a body and a ramus. The body forms two fifths of the acetabulum. The ischial spine, a triangular eminence, projects from the dorsal border. Above the spine is the greater sciatic notch. Below the spine is the lesser sciatic notch. Dorsal to the obturator foramen is a large roughened swelling, the ischial tuberosity. The pubis forms the front portion of the acetabulum. The two pubic bones articulate in the midline at the pubic symphysis.

### The Femur

The femur (thigh bone) is the longest, largest, heaviest, and strongest of all skeletal bones (see Figure 9b). At the upper end are the head, neck, and the greater and lesser trochanters. The head is large and globular. The neck connects the head to the body and is placed at approximately a right angle to the shaft. The greater trochanter is the large superior projection on the lateral

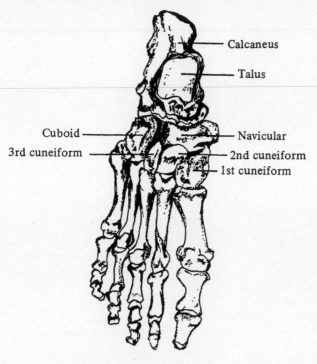

Calcaneus

Talus

Cuboid

Navicular

3rd cuneiform

2nd cuneiform

1st cuneiform

Figure 8c: View of the dorsal surface of the right foot.

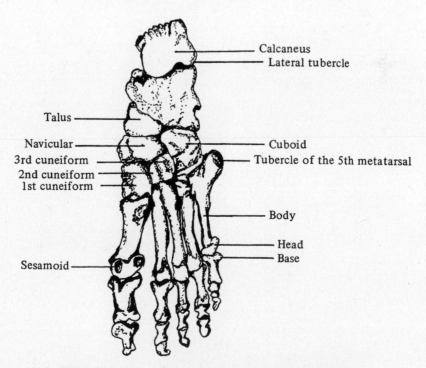

Calcaneus

Lateral tubercle

Talus

Navicular

Cuboid

3rd cuneiform

Tubercle of the 5th metatarsal

2nd cuneiform

1st cuneiform

Body

Head

Base

Sesamoid

Figure 8d: View of the planter surface of the right foot.

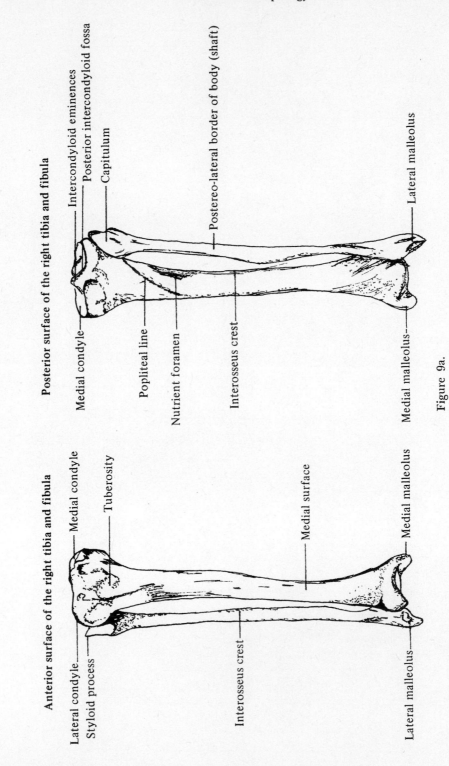

**Posterior surface of the right tibia and fibula**

Intercondyloid eminences

Posterior intercondyloid fossa

Capitulum

Postereo-lateral border of body (shaft)

Lateral malleolus

Medial condyle

Popliteal line

Nutrient foramen

Interosseus crest

Medial malleolus

Figure 9a.

**Anterior surface of the right tibia and fibula**

Medial condyle

Tuberosity

Medial surface

Medial malleolus

Lateral condyle

Styloid process

Interosseus crest

Lateral malleolus

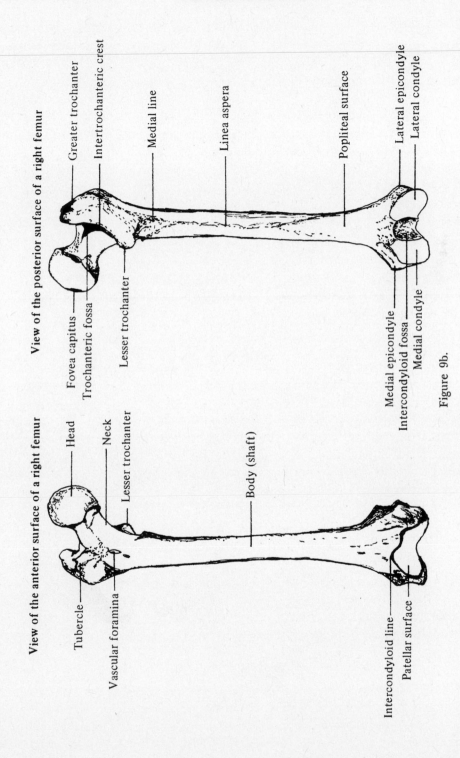

View of the anterior surface of a right femur

View of the posterior surface of a right femur

Head
Neck
Lesser trochanter
Tubercle
Vascular foramina
Body (shaft)
Intercondyloid line
Patellar surface

Greater trochanter
Intertrochanteric crest
Medial line
Linea aspera
Popliteal surface
Lateral epicondyle
Lateral condyle
Fovea capitus
Trochanteric fossa
Lesser trochanter
Medial epicondyle
Intercondyloid fossa
Medial condyle

Figure 9b.

side of the shaft at its junction with the neck. The lesser trochanter is the smaller, conical eminence on the inner side of the shaft just below the neck. A well-marked ridge or crest, the linea aspera, runs longitudinally on the posterior part of the shaft.

The distal end of the femur forms the medial and lateral condyles. They are joined together anteriorly but are separated posteriorly. Between the two condyles posteriorly is a deep notch, the intercondylar fossa. The epicondyles are two rough prominences on the medial and lateral surfaces of the condyles. The medial epicondyle is larger and more prominent than the lateral.

### Patella

The patella or kneecap is a large sesmoid bone forming the prominence on the front of the knee when the leg is extended. It is flat and triangular in shape. The anterior surface is convex, while the posterior surface is smooth, oval, and divided into two concave articular facets. The apex is pointed downward and the superior border is thick and rounded.

### Tibia

The tibia (see Figure 9a) or shin bone is the larger bone of the lower leg. The thickened proximal end supports the medial and lateral articular surfaces for the condyles of the femur. Between these two surfaces is the intercondylar eminence. On the anterior surface, just below the proximal end, is the tibial tuberosity. Immediately beneath the outer ridge of its lateral condyle, the tibia has an articular facet for the fibula. The distal end of the tibia has a projection on its medial side, the medial malleolus, which forms the prominence on the inner side of the ankle. The lateral side of the distal end articulates with the fibula and the distal surface with the talus.

### Fibula

The fibula (see Figure 9b) is a slender bone on the lateral side of the leg. The head articulates with the lateral condyle of the tibia just beneath the lateral ridge. The fibula ends below in the lateral malleolus, the prominence of the outer side of the ankle.

### The Foot

There are twenty-six separate bones in the foot (see Figure 8a,b) divided into three main groups: tarsals, metatorsals, and phalanges. Of the tarsals, the talus is the superior bone which articulates with the tibia and fibula. It is the second largest of the tarsal bones. Below the talus is the calcaneus, which is the largest of the tarsal bones. It forms the heel. In front of these on the lateral side is the cuboid, on the medial side, the navicular, and in front of the navicular, the three cuneiform bones in a row. Anterior to the tarsals lie the five metatarsal bones. The bones of the medial three articulate mainly with the three cuneiform bones, and those of the lateral two with the cuboid. The first metatarsal is thick and short. The second is the longest of the five. The third and fourth are smaller and very similar. The fifth metatarsal is recognized by a rough eminence or tuberosity on the lateral side of its base. The phalanges are similar in arrangement and in number to those of the hand, except that the shafts are round in cross section. There are two phalanges in the great toe and three in each of the other toes.

# CHAPTER III

# DENTITION

THE UTILITY OF DENTAL morphology in anthropological studies has been recognized for many years. The dentition of extinct and living human and nonhuman groups is useful as an indicator of population affinity, adaptation, and behavior. Because they are one of the hardest materials in nature, teeth preserve well and, therefore, provide evidence of evolutionary changes through time. Their functions are known and can be identified. Teeth possess features that have a high genetic component in their expression, are little effected by environmental factors, and, therefore, have proven useful in the study of genetic admixture, dental morphology, and in establishing biological relationships between various groups of human and nonhuman primates. Teeth provide evidence of behavioral patterns and biocultural interaction, e.g. incidence in dental decay may suggest diet variation and the presence of enamel hypoplasia might be correlated with periods of malnutrition or of disease during childhood. In addition, teeth are the only hard part of the body that can be observed directly in the living without resorting to radiography. They are often the only recovered part of the skeleton and, therefore, may be of critical value for micro- and macro-evolutionary, as well as forensic, studies.

Teeth, however, have some disadvantages. They are severely modified by attrition. Dental wear often obscures surface morphology and obliterates lingual ridges, cusp configuration, groove patterns, etc., making observation difficult and often virtually impossible. Very little is known of the evolutionary significance of tooth morphology as regards structure and function. Their apparent multifactorial modes of inheritance make dental traits difficult to ascertain. Some discrete dental traits, e.g. Carabelli's cusp and protostylid, show continuous expressivity ranging from lines and pits to grooves and cusps and, therefore, are nearly impossible to classify and compare. For example, a trait may have an expression so low that its classification may be obscured and/or confused with other surface irregularities on the crown. Environmental and culturally induced alterations through processes such as decay, calculus build up, filing, and removal also handicap their utility in anthropological studies.

## ANATOMY OF THE PERMANENT TEETH

A tooth is composed of four different tissues: (1) enamel, a hard, brittle substance covering the crown; (2) dentin, a bonelike substance which forms the body of the tooth; (3) cementum, a bonelike substance which covers the tooth root; and (4) pulp, which occupies the central cavity of the tooth (Morrey and Nelsen, 1970). Enamel, dentin, and cementum are hard tissues. The pulp, a soft tissue, provides the blood and nerve supply to the tooth. The teeth are held in place by the alveolar bone or process.

The crown of a tooth may have an incisal ridge or edge as in the central and lateral incisors, a single cusp as in the canines, or two or more cusps as in the premolars and molars. The root of the tooth may be single (incisors and canines), double (premolars), or triple (molars). Occasionally four separate roots may be found in the upper molars.

In the incisors and canines the surfaces toward the lips are called labial, and in the premolars and molars are called buccal. Together, they are known as facial surfaces. The surfaces of the teeth facing adjoining teeth in the same dental arch are called mesial toward the midline and distal away from the midline.

### Upper (maxillary) Incisors

The maxillary central incisors are the shearing and cutting teeth. They are the widest of the anterior teeth and the lingual surface is irregular and less convex than the lateral incisors. The lateral incisors are smaller in all dimensions except root length and are more variable in form than any other tooth except the third molars. A pointed form of the lateral incisors, "peg shaped," is occasionally present. Other characteristic features include large pointed tubercles as part of the cingulum, developmental grooves, twisted roots, and distorted crowns. The labial aspect of the lateral incisors has more curvature than the central and is narrower.

### Lower (mandibular) Incisors

The mandibular incisors are the smallest teeth in the dental arch. The central incisors are smaller than the lateral, show uniform development, and are rarely deformed. Unlike the central and lateral upper incisors, the lingual surfaces of the lower incisors are very smooth. Mandibular central and lateral incisors are very similar, making them hard to distinguish in recovered specimens where they have been separated from the dental arches.

### Canines

Both upper and lower canines are similar in form and in function. They are the longest teeth in the mouth, and their crowns are usually as long as those of the maxillary central incisors although their roots are usually longer. Canines have a single, well-developed cusp. Their crowns and roots are markedly convex. Because of the labiolingual thickness of the crown, root, and the anchorage in the alveolar process of the jaws, they are the most stable of all teeth. The lingual surface of the crown is smoother and has less cingulum development and less bulk to the marginal ridges in the mandibular canines.

### The Maxillary Premolars

One of the major differences between the anterior (incisors and canines) teeth and premolars is the development in the latter of a well-developed lingual cusp. This cusp arises from the lingual lobe which is represented by the cingulum in the incisors and canines. The buccal cusp is long and sharp in the first maxillary premolars. The crowns and roots of the maxillary premolars are shorter than those of the maxillary canines. When premolars have two roots, one is placed buccally and one lingually.

### The Mandibular Premolars

The first premolar has a large well-formed buccal cusp and a nonfunctioning lingual cusp. The first premolar is always the smaller of the two mandibular premolars, whereas the opposite is true in many cases of the maxillary premolars. The second premolar is more rounded than the first and usually has a single root. The buccal cusp is not as long as that of the first premolar and is less pointed. The form of both mandibular premolars often does not conform to the implications of the term bicuspid, which implies two functioning cusps. Both mandibular premolars exhibit more variability on their occlusal surface than the maxillary premolars. The single root of the second premolar is larger and longer than that of the first premolar. Their roots are seldom bifurcated. The lingual cusps of the mandibular second premolars are well developed and function by being supplementary to the mandibular first molar.

### The Maxillary Molars

In general, the crown of the first maxillary molar is wider buccolingually than mesiodistally and is normally the largest tooth in the upper jaw. It has four large cusps: mesiobuccal, distobuccal, mesiolingual, and distolingual. A fifth cusp, the Carabelli's complex or trait, is often present. This may appear as a pit, tubercle, or a well-developed cusp. This cusp is lingual to the mesiolingual cusp, which is the largest of the cusps. The first molar has three well-developed and separate roots: mesiobuccal, distobuccal, and lingual. The lingual is the largest and longest, the mesiobuccal is not as long but is broad, and the distobuccal is the smallest.

The maxillary second molar supplements the first molar in function. In its morphology, it may resemble the first, third, and occasionally a combination of both. The distolingual cusp is poorly developed, resulting in a heart-shaped form of the occlusal surface typical of the third molar. The roots are similar to those of the first molar. Carabelli's trait may be present, but in a much lower frequency than that of the first molar.

The maxillary third molar varies in size, contour, and relative position. Its basic design is similar to the second molar. The crown is smaller, and the roots are shorter and have a tendency to fuse. The third molar is heart-shaped because the distolingual cusp is very small, poorly developed, or absent. Occasionally, they may be so deformed that they no longer resemble either first or second molars.

### The Mandibular Molars

Each of the mandibular molars has two roots, one mesial and one distal. Their crowns are roughly quadrilateral, being somewhat longer mesiodistally than buccolingually, which is the case in the maxillary molars.

The mandibular first molar is the largest of all molars. It has five well-developed cusps: two buccal, two lingual, and one distal. The roots are widely separated at the apices. The mesial root is broad and curved distally. The distal root is rounder, broad at the cervical portion, and pointed in a distal direction.

Although similar in function, the mandibular second molar differs in some detail in its anatomy. The crown of the mandibular second molar has four well-developed cusps: two buccal and two lingual. A fifth cusp is not usually present. The tooth has well-developed roots, one mesial and one distal. These roots are broad buccolingually but not as broad as those of the first molar nor are they as widely separated.

The third mandibular molar is variable both in form and position. It is seldom fully developed. The crown is irregular in form, with undersized roots that are usually fused and/or malformed. Generally speaking, it conforms to the general form of the second more than to the first molar. Occasionally a third molar may have five or more cusps. Due to a lack of space to accommodate them, third molars are often completely or partially impacted.

### TERMINOLOGY

Students should be familiar with certain definitions and terminology. The following terms are modified after Black (1902) and Wheeler (1968).

ALVEOLAR PROCESS: The process of the mandible and maxilla which holds the roots of the teeth.

ALVEOLUS: A socket or cavity in the alveolar process of both the maxilla and mandible in which the root of the tooth is anchored.

ANGLE: The area or point of junction of two intersecting borders or surfaces.

APEX: The terminal end of the root.

APICAL FORAMEN: An opening in the apex of the root through which the nerves and blood vessels pass.

BICUSPID: A tooth with two cusps. In the anthropological literature, bicuspid refers to the premolars.

BUCCAL SURFACE: The side of the tooth adjacent to the cheek.

BUCCOLINGUAL: From the cheek toward the tongue.

CEMENTUM: A tissue resembling bone which forms the outer surface of the roots of the teeth.

CINGULUM: The lingual lobe of an anterior tooth. A shelf or swelling which is found on the tooth just above the cervical line and is the site of the development of many supernumerary cusps.

CROWN: The part of the tooth covered by enamel.

CUSP: A pronounced eminence or elevation on the crown surface of the tooth.

CUSPID: A tooth with one cusp (canine).

CUTTING EDGE: The edge formed by the junction of the labial and lingual surfaces of the incisors and canines.

DENTIN: The tissue which forms the main body of the tooth. It surrounds the pulp cavity and underlies the enamel of the crown and the cementum of the roots.

DISTAL: Away from the midline of the arch.

ENAMEL: The hard tissue covering the crown of the tooth.

FISSURE: A fault in the surface of the tooth caused by imperfect joining of the enamel of the different lobes.

FOSSA: A round or angular depression in the surface of the tooth, found most often on the occlusal surfaces of the molar teeth and the lingual surfaces of the incisors.

GINGIVA: The portion of the gum tissue enveloping the necks of the teeth from the attachment at the gingival line.

GROOVE: A line or narrow depression between the main parts of the occlusal surfaces of the tooth.

INCISOR: A tooth with one cutting edge.

LABIAL: Pertaining to the lips. Toward the lips.

LABIAL SURFACE: The surface of the tooth adjacent to the lips. Only incisors and canines have labial surfaces.

LABIALLY: A direction toward the lips.

LABIOLINGUAL: From the lips toward the tongue.

LINGUAL: Next to or toward the tongue.

MAMMELONS: Three rounded prominences seen on the cutting edges of the incisors when they first erupt.

MARGINAL RIDGES: Ridges or elevations of enamel on the margins of the occlusal surface of molars and premolars and on the mesial and distal margins of the lingual surface of the incisors and canines.

MEDIAN LINE: The anteroposterior perpendicular central line of the body.

MESIAL: Toward the midline. The surfaces of the tooth toward the median line are called mesial surfaces.

MESIAL ANGLE: The junction of the mesioincisal and of the mesio-bucco occlusal angle.

MESIALLY: Toward the median line.

MESIOBUCCAL ANGLE: The angle formed by the union of the mesial and buccal surfaces of the premolars and molars.

MESIODISTAL: From mesial to distal.

MESIOLABIAL ANGLE: The angle formed by the union of the mesial and labial surfaces of the incisors and canines.

MESIOLINGUAL ANGLE: The angle formed by the union of the mesial and lingual surfaces of a tooth.

NECK: The portion of the tooth which forms the junction of the crown and root.

OCCLUSAL SURFACE: The surface of the premolars and molars that comes in contact with the teeth of the opposite jaw when the mouth is closed.

PITS: A small pin-point depression in the enamel.

PULP: The soft tissue that fills the pulp chambers and root canals of the teeth and contains the nerves and blood vessels.

RIDGE: A long linear elevation on the surface of the tooth. Normally a ridge is named after its position, i.e. incisal ridge, buccal ridge, marginal ridge, etc.

SULCUS: A long depression or valley in the surface of the tooth between ridges and cusps.

TUBERCLE: A small rounded elevation on the surface of the tooth. They are normally deviations from normal tooth form.

## DENTAL CROWN MORPHOLOGY

### Shovel-Shaped Incisors

The term shovel-shaped was first introduced by Muhlreiter in 1870. It refers to a condition resulting from a combination of a concave lingual surface and elevated marginal ridges of the upper and lower incisor teeth.

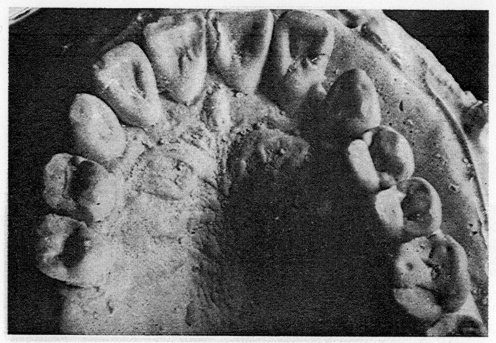

Figure 10a: Shoveling of the upper central and lateral incisors of an adult male American Indian.

Hrdlička (1911) first noted that shoveling was pronounced in the incisors of American Indians. In 1920 and 1921, he reported a high incidence of well-defined shovel-shaped incisors in Mongoloids (Chinese, Japanese, Eskimos, and American Indians), a low incidence in Negroes, and a still lower incidence among Caucasians. Nelson (1938), Goldstein (1948), Pedersen (1949), and Dahlberg (1945, 1949), have substantiated Hrdlička's findings and demonstrated that shovel-shaped teeth are characteristic of the Mongoloid stock. Weidenreich (1937) used the marked shovelling of the incisors of *Sinanthropus pekinensis* to suggest genetic continuity to modern Mongoloid populations.

Hrdlička (1920) classifies shoveling into four classes or grades:

(1) *Shovel*—The enamel rim with well-developed fossa.

(2) *Semishovel*—Enamel rim still distinct, shallower fossa.

(3) Distinct traces of enamel rim, but which could not be classified as semishovel.

(4) *No shovel*—No traces of rim or fossa, or very faint.

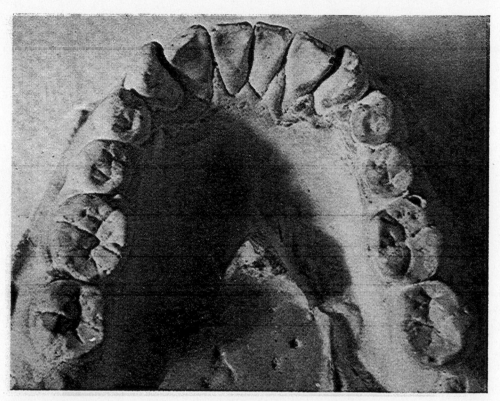

Figure 10b: Shoveling of the lower central and lateral incisors of an adult male American Indian.

## Carabelli's Complex

Carabelli's complex or trait was first described by Von Carabelli in 1842, as an accessory cusp on the lingual surface of the maxillary molars. The trait varies considerably in its occurrence, size, and location. The order of its occurrence in diminishing frequency is as follows: deciduous second molar, first, second, and third molars. The size varies from a well-defined cusp to a small line or deflected groove. Often, instead of a cusp, a fissure may be present. It may occur unilaterally or may be symmetrical. Its location on the deciduous second molar and first permanent molar is always on the mesial half of the lingual surface, but on the second permanent molar it is more distally located. (Figure 11).

The cusp of Carabelli occurs in low incidence in Mongoloid and related groups and in a much higher incidence in Caucasians and Negroes. A

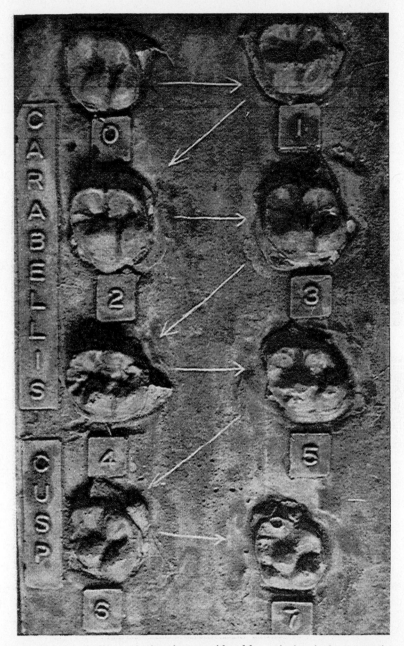

Figure 11: Carabelli's trait showing considerable variation in its expression.

comparatively low incidence of Carabelli's trait in populations of Mongoloid stock has been reported for Mongols, (Batujeff, 1896), Chinese (De Terra, 1905), Japanese (Hachisuka, 1937), Pecos Indians (Nelson, 1938), East Greenlandic Eskimos (Pedersen, 1949), Northwest and Labrador

Eskimos, and Pima and Blackfoot Indians (Dahlberg, 1949). White admixture East Greenland Eskimos show the cusp or pit to be present in 29 percent of the population (Pedersen, 1949). In more isolated areas where admixture has been at a minimum, the incidence of the trait is almost nil (Pedersen, 1949).

The genetics of Carabelli's cusp are not well established, although many dental anthropologists claim that the trait is inherited. Pedigree analysis by Kraus (1951) shows the trait to be inherited as a Mendelian dominant. Kraus assumes the existence of three genotypes with three corresponding phenotypes: cc = absence of the trait; Cc = intermediate expression of the trait; and CC = pronounced tubercle. The number of types (different grades of the same trait), however, suggest a much more complex genetic pathway and all attempts to characterize the genetics of Carabelli's cusp by any simple Mendelian mode have, thus far, failed.

### Groove Pattern and Cusp Number of the Mandibular Molars

In 1916, William K. Gregory discovered that man, the great apes, and the Dryopithecinae have a basically similar arrangement of cusps and grooves of the permanent mandibular molars. This configuration is known as the Dryopithecus "Y5" pattern. The typical "Y" pattern is recognized by the formation of a Y from the three main buccolingual grooves between the five main cusps. The creses of cusps one and four are separated and those of two and three remain in contact (Figure 12).

The degree of retention of the ancestral groove configuration is not the same in all human groups nor in all mandibular molars. Goldstein (1948) has shown that the deciduous second molars retain the Y pattern more frequently than the permanent molars of the same individual. Modification of the Y pattern occurs either by changing to an "X" by retaining the five cusps or to a "+" pattern by the reduction of the five cusps to four. In general, the first mandibular molar is the most conservative, the second is most frequently modified to an X or + pattern, and the third occupies an intermediate range. According to Hellman (1928), modification of both cusp number and groove configuration occurs to a more marked degree in Caucasian than in Negro or Mongoloid populations.

### Number of Cusps in the Maxillary Molars

The number of cusps in the upper (maxillary) permanent molars varies from four to three. The first permanent molar is the most conservative, usually having four cusps. The number of cusps is more variable in the third than in the first and second molars. Among the Aleuts, Texas Indians, and East Greenland Eskimos the quadricuspal form of the second molars is

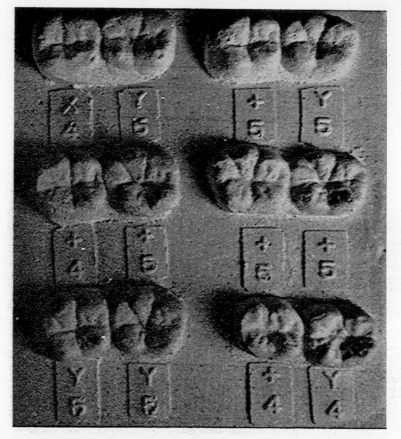

Figure 12: The "Y", Y5, X, and + pattern of lower molars.

found in about 60 to 70 percent, while in Australian aborigines the quadri-cuspal form is almost 100 percent (Moorrees, 1957). One must be very careful in using different classifications by different authors. Often comparisons may be limited. Hellman (1928) noticed that Mongoloids appear to be more conservative in cusp reduction than Caucasians or Negroes.

### Supernumerary and Missing Teeth

Hyperodontia, the increase in the number of teeth over the normal number, occurs mainly in the incisor region, but extra teeth may be present anywhere in the mandible or maxilla. The incidence varies within and between different human groups and ranges in frequency from 0.3 to 2.7 percent according to Pedersen (1949). Goldstein (1932) and Pedersen (1949) find Eskimos to have a high incidence of missing third molars. Moorrees (1957) found 40 percent of the Aleuts he studied to have missing upper and lower third molars. It is important that students differentiate between congenitally missing third molars and those lost antemortem where resorption of the alveolar bone has taken place. Such conditions may be misleading in the final interpretation of data.

## Supernumerary Cusps

Bolk (1916) describes extra cusps occurring on the buccal surface of the second and third molars, which he terms "paramolar cusps". He suggests that these cusps are derived from supernumerary teeth fused during development to the permanent teeth. Bolk further suggests that these cusps are remnants of lost posterior teeth of the deciduous series and, therefore, will not be present on the first permanent molar. Dahlberg (1945) reports the presence of paramolar cusps (parastyle) on the first permanent molars, thereby refuting Bolk's hypothesis on their origin. Dahlberg (1950) used the term paramolar cusp to refer to all anomalous cusps on the buccal side of both the maxillary and mandibular premolars and molars. Of this group, Dahlberg distinguishes a subgroup, the protostylids, which are restricted to the mesial portion of the buccal surfaces of the mandibular molars.

## DENTAL PATHOLOGY
### Dental Caries

Dental caries are the most widespread dental disease in the world today. They are pathological conditions of the teeth in which the enamel or dentine is decalcified and the remaining organic material disintergrated (Fisher, Kuhm, and Adami, 1931). They usually develop in one or more regions of the tooth at the occlusal surface or the dentoenamel junction. In the anterior teeth the labial surface is usually most affected.

The differential presence of dental caries in the various tooth groups has been attributed to differences in anatomical forms. According to Moorrees (1957), molar teeth possess larger crown dimensions than any of the tooth groups and, therefore, more surface area. Molar teeth are the grinders and possess crevices which collect and hold food particles. They also have more interproximal space where food can accumulate.

Carbohydrates have been blamed most often for the initiation of the carious process. Carbohydrate substances provide a fermentable substrate which leads, through bacterial activity, to the formation of acids on the surface of the teeth with subsequent decalcification of the enamel. A widely accepted explanation of the etiology of dental caries is Miller's (1883a, 1883b) "Chemico-parasitic theory". According to Miller, acids formed by bacteria from fermentable food debris (carbohydrates) are largely responsible for the breakdown of the coronal tissue of the teeth. Sognnaes (1948a, 1948b) made the important discovery that dental caries can be produced more rapidly in experimental animals when the "caries-producing rations" were given to the mother before or at conception and up to the time of weaning, thus exerting influence during the developmental period of the teeth. Sognnaes (1948b) shows that the incidence of dental caries diminished following restriction of carbohydrates during World War II.

### Periodontal Disease

This is an infection of the alveolar bone and of the soft tissues surrounding the teeth. Periodontal disease causes recession of the alveolar bone which results in loosening of the teeth and their eventual loss. The exact etiology of this disease is not known. Nutritional imbalance, calculus deposits, poor hygiene, and attrition may singly or in combination contribute to this pathology.

### Dental Abscess

An abscess is a collection of pus surrounded by denser tissue (Brothwell, 1972). It is commonly found as a cavity within the alveolus near the root apex. The abscess may form in association with general periodontal infection, tooth wear, or dental caries. The incidence of abscesses, similar to those of dental caries and periodontal diseases, vary from individual to individual and from one human group to the other. Leigh (1925) found a low incidence among the Sioux Indian tribes with high protein diet as compared to a high incidence among Pueblo Indians who subsist normally on a high carbohydrate diet. The frequency ranges from 16 percent in Sioux to 52 percent in Zuni Pueblo Indians. Similarly, El-Najjar (1974) found a higher incidence among the Canyon de Chelly Pueblo Indians than among the hunting and gathering Basketmakers who occupied the canyon at an earlier date.

### Dental Enamel Hypoplasia

Dental enamel hypoplasia is a developmental enamel defect in the deciduous and permanent teeth. It results in structural changes, seen as transverse lines, pits, and grooves, on the enamel surface. Enamel hypoplasia may range from small localized defects to multiple defects. Occasionally the whole enamel surface may be affected. The most common variety of enamel hypoplasia involves a number of teeth in which formation of the enamel matrix takes place over the same period. The causative agent affects that zone of enamel which is being produced during its onset. Whatever the etiology, hypoplasia can only be produced if the disturbance coincides with a period of active enamel matrix formation.

Robinson (1952) found enamel hypoplasia in 28 percent of the forty-seven teeth of the Australopithecus genus, parathropus. Sognnaes (1956) reports an irregular microstructure in most of the Upper Pliestocene Mount Carmal specimens. This is not surprising since metabolic disturbances of some type, whether nutritionally or disease induced, could easily go back before the origin of man. This becomes increasingly convincing if one examines the high probability of seasonal dietary inadequacy owing to the hunting and gathering subsistance pattern.

The etiology of enamel hypoplasia is not precisely known. It has been attributed to vitamin D deficiency (Gottlieb, 1920), vitamin A deficiency (Boyle, 1933), hereditary factors (Butting, 1929), and congenital syphilis (Braur and Blackstone, 1924). In addition to the above causative agents, factors such as maternal hyperparathyroidism (Van Arsdel, 1955), hemolytic anemia (Watson, Massler, and Perlstein, 1964), premature birth (Grahnen, Sjolin, and Stenstorm, 1974), and hypocalcemia (Levine, 1974), which may affect the individual prenatally or postnatally, have increased the overwhelming etiological range of this pathology.

### Antemortem Tooth Loss

The most likely cause of antemortem tooth loss is probably related to periodontal diseases, dental caries, and nutritional deficiencies. Shaw (1962) states that acute protein deprivation in the albino rat can cause a degeneration of the connective tissue components of the gingiva and the periodontal membrane, periodontal ligaments, osteoporosis of the alveolar bone, and retardation in the formation of the cementum. According to Kerr (1962), vitamin C deficiency enhances gingival bleeding due to local factors because of altered capillary permeability. It also prevents repair of the periodontium in the face of chronic destructive periodontal disease, so that the disease may progress much more rapidly in the individual with vitamin C deficiency.

### Attrition

Attrition is the gradual wearing away of the hard parts of the teeth. When food is abrasive or contains extraneous abrasive material introduced in its preparation, the degree of wear on the occlusal surface increases. Fisher et al. (1931) classify dental wear as follows:

0—the enamel of cusps is somewhat worn without exposure of the underlying dentin;

1—the cusps are worn away enough to obliterate the sulci between them;

2—the underlying dentin has become visible;

3—the pulp is exposed;

4—abrasion has continued so that the root stumps have become functional.

The wearing of the tooth surface appears to be a normal result of tooth structure, function, eating habits, and food preparation.  The degree of attrition is also determined by the hardness of the teeth, condition of the supporting bone, periodontal tissues, and the habits of mastication.

# CHAPTER IV

# RECONSTRUCTION OF THE INDIVIDUAL FROM THE SKELETON

THIS SECTION IS DESIGNED to provide the student with guidelines to reconstruct as much information as possible from the skeleton of an individual, including age, race, sex, and stature. This is by no means all that can be determined from the skeleton, but how much is learned beyond these four depends on the imagination, curiosity, and expertise of the investigator, and the condition and completeness of the skeleton with which he is working. The following is practical information which can be employed in typical cases the anthropologist encounters. Some of the techniques presume a nearly complete skeleton for the application of the method outlined, or at least that certain parts of the skeleton be present and in good condition. Since the skeleton often does not meet these criteria, alternative methods are presented so that at least a well-founded estimate may be made.

The order of presentation is as follows: age, race, sex, and stature. Reconstruction should proceed in this order since each is influenced by those which preceed it. The skeleton of an aged individual may have become modified by various processes so that it resembles an individual of a different race or sex. Stature decreases with age. Age, and especially race, influence the expression of sexual criteria. The first three must be known in order to enter the correct tables to estimate stature and make the appropriate adjustment for age. Using the methods presented here, one should be able to assess age, sex, and stature in any skeleton complete enough to permit such assessment.

There is no substitute for experience. This is not a "cookbook" for use by the uninitiated since many of the methods presented will require modification in certain cases, and many of them amount to an art which can only be acquired by encountering such cases previously or by examination of a large number of skeletons.

## ESTIMATION OF AGE

Age estimation from the human skeleton is, in most cases, about as difficult as estimation of age from living physiognomy. Accuracy, as well as certainty, decreases with the advancing age of the individual, be that individual living or dead. Also, as with the living body, different parts of the skeleton are most informative at different ages in the life of the deceased. To further confound the anthropologist, it is necessary to estimate first the approximate age of the individual at the time of death in order that the most appropriate part of the skeleton be utilized in the detailed assessment of age. Fortunately, this is not as difficult as it sounds since the criteria which are the hallmarks of different age groups are usually readily apparent to an observer familiar with the methods used to assess age.

The following classification based broadly on the methods available for age estimation in different age categories is useful to the physical anthropologist working with human bone.

## Neonate

This is the period before the eruption of the deciduous dentition. This stage is accompanied by very small bones and lack of fusion of many elements of the skeleton, such as neural arches of the vertebrae, segments of the pelvis, halves of the frontal bone, epiphyses, etc. The crypts of the unerupted teeth are apparent in the jaws. It is very difficult to estimate age in so young a skeleton with precision. The stature obtained from the Olivier and Pineau (1957) methods cited in the section on stature may be used to estimate very roughly the age of a neonate according to Table I. Because of variation in size from the norm of any given fetus, this table, according to Olivier, may be in error by four to five weeks near the beginning to about ten weeks near the end.

## Infancy/Early Childhood

Most of the criteria of skeletal immaturity cited above continues during much of this period. However, during this time the halves of the frontal bone normally fuse into a single bone, as well as other changes occurring. An obvious marker for this age group is the erupting dentition which

TABLE I
FETAL AGE RELATED TO TOTAL FETAL STATURE*

| Fetal stature (cm) | Age in lunar months |
|---|---|
| 23.80 | 5 |
| 30.69 | 6 |
| 36.52 | 7 |
| 41.58 | 8 |
| 46.03 | 9 |
| 50.02 | 10 |

*From G. Olivier, *Practical Anthropology*, 1969. Courtesy of Charles C Thomas, Publisher, Springfield, Illinois.

serves as a rather reliable guide to age. The eruption sequence is summarized in the section on Late Childhood. The appearance of ossification centers aid in age estimation during both this and the neonate period.

TABLE II

AGE ORDER OF APPEARANCE OF OSSIFICATION CENTERS AFTER ABOUT
5 YEARS. GIVEN IN YEARS AND MONTHS*

| center | white male | white female |
|---|---|---|
| Humerus, medial epicondyle | 5:2 | — |
| Ulna, distal | 5:6 | — |
| Calcaneal epiphysis (tuber) | 6:2 | — |
| Talar epiphysis | 8:0 | 6:10 |
| Humerus, trochlea | 8:4 | 7:2 |
| Olecranon | 8:8 | 6:8 |
| Femur, lesser trochanter | 9:4 | 7:7 |
| Pisiform | 9:10 | 7:1 |
| Sesamoid (flexor hallux brevis) | 10:4 | 8:2 |
| Humerus, lateral epicondyle | 10:5 | 8:3 |
| Tibial tubercle | 10:10 | 9:0 |
| Metatarsal V, proximal | 11:0 | 8:7 |
| Sesamoid (flexor pollex brevis) | 11:8 | 9:4 |
| Rib I, tubercle | 13:3 | 10:0 |
| Ilium, anterosuperior spine | 13:4 | 9:3 |
| Thoracic vertebra I, transverse process | 13:4 | 11:4 |
| Acromion | 13:5 | 11:4 |
| Iliac crest | 13:5 | 12:0 |
| Coracoid angle | 13:10 | 11:3 |
| Ischial tuberosity | 15:0 | 13:2 |
| Clavicle, medial | 15:0+ | 14:6 |

*Krogman 1962: Table 26.

## Late Childhood

During this period, the permanent dentition begins to erupt. As with the period of eruption of the deciduous teeth, aging in these later childhood years is based on the appearance of the permanent teeth, which occurs with fair regularity. The beginning of this period is marked by the appearance of the first permanent tooth, although the dentition will be a mixture of permanent and deciduous teeth for some years to come. The most commonly used standards for age estimation of subadults using dental development, at least in this country, are probably those provided by Schour and Massler (1940). The standards are not without imperfection in that there is more variability in age of tooth eruption than they allow, but usually it will be very close for most individuals. The chart is available from the American Dental Association in Chicago and is very useful. The eruption sequence detailed on the chart is as follows.

TABLE III

NORMAL VARIABILITY IN THE ERUPTION OF THE HUMAN PERMANENT DENTITION. AGE IN YEARS*

| Order of Appearance | TOOTH | | MALES | FEMALES | Sexual Difference |
|---|---|---|---|---|---|
| | Maxilla | Mandible | | | |
| 1 | — | M₁ | 4.64 – 7.78 | 4.37 – 7.51 | .27 |
| 2 | M¹ | — | 4.83 – 7.97 | 4.65 – 7.79 | .18 |
| 3 | — | I₁ | 5.01 – 8.07 | 4.73 – 7.79 | .28 |
| 4 | I¹ | — | 5.88 – 9.06 | 5.61 – 8.79 | .27 |
| 5 | — | I₂ | 5.98 – 9.42 | 5.62 – 9.06 | .36 |
| 6 | I² | — | 6.75 – 10.59 | 6.28 – 10.12 | .47 |
| 7M 8F | Pm¹ | — | 7.52 – 13.28 | 7.15 – 12.91 | .37 |
| 8M 7F | — | C | 8.30 – 13.28 | 7.37 – 12.35 | .93 |
| 9 | — | Pm₂ | 7.94 – 13.70 | 7.30 – 13.06 | .64 |
| 10 | Pm² | — | 8.10 – 14.26 | 7.80 – 13.96 | .30 |
| 11 | — | Pm₂ | 8.18 – 14.76 | 7.60 – 14.18 | .58 |
| 12 | C | — | 9.00 – 14.38 | 8.29 – 13.67 | .71 |
| 13 | — | M₂ | 9.45 – 14.79 | 8.99 – 14.33 | .46 |
| 14 | M² | — | 9.99 – 15.37 | 9.58 – 14.96 | .41 |
| 15 | — | M₃ | 16.5(?) – 27.0(?) | 16.5(?) – 27.0(?) | slight |
| 16 | M³ | — | 16.5(?) – 27.0(?) | 16.5(?) – 27.0(?) | slight |

*From V.O. Hurme, Time and sequence of tooth eruption, *J Forensic Sci*, 2:377-388, 1957. Reprinted with permission from the *Journal of Forensic Sciences*, 2:377-338, 1957, published by Callaghan & Company, 6141 North Cicero Avenue, Chicago, Illinois 60646.

### Deciduous Dentition

6 mos. (± 2) Beginning eruption of the maxillary central incisors and all mandibular incisors.

9 mos. (± 3) Eruption of maxillary lateral incisors. Completion of incisor set.

1 year (± 3 mos.) Beginning eruption of mandibular premolar.

18 mos. (± 3 mos.) Eruption of maxillary premolar, beginning eruption of canines and molars.

2 years (± 6 mos.) Completion of the above except the molars which are not completely finished erupting.

3 years (± 6 mos.) Completion of deciduous dentition.

### Mixed Dentition

6 years (± 9 mos.) Beginning eruption of first permanent molar. All deciduous teeth are retained at this age.

7 years (± 9 mos.) Loss of maxillary central deciduous incisors as well as all mandibular incisors. Beginning eruption of maxillary central permanent incisors and all maxillary incisors with the centrals in more advanced state of eruption than the laterals. Completion of first permanent molar eruption.

8 years (± 9 mos.) Beginning eruption of maxillary lateral incisors. Loss of deciduous maxillary lateral incisors.

9 years (± 9 mos.) Completion of eruption of permanent incisors. At this age, the dentition consists of the permanent incisor set as well as the permanent first molars, plus the deciduous canines, premolars, and molars.

10 years (± 9 mos.) Beginning eruption of maxillary and mandibular first premolars and of mandibular canines. The deciduous premolars and the mandibular canines are lost.

### Permanent Dentition

11 years (± 9 mos.) All deciduous teeth have been shed. Beginning eruption of all canines and second premolars.

12 years (± 6 mos.) Completion of all permanent dentition mesial to first molar. Beginning eruption of second molar.

15 years (± 6 mos.) Completed eruption of second molars.

21 years (quite variable) Eruption of third molars, completing the permanent dentition. In some individuals this tooth never appears.

Kerley (1965, 1973) notes that it is possible to estimate age fairly closely by examining certain features of the teeth microscopically. He cautions, however, that this is best done by a forensic dentist because of the special techniques involved.

Figure 13: An immature tibia showing the caps (epiphyses) not yet united to the shaft (diaphysis).

## Adolescence

This period is marked by cessation over a period of time of length increase of most of the long bones, signalled by the fusion of the bony "cap" (epiphysis) of the bone to the shaft (diaphysis). This fusion, termed epiphyseal union, occurs with sufficient regularity to serve as an age marker. Each epiphysis fuses with the shaft of the bone at a particular age, but the entire process from the first epiphyseal union to the last extends over many years, from puberty to full skeletal maturity.

McKern and Stewart (1957) define five grades of epiphyseal union. These are: Unobservable (0), Beginning (1), Active (2), Recent (3), and Complete union (4). These grades are used in tables that are drawn from their publication.

## Young Adult

Aging during this period begins to turn from details of development to details of degeneration.

Formerly, cranial suture closure was used as an age criteria for adults. However, the observations of McKern and Stewart on Korean War dead have negated the value of this method. They state that, "the irregular pattern does not indicate or support a reliable terminal age of closure within the ages represented" (McKern and Stewart, 1957). This indicates that closure of cranial sutures is erratic at best up to at least age forty-five. McKern and Stewart also state that "an exception is the basilar suture which is completely closed at the age of twenty-one. It has been known that

TABLE IV

AGE DISTRIBUTION OF COMPLETE UNION FOR THE LONG BONE EPIPHYSES OF GROUP I, IN PERCENT.*

| Age | No. | Humerus: med. epicond. | prox. Radius: | Ulna: prox. | head | Femur: grt. troch. | lsr. troch. | Tibia: dist. | Fibula: dist. |
|-----|-----|------|------|------|------|------|------|------|------|
| 17-18 | 55 | 86 | 93 | 90 | 88 | 88 | 88 | 89 | 89 |
| 19 | 52 | 96 | 100 | 100 | 96 | 98 | 98 | 98 | 94 |
| 20 | 45 | 100 | | | 100 | 100 | 100 | 100 | 100 |

Total = 152

*From T.W. McKern and T.D. Stewart, *Skeletal Age Change in Young American Males*, 1957. Courtesy of Headquarters Quarter-master Research and Development Command, Natik, Massachusetts.

TABLE V

AGE DISTRIBUTION FOR STAGES OF EPIPHYSEAL UNION IN THE LONG BONES IN PERCENT.*

**UPPER EXTREMITY**

| Age | No. | Humerus (prox.) Stages | | | | | Radius (dist.) Stages | | | | | Ulna (dist.) Stages | | | | |
|---|---|---|---|---|---|---|---|---|---|---|---|---|---|---|---|---|
| | | 0 | 1 | 2 | 3 | 4 | 0 | 1 | 2 | 3 | 4 | 0 | 1 | 2 | 3 | 4 |
| 17-18 | 55 | 14 | 5 | 25 | 35 | 21 | 22 | 3 | 14 | 32 | 29 | 29 | 1 | 11 | 24 | 35 |
| 19 | 52 | 5 | 2 | 10 | 58 | 25 | 7 | — | 5 | 48 | 40 | 7 | — | 5 | 32 | 56 |
| 20 | 45 | 2 | 2 | 4 | 40 | 52 | 4 | — | 2 | 24 | 70 | 4 | 2 | — | 24 | 70 |
| 21 | 37 | | | 2 | 27 | 71 | | | | 19 | 81 | | | | 10 | 90 |
| 22 | 24 | | | | 12 | 88 | | | | 12 | 88 | | | | 8 | 92 |
| 23 | 26 | | | | 4 | 96 | | | | | 100 | | | | | 100 |
| 24+ | 136 | | | | | 100 | | | | | | | | | | |

Total = 375

**LOWER EXTREMITY**

| Age | No. | Femur (dist.) Stages | | | | | Tibia (prox.) Stages | | | | | Fibula (prox.) Stages | | | | |
|---|---|---|---|---|---|---|---|---|---|---|---|---|---|---|---|---|
| | | 0 | 1 | 2 | 3 | 4 | 0 | 1 | 2 | 3 | 4 | 0 | 1 | 2 | 3 | 4 |
| 17-18 | 55 | 16 | 2 | 3 | 18 | 61 | 2 | 2 | 7 | 23 | 66 | 14 | — | 3 | 12 | 71 |
| 19 | 52 | 4 | — | 1 | 9 | 86 | 1 | — | 1 | 17 | 81 | 4 | — | 6 | 4 | 86 |
| 20 | 45 | | | 2 | 9 | 89 | | | | 13 | 87 | | | 2 | | 98 |
| 21 | 37 | | | | 8 | 92 | | | | 5 | 95 | | | | 5 | 95 |
| 22 | 24 | | | | | 100 | | | | 4 | 96 | | | | | 100 |
| 23 | 26 | | | | | | | | | | 100 | | | | | |
| 24+ | 136 | | | | | | | | | | | | | | | |

Total = 375

*From T.W. McKern and T.D. Stewart, *Skeletal Age Change in Young American Males*, 1957. Courtesy of Headquarters Quartermaster Research and Development Command, Natik, Massachusetts.

TABLE VI

EPIPHYSES OF THE ILIAC CREST: AGE DISTRIBUTION OF STAGES OF UNION.*

| Age | No. | 0 | 1 | 2 | 3 | 4 |
|-----|-----|----|----|----|----|-----|
| 17 | 10 | 40 | 10 | 10 | 40 | — |
| 18 | 45 | 18 | 16 | 26 | 20 | 20 |
| 19 | 52 | 5 | 4 | 27 | 28 | 36 |
| 20 | 45 | 2 | 6 | 4 | 24 | 64 |
| 21 | 37 | — | 5 | 8 | 13 | 74 |
| 22 | 24 | — | — | 4 | 4 | 92 |
| 23 | 26 | — | — | — | — | 100 |

| Age | No. | 0 | 1 | 2 | 3 | 4 |
|-----|-----|----|----|----|----|-----|
| 17 | 10 | 50 | 10 | 20 | 10 | 10 |
| 18 | 45 | 52 | 13 | 12 | 12 | 11 |
| 19 | 52 | 14 | 24 | 13 | 17 | 32 |
| 20 | 45 | 11 | 13 | 9 | 23 | 44 |
| 21 | 37 | 10 | 6 | 3 | 25 | 56 |
| 22 | 24 | 4 | — | — | 4 | 92 |
| 23 | 26 | — | — | 4 | 4 | 92 |
| 24-25 | 27 | — | — | — | — | 100 |

*From T.W. McKern and T.D. Stewart, *Skeletal Age Changes in Young American Males*, 1957. Courtesy of Headquarters Quartermaster Research and Development Command, Natik, Massachusetts.

TABLE VII

AGE DISTRIBUTION OF THE STAGES OF UNION FOR THE MEDIAL CLAVICULAR EPIPHYSIS, IN PERCENT.*

| age | no. | 0 | 1 | 2 | 3 | 4 |
|-----|-----|----|----|----|----|-----|
| 17 | 10 | — | — | — | — | — |
| 18 | 45 | 90 | 10 | — | — | — |
| 19 | 52 | 79 | 13 | 8 | — | — |
| 20 | 45 | 69 | 28 | 11 | 2 | — |
| 21 | 37 | 36 | 43 | 13 | 8 | — |
| 22 | 24 | 4 | 27 | 39 | 30 | — |
| 23 | 26 | — | 11 | 43 | 13 | 8 |
| 24-25 | 27 | — | 3 | 10 | 52 | 37 |
| 26-27 | 25 | — | — | — | 36 | 64 |
| 28-29 | 18 | — | — | — | 31 | 69 |
| 30 | 11 | — | — | — | 9 | 91 |
| 31 | 54 | — | — | — | — | 100 |

*From T.W. McKern and T.D. Stewart, *Skeletal Age Changes in Young American Males*, 1957. Courtesy of Headquarters Quartermaster Research and Development Command, Natik, Massachusetts.

TABLE VIII
ORDER OF FUSION OF EPIPHYSES.*

| | |
|---|---|
| At 4 years | In females, fusion of greater tubercle to head of humerus. |
| At 5 years | In males, fusion of greater tubercle to head of humerus. |
| At 7 years | In females, fusion of rami of ischium and pubis. |
| At 9 years | In males, fusion of rami of ischium and pubis. |
| At 13 years | In females, fusion of ilium, ischium, and pubis at acetabulum. |
| | In males, fusion of trochlea to lateral epicondyle. |
| At 14 years | In females, fusion of olecranon, upper radius, head of femur, distal tibia, and fibula. |
| At 15 years | In females, fusion of medial epicondyle, proximal tibia. |
| | In males, fusion of ilium, ischium, and pubis at acetabulum. |
| At 16 years | In males, fusion of lower conjoint epiphysis of humerus, medial epicondyle, olecranon, head of radius. |
| At 17 years | In both sexes, fusion of acromian of scapula. |
| | In females, fusion of upper conjoint epiphysis of humerus, distal ulna, distal femur, proximal fibula. |
| | In males, fusion of head of femur, greater trochanter, distal tibia and fibula. |
| At 18 years | In females, fusion of distal radius. |
| | In males, fusion of proximal tibia. |
| At 19 years | In males, fusion of upper conjoint epiphysis of humerus, distal radius and ulna, distal femur, proximal fibula. |
| At 20 years | In both sexes, fusion of iliac crest. |
| | In males, fusion of tuber ischii. |
| At 21 years | In both sexes, clavicle. |
| | In females, fusion of tuber ischii. |

*Modified from H. Flecker, Roentgenographic observations, *Journal of Anatomy,* 67:118-164, 1932/33.

this suture closes rapidly and completely but no evidence has been presented heretofore on the terminal data" (McKern and Stewart, 1957). This last is, then, a reliable indicator of the attainment of at least the age of twenty-one if fusion has occurred.

TABLE IX
AGE DISTRIBUTION OF STAGES OF CLOSURE IN THE BASILAR SUTURE, IN PERCENT*.

| Age | No. | 0 | 1 | 2 | 3 | 4 |
|---|---|---|---|---|---|---|
| 17-18 | 55 | 3 | 2 | 7 | 10 | 78 |
| 19 | 52 | — | — | — | 3 | 97 |
| 20 | 45 | — | — | — | 2 | 98 |
| 21 | 37 | — | — | — | — | 100 |
| 22 | 24 | — | — | — | — | 100 |

*From T.W. McKern and T.D. Stewart, *Skeletal Age Changes in Young American Males,* 1957. Courtesy of Headquarters Quartermaster Research and Development Command, Natik, Massachusetts.

McKern and Stewart (1957) point out that the main eruption period for third year molars is seventeen to twenty-two years, but note that some unerupted and erupting third molars are found as late as thirty-five years.

It has been shown (McKern and Stewart, 1957) that, rather than emphasize complete skeletal coverage, reliable age estimates can better be derived from the combined maturational activity of a small number of critical growth areas. In other words, the age status of a given skeleton can be predicted from the sum of the scores for the epiphyseal activity in the following *critical* areas:

> medial end of clavicle
> iliac crest
> distal end, femur
> head, femur
> head, humerus
> medial epicondyle, humerus
> distal end, radius
> lateral joints, sacrum
> 3-4 joint, sacrum

The pubic symphysis is formed by the meeting of the right and left innominate bones at the midline in front. This area has proven to be the best for age estimation in young adults after closure of the various epiphyses is completed until about the age of forty-five years. Aging is done by comparison of the face of the pubic symphysis with standard casts of symphyses known to be characteristic of certain ages. This technique is more reliable for males than females due to less regular change and more rapid degeneration in females, probably due to trauma to this area associated with childbirth. The resulting age estimate is correspondingly less precise.

The technique described by McKern and Stewart (1957) was established based upon bones of young American males whose bodies were identified and repatriated following the Korean War. Because of the sample composition, their technique is limited to use in relatively young males. It is a modification of Todd's (1920) method which Brooks (1955) has shown to have certain deficiencies.

McKern and Stewart (1957) consider three components of the pubic symphysis each divided into five developmental stages.

### I. Dorsal Plateau

    0. Dorsal margin absent.
    1. Slight margin formation appears in the middle third of dorsal border.
    2. Dorsal margin extends along the entire dorsal border.

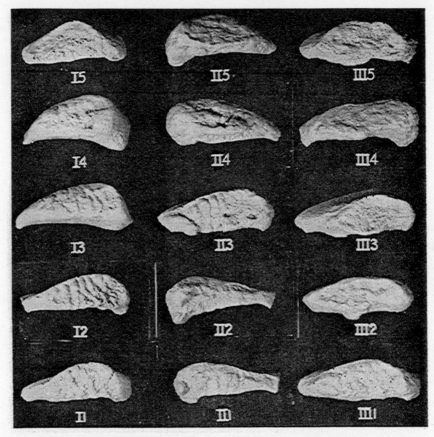

Figure 14: Photograph of the casts of pubic symphyses of McKern and Stewart used to estimate age in adult males.

3. Filling in of grooves and resorption of ridges to form a beginning plateau in the middle third of the dorsal demiface.
4. The plateau, still exhibiting vestages of billowing, extends over most of the dorsal demiface.
5. Billowing disappears completely and the surface of the entire demiface becomes flat and slightly granulated.

## II. *Ventral Rampart*

0. Ventral beveling absent.
1. Ventral beveling present only at superior extremity of ventral border.
2. Bevel extends inferiorly along ventral border.
3. Ventral rampart begins by means of bony extensions from either or both extremities.

4. Rampart extensive but gaps still evident along the earlier ventral border, most evident in the upper two-thirds.
5. Rampart complete.

### III. Symphyseal Rim

0. Rim absent.
1. Partial dorsal rim present, usually at the superior end of the dorsal margin. It is round and smooth in texture and elevated above the symphyseal surface.
2. Dorsal rim complete and ventral rim beginning to form. No particular beginning site.
3. Rim complete. Enclosed symphyseal surface finely grained in texture and irregular or undulating in appearance.
4. Rim begins to break down. Face becomes smooth and flat and rim no longer round but sharply defined. Some evidence of lipping on the ventral edge.
5. Further breakdown of the rim, particularly along the superior ventral edge, with rarefaction of the symphyseal face. Also, disintegration and erratic ossification along the ventral rim.

All three components progress steadily through the five stages as age increases. Each component is scored separately to determine the grade into which it falls. When all three components have produced grade scores, these are added together and, with the resultant number, one enters a table to determine the age and standard deviation appropriate to that score. For example, if the scores produced for the three components are as follows:

$$I. \quad 4$$
$$II. \quad 3$$
$$III. \quad \underline{4}$$
$$11$$

the total score, 11, would be sought in Table X. The score 11 indicates a mean age of 29.18, with a standard deviation of 3.33, which means there is a 66 percent likelihood that the (correct) age is within $\pm$ 6.66 years. The observed range in ages for this score is 23 to 39 years.

Using methods similar to those of McKern and Stewart, Gilbert and McKern (1973) have devised a method for aging female skeletons using the pubic symphysis. Gilbert and McKern also use three components divided into five phases. The components and grades are described (Gilbert and McKern, 1973) as follows:

Component I
0. Ridges and furrows very distinct, ridges are billowed, dorsal margins undefined.

TABLE X
TABLE OF AGE ESTIMATION TO BE USED WITH CASTS OF THE MALE
PUBIC SYMPHYSIS.*

| Score | Age | S.D. | Range |
|-------|------|------|-------|
| 0 | 17.29 | .49 | -17 |
| 1-2 | 19.04 | .79 | 17-20 |
| 3 | 19.79 | .85 | 18-21 |
| 4-5 | 20.84 | 1.13 | 18-23 |
| 6-7 | 22.42 | .99 | 20-24 |
| 8-9 | 24.14 | 1.93 | 22-28 |
| 10 | 26.05 | 1.87 | 23-28 |
| 11-13 | 29.18 | 3.33 | 23-39 |
| 14 | 35.84 | 3.89 | 29- |
| 15 | 41.00 | 6.22 | 36- |

*From T.W. McKern and T.D. Stewart, *Skeletal Age Changes in Young American Males,* 1957. Courtesy of Headquarters Quartermaster Research and Development Command, Natik, Massachusetts.

1. Ridges begin to flatten, furrows fill in, and a flat dorsal margin begins in middle-third of demiface.
2. Dorsal demiface spreads ventrally, becomes wider as flattening continues, dorsal margin extends superiorly and inferiorly.
3. Dorsal demiface is quite smooth, margin may be narrow or indistinct from face.
4. Demiface becomes complete and unbroken, is broad and very fine grained, may exhibit vertical billowing.
5. Demiface becomes pitted and irregular through rarefaction.

Component II

0. Ridges and furrows very distinct. The entire demiface is beveled up toward the dorsal demiface.
1. Beginning inferiorly, the furrows of the ventral demiface begin to fill in, forming an expanding beveled rampart, the lateral edge of which is a distinct, curved line extending the length of the symphysis.
2. Fill in of furrows and expansion of demiface continue from both superior and inferior ends, rampart spreads laterally along its ventral edge.
3. All but about one third of the ventral demiface is filled in with fine-grained bone.
4. The ventral rampart presents a broad, complete fine-grained surface from the pubic crest to the inferior ramus.
5. Ventral rampart may begin to break down assuming a very pitted and perhaps cancellous appearance through rarefaction.

Component III

0. The rim is absent.
1. The rim begins in the middle-third of the dorsal face.
2. The dorsal part of the symphyseal rim is complete.

3. The rim extends from the superior and inferior ends of the symphysis until all but about one third of the ventral aspect is complete.
4. The symphyseal is complete.
5. The ventral margin of the dorsal demiface may break down so that gaps appear in the rim, or it may round off so that there is no longer a clear dividing line between the dorsal demiface and the ventral rampart."

The score is used to enter Table XI to obtain the age.

TABLE XI

TABLE OF AGE ESTIMATION TO BE USED WITH CASTS OF THE FEMALE PUBIC SYMPHYSIS.*

| Score | Mean Age | Age Range | S.D. |
|-------|----------|-----------|------|
| 0 | 16.00 | 14-18 | 2.00 |
| 1 | 19.80 | 13-24 | 2.76 |
| 2 | 20.15 | 16-25 | 4.97 |
| 3 | 21.50 | 18-25 | 5.36 |
| 4-5 | 26.00 | 22-29 | 5.70 |
| 6 | 29.62 | 25-36 | 6.86 |
| 7-8 | 32.00 | 23-39 | 5.54 |
| 9 | 33.00 | 22-40 | 9.00 |
| 10-11 | 36.90 | 30-47 | 7.73 |
| 12 | 39.00 | 32-52 | 8.54 |
| 13 | 47.75 | 44-54 | 7.57 |
| 14-15 | 55.71 | 52-59 | 8.07 |

*From B.M. Gilbert and T.W. McKern, A method for aging the female Os pubis, *Am J Phys Anthropol, 38*:31-38, 1973.

As is readily apparent by examination of the tables, the method used to age female pubic symphyses has much wider standard deviations than that used for males and, therefore, less likelihood of an absolutely accurate estimation of age for female skeletons. The reason for the sexual difference is attributed to childbirth trauma to the pubic symphysis in females (Gilbert, 1973).

**Older Adult**

Skeletal age beyond about forty-five years is the most difficult to estimate with precision. The tendency toward degeneration of the teeth and skeleton which began in the young adult continues, but without regularity. By this age arthritis has almost always appeared in the vertebrae, but its severity is not a reliable age indicator since it varies with the individual. The teeth will generally exhibit wear facets, although the degree of wear is a function of diet and individual habits. The apices of the cusps may only be blunted,

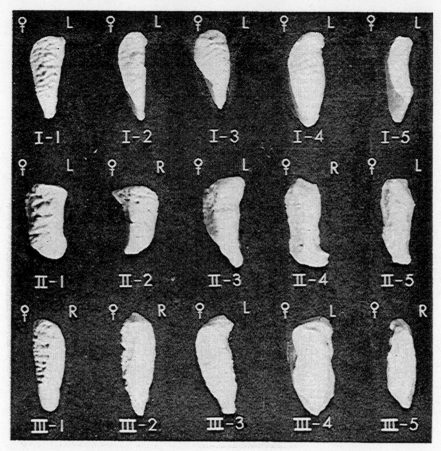

Figure 15. Photograph of the casts of pubic symphyses used in the Gilbert and McKern method to estimate age in adult females.

or the tooth crown may be worn to the gumline. By the middle forties one or more teeth are often lost through accident or disease, although this again varies with the individual. One individual may have a full complement of thirty-two teeth at age sixty, while another member of the same population may be completely edentulous. No precise method of age determination by gross inspection is known for the older adult skeleton. Microscopic examination of thin sections of adult bone will provide a precise estimation of age in this older age group.

Kerley's (1965) methods for aging older skeletons (or younger, for that matter) involves examining thin sections from the midshafts of long bones under a low powered microscope looking for structural changes associated with age in the outer third of the cortex. The changes can be used to age bone to at least age ninety-five, with accuracy of ± 10 years for all specimens and ± 5 years in 87.3 percent of cases examined. Kerley notes that accuracy is highest in younger specimens.

Bone sections are examined for:
1. the number of osteones
2. the number of fragments of old osteones
3. the percentage of circumferential lamellar bone
4. the number of non-Haversian canals.

Items one and two increase with advancing age, three and four decrease with age, disappearing completely around age fifty-five. Charts for age estimation and a sample data form are available in the original article.

McKern and Stewart suggest that

the innominate bone is the most critical area of the skeleton. The combination of pubic symphysis, iliac crest, ischial tuberosity, and ramus will immediately place the skeleton in its proper age group. If the pubic symphysis, which is a good indicator of age over much of the life span, is damaged or missing, the remaining age areas of the innominate will give the observer a clue as to his next most reliable source of age information. For example, if the iliac crest suggests an adolescent, the basilar suture and the epiphyses of the elbows can be turned to for both clarification and supportive evidence. On the other hand, if the iliac crest exhibits the pattern of a young adult, the epiphyses of the shoulders, wrists, and knee joints as well as the medial end of the clavicle will help establish an exact age estimate (McKern and Stewart, 1957).

Schranz (1959) calls attention to a method of age estimation more widely used at this time in Europe than in the United States, based on age changes in the trabeculae of the proximal humerus. Schranz combines his own work with that of other authorities (Wacholz, 1894; Bruno, 1934; Hansen, 1954) and produces the following comments on the age changes:

15 to 16 years: The metaphysis is cartilaginous.

17 to 18 years: Union is beginning between the diaphysis and the epiphysis. The internal structure of the diaphysis is archlike.

19 to 20 years: Union of the epiphysis and the diaphysis is nearly complete. Internally, the structure of the epiphysis is arranged radially, while that of the diaphysis remains arched.

21 to 22 years: Union of the two parts is complete. The internal structure remains the same.

23 to 25 years: The internal structure of the epiphysis is less radial. The diaphyseal structure remains arched. The medullary cavity is widely separated from the surgical neck.

26 to 30 years: The arrangement of the trabeculae in the epiphysis is becoming less radial, that of the diaphysis remains arched. The medul-

lary cavity approaches, but has not yet reached the surgical neck of the bone.

31 to 40 years: The internal structure of the epiphysis is no longer radial, while that of the diaphysis has become more columnar. The medullary cavity approaches the surgical neck.

41 to 50 years: The columnar structure of the diaphysis is discontinuous. The cone of the medullary cavity reaches the surgical neck with occasional lacunae in the epiphyseal structure at the epiphyseal line.

51 to 60 years: The lacunae become more common, and pea-size cavities appear in the trabeculae of the epiphysis.

61 to 74 years: The cortex of the bone is thin, and externally it is roughened. The characteristic features of the structure of the diaphysis disappear. The cavity of the medulla reaches the epiphyseal line. Bean-sized or larger lacunae appear in the trabeculae of the epiphysis.

74 plus-years: The tuberculum majus is much less prominent and little spongy tissue remains in the medullary cavity.

Schranz cautions that x-ray pictures are not very useful for estimation of the condition of the trabeculae and it is necessary to saw the bone lengthwise for visual examination. He also notes that it is necessary to know the sex of the individual from whom the bone came since the age changes occur at different times in the sexes. Females are about two years advanced over males at puberty, five years at maturity, and seven to ten years in old age. Schranz also notes that atypical cases do occur, but only rarely. These involve premature appearance of lacunae. Other criteria will provide a true age estimate in these cases. The bone must be thoroughly macerated to permit accurate observation of details of the internal structure.

## RACE IDENTIFICATION

Race is difficult to determine from the human skeleton, both due to the lack of definite racial criteria in many cases, and also due to the lack of precise definitions of what a race is and how it is recognized. Like age, race in the skeleton is no more easily recognized than from the physiognamy of the living. In many cases there is little doubt that an individual belonged to the Negro, Caucasian, or Mongoloid racial stock, but for other individuals the classification is uncertain. In cases where an individual is a blend of two or more racial stocks the problem can become exceedingly difficult (Gill, 1976). With experience, it is sometimes possible to state that a given skeleton resembles a northern European rather than just Caucasian. This latter is very chancy due to the variation which occurs normally in

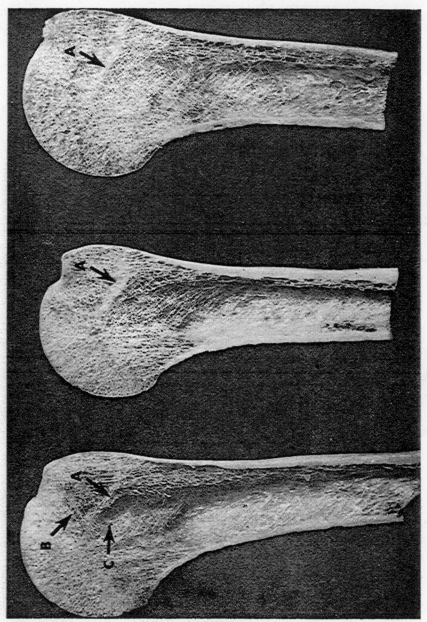

Figure 16: Internal structure of the humerus in cross section. The persistent epiphyseal line is indicated at point A, although all three bones are from individuals in excess of fifty years of age. In the specimen on the left, point B indicates a lacuna in the structure of the epiphysis and point C shows the medullary cavity at the epiphyseal line. According to these and other characteristics of this bone, this individual was in the 61 to 74 year age range using the system of Schranz.

Caucasians, or any other racial stock. Still, a very tall Caucasian whose face comes to a vertical ridge in the midline does not resemble a Mediterranean type.

Here is a very brief summary of the traits which tend to distinguish Negroes from Caucasians from Mongoloids.

## Negro

A rounded forehead, "pedomorphic skull" with few knobs, and light muscle markings characterize the Negro skull, but the most diagnostic feature is the guttered nasal sill. Instead of the sharp ridge of the nasal sill usually found in Caucasians and often in Mongoloids, the Negro nasal sill is usually rounded. In addition, a "gutter" or trough is often found running laterally about 5 mm inside the nostril. The guttered nasal sill tends to persist in the skulls of Negroes who are known to be mixed with Caucasians or Mongoloids, as is often the case with American Negroes. Another persistant trait in skulls of phenotypic Negroes is alveolar prognathism. The part of the jaw in which the roots of the teeth are imbedded, the alveolar process, protrudes forward of a line perpendicular to the Frankfort horizontal plane and passing through glabella. Prognathism may also be found in some American Indian skulls, although usually to a lesser degree than in Negroes. It is almost never present in Caucasians. Negro orbits tend to be square, and the nasal aperture flared. The palate may be approximately rectangular, or narrow and pointed. The skull of Negroes tends to be long (meso– or dolichocranic) rather than round, a trait which may be modified by racial mixture.

## Caucasian

The Caucasian face comes to a sharp vertical line in the sagittal plane, producing a "hatchet face." The malars recede, and the skull tends to be long rather than round. The nasal root depression is usually well marked. The superior ends of the nasal bones often seem to disappear beneath an overhanging projection at glabella. This is typical of northern European males and less so of Mediteraneans and females in general. The Caucasian face is orthognathous, meaning that it recedes behind a line perpendicular to the Frankfort horizontal passing through glabella. Muscle markings may be pronounced. The orbits tend to be rounded, the nasal aperture narrow and elongated. The palate is usually triangular. The postcranial bones are usually heavy compared to other races.

## Mongoloid (Including American Indians)

The Mongoloid skull is often, but not always, round rather than long. The malars project making the face appear flat. Muscle markings may or may not be pronounced. The diagnostic trait from Mongoloids is the shape of the incisor teeth. The incisors, especially the maxillary central incisors, are often "shovel shaped," that is, have a ridge of enamel on the lingual surface running vertically on the mesial and lateral edges. This trait may occur also in other races, but rarely does. The face may display some alveolar prognathism, but not usually as marked as in Negroes. The orbits may be roughly triangular. The nasal aperture tends to be rounded. The palate is parabolic or horseshoe shaped.

Study of the foregoing features of different races, and examination of a number of skulls of each race, is the only way to learn to detect the marks of race in the skull. Some of the features may not be present in a given skull although that skull belonged to a member of a race which should show those features. Similarly, there are other features useful in race estimation which are part of the mental picture acquired by the investigator through experience, but are difficult to codify and set down on paper. For instance, Negroes often seem to show crenulations on the occlusal surfaces of the molar teeth, although this has not been demonstrated conclusively. Just as it is difficult to say why you believe certain people look Jewish or Italian, so it is difficult to estimate race in the skeleton, more so for some races than others. To test this, estimate race in the faces of the people you see one day, then check yourself by asking them about their ethnic ancestry. You will find that you are wrong discouragingly often, particularly when you try to estimate subdivisions such as Nordic, Alpine, etc. You will usually be right as long as you stick to the three major stocks. You will find that you can improve with practice.

Howells (1970) presented a method for race identification from human crania using statistical analysis, as did Giles and Elliot (1962). Neither method is without problems (Birkby, 1966), but may be useful in some cases when the inspection methods outlined here do not produce satisfactory results.

## ESTIMATION OF SEX

In order to estimate sex from the skeleton, it is useful to know something about the population from which a skeleton is derived, since there are regional and racial variations in the development of sexual characteristics in the skeleton (Stewart, 1947:128). Accurate sex estimation is also contingent upon the bones available to the observer, since some bones show a good deal more about the sex of the deceased than others. For instance, in the pelvis, a great number of objective observations have been described for sex assessment (Krogman, 1962). Other bones can aid in the assessment of sex to varying degrees. Bones such as the clavicle, the calcaneus, or the radius and ulna may in some cases be useful. Other bones, such as those of the fingers, vertebrae, ribs, etc., have provided almost no useful information as far as the determination of sex. This is not to say that such information will not someday be produced, only that it has not yet. It is here that the mental template of the observer becomes crucial, since he will have formed an idea of the size and morphology appropriate to each sex in a normal individual.

Bones of immature individuals (preadolescent) are almost useless in sex determination due to the fact that the secondary sexual characteristics do not appear in the bone except under the influence of estrogens and androgens at puberty (Weiss, 1972). Preadolescent children show very little dimorphism in the dimensions or configuration of the body outside the external genitalia. However, it may be true that there are characteristics to be observed in these bones. Boucher (1955, 1957) has observed sexual differences in the pelvis of infants, although her technique requires that the body either be intact and that measurements and estimations be based on X rays, or the use of skeletons with the cartilage intact. There are a number of bones in the human skeleton which offer intuitive clues to the experienced observer. Examples of this sort include the robustness and size of the clavicle, although it seems to have very little reliable measureable sexual dimorphism, while the sternum is of variable reliability, often being excellent. Each observer develops his own favorite criteria for sex estimation. While one observer will first examine the skull for mastoid size and muscular relief, another will look first for prominence of the brow ridge and sharpness of the orbital rim. Neither is incorrect, although one observer may prove to be more reliable than another because of the particular configuration he seeks before he is satisfied that his determination is accurate. This section will make the observer aware of some of the criteria to be observed from which he is to form his considered opinion. Most sexual criteria in bone are a matter of degree rather than absolute difference. This being the case, it is essential that the student of sex determination become thoroughly acquainted with the fairly typical male skeleton and the fairly typical female skeleton. Handling and experience with these bones will commit to his memory the mental template referred to above. Without this it is impossible to be accurate to any degree since absolute criteria seldom exist. It is necessary for the observer to have an internal awareness of the degree of variation which may be anticipated in each trait, and its variation from one population to another.

## The Pelvis

The most reliable part of the human skeleton for the assessment of sex is the pelvis. The best criteria for the assessment of sex are two angles of the innominate, the sciatic and the subpubic. In a single innominate the entire sciatic angle is present, and half of the subpubic. In the female, the two angles are much more obtuse than in the male. A "rule of thumb" for the estimation of sex from these angles is: Either angle in the female approximates the angle between the thumb and index finger when they are fully extended; in the male, the angles are more nearly like that between the index and second fingers when they are widely separated in the "V for victory" sign of Winston Churchill. If both innominates are present for an individual, the subpubic angle can be restored by approximating the two faces of the pubic symphysis. However, very often only one innominate survives. In this case, examination of the ischiopubic ramus may suffice. In the female, this element will almost always be concave, while in the male it is usually straight or convex. The complete angle can be reconstructed mentally by observing the angle made by the face of the pubic symphysis relative to the inferior border of the ischiopubic ramus.

Bass gave a different thumb rule for the subpubic angle and observed that: "when the index finger is held perpendicular to the pubic symphysis the thumb can be moved only slightly, if at all, with a male innominate, but has ample room for movement on a female innominate" (Bass, 1971). He said the same rule applies to the sciatic angle.

According to Phenice (1967), three characteristics of the female pubis and ischiopubic ramus serve to distinguish the sexes in over 95 percent of the cases. The *ventral arc* is a slightly elevated ridge of bone which takes a course across the ventral surface of the female pubis. In the male there is no ventral arc, but a ridge may appear on the ventral surface. A ridge on the male pubis rarely appears as the ventral arc of the female. This is particularly true if the pubis is properly oriented for observation, with the ventral surface directly facing the observer and the symphyseal surface in an a-p plane. The *subpubic concavity* is a lateral curvature inferior to the symphysis in the female. This is best observed on the dorsal surface of the bone. In the male there is rarely a subpubic concavity. The medial aspect of the ischiopubic ramus in the female presents a ridge or a narrow surface immediately below the symphyseal surface, while in the male the medial aspect of the ischiopubic ramus is a broad surface.

Genovés (1962) suggested the use of the following for sex estimation from the pelvis:

1. size of the middle of the pubis from the midpoint of the anterior border of the pubic symphysis to the nearest medial border of the obturator foramen—males are smaller
2. the least inferior breadth of the ilium. This is the least distance between the supra-acetabular point and the anterior border of the

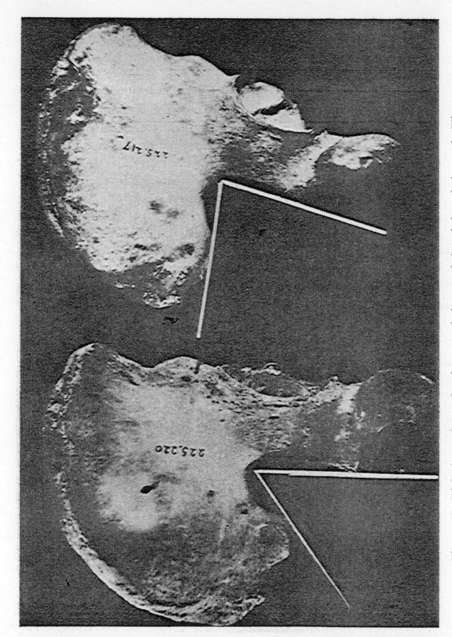

Figure 17: Right innominate showing sexual characteristics of the sciatic notch. The one on the left is male, on the right a female.

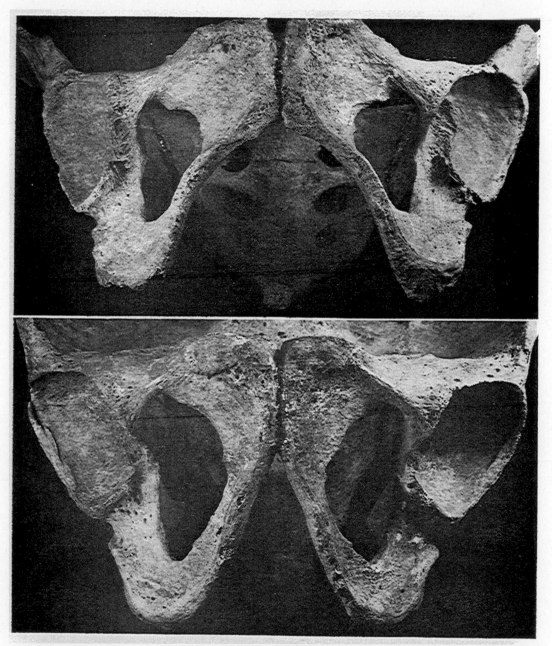

Figure 18: The subpubic angle of the pelvis, with a pronounced female above and a typical male below.

sciatic notch—males are broader

3. maximum vertical diameter of the acetabulum. This is taken approximately perpendicular to the maximum horizontal diameter, that is, perpendicular to the ascending ramus of the pubis—the male diameter is greater

4. ridge from the anterior border of the auricular surface leading directly to the anterior border or apex of the sciatic notch—females lack this ridge

5. relative massiveness of the superior area of the medial portion of the pubis or the pubic crest—males are more massive.

The preauricular sulcus is a groove occurring immediately lateral to the sacroiliac joint on the anterior surface of the ilium. In a study of the sulcus, Houghton (1974) defined two forms of the groove which he calls GP, or groove of pregnancy, and GL, or the imprint of a strong ligament on the

Figure 19: Left sacroiliac joint of a female pelvis. The arrow indicates a preauricular sulcus of the sort defined by Houghton as a GP, or groove of pregnancy.

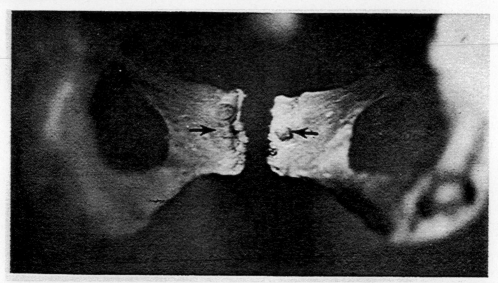

Figure 20: Dorsal view of the same pelvis shown in figure 19 showing parturition pits.

bone which occurs in both the male and the female pelvis. He said that GP appears to be formed by the coalescence of a series of pits. GL is a narrow, short, straight-edged (sometimes roughened) and shallow groove. He noted that the essential feature of GL is the even, flat floor of the groove. "In distinguishing between GP and GL it is most helpful to ask the question 'Is this groove unequivocally GP?' If the answer is 'No', if the pits or scoops on the bone are not unequivocally present, the groove is GL." (Houghton, 1974). Obviously, a GP can occur only in females while GL is the variant which may occur in either sex. This eliminates some confusion which has been associated with the meaning of the preauricular sulcus.

Another kind of pitting occurring in the innominate is parturition or postpubic pits. This is one or usually more deep pits found on the posterior surface of the pubic bone roughly parallel to the edge of the pubic symphysis. Angel (1969) and Stewart (1957, 1970) agree that these pits are associated with childbirth trauma and therefore are diagnostic of female pelves.

Nemeskeri (1972) has published a five-stage scheme for estimation of the number of pregnancies a female has experienced. The method is based upon observed degenerative changes in pubic symphyses in adult female innominates which are assumed to be attributable to pregnancy. Nemeskeri observed that the number of pregnancies he attributed to each stage remain to be verified by control investigations in autopsy material.

Nemeskeri's (1972) five stages are:

    1. Sharp sites of muscle insertion extending spirally downward and separated

by pits at the anterior medial margin of the pubis (1-2 childbirths).

2. Low, well-defined, pearllike exostoses along the downward extending lines of muscle insertion; at the posterior surface of the pubis there are already very distinct transverse impressions and several haemorrhagic pits (3-4 childbirths).

3. Initially sharply defined lines of muscle insertion on the anterior and posterior surfaces of the pubis become thicker and labiated and the pits between them become deeper; the haemorrhagic pits may merge and form cysts (4-5 childbirths).

4. Multiple labiated and thickened lines of muscle insertion with exostoses appearing coalesced in the form of thick protuberances; the coalesced cysts forming a uniform haemorrhagic cavity at the posterior surface, the surface being quite irregular (6-8 childbirths).

5. Pubic region already so highly deformed and differentiated, that a further classification into stages is not possible (more than 8-10 childbirths).

Ullrich (1975) modified the five stages of Nemeskeri somewhat, placing emphasis only on the posterior face of the pubis. The modifications of Ullrich are also impressions and are not necessarily more reliable than those of Nemeskeri. As far as knowledge of parturation changes at the pubic symphysis now goes, it is probably true that the changes noted in the form of pitting and degeneration are associated with childbirth trauma and marked changes do indicate that such trauma has occurred repeatedly. Whether or not the degrees of change are directly correlated with the number of pregnancies a woman has undergone is uncertain since a particularly difficult delivery might mark the pubis as much as several less traumatic ones. Still, it seems likely that marked degeneration in that area would support a hypothesis of the female being a multipara, while a pubis which is only slightly marked would suggest a woman who has had only one or a few births. No doubt in time appropriate studies will be made which will clarify the question.

Ullrich (1975) also drew attention to changes in the sacroiliac region. He suggested that the preauricular sulcus becomes more extensive and marked with succeeding births and noted degenerative changes on the anterior auricular margin of the sacrum which he believed to be correlated with expansion of the sacroiliac joint and trauma to the ligamentous insertions during delivery. Whatever the relationship between the number of births and the degree of trauma, the presence of degenerative changes at these points seems to be a reliable indicator of the female sex. Ullrich (1975) wrote an excellent summary of changes associated with pregnancy and childbirth in the dorsal aspect of the pubis and the sacroiliac region.

Inspection data of Olivier (1969) included several observations. In men, the body of the pubis is generally triangular; its inferior ramus is convex downwards; the symphysis is higher; the obturator foramen is ovoid; the ischia are closer together; all bony parts are thicker and heavier. In women, the body of the pubis is usually rectangular with small fossae on its anterior surface near the symphysis; the inferior ramus of the pubis is concave downward; the symphysis is lower; the obturator foramen is rather triangular; the conjoint (or ischio pubic) rami and the ischial tuberosities are turned down and out.

Sex estimation from the sacrum is, in our experience, risky. In general, the sacrum is more curved in males when viewed in profile, the shape of the bone is long relative to its height in males while it is more nearly square in females, and the ala are wider relative to the width of the articular surface of the first sacral body. Anderson (1962) suggested that, in females, the width of the articular area of the first sacral body is equal in width to each ala, while in males the body is wider than the ala. This is often not true, but when it occurs it surely indicates a female.

## The Skull

After the pelvis, the skull is the most important area for sex estimation. A number of marks of sex exist upon the skull, but a certain amount of caution must be used since the degree of sexual dimorphism evident there varies both between and within major racial divisions of man.

Generally, the marks of sex on the skull may be summarized by saying that males are more robust than females. If smoothness and roundness characterize the female form in general, and squareness and roughness the male, the same may be said for the osseous skull. However, there are subdivisions of mankind where no skull exists which would be classified "male" in another, more robust division. For example, the prehistoric American Indians of the archeological group called *Fourche Maline,* an Archaic group from eastern Oklahoma, are exceedingly gracile to the extent that familiarity with the whole range of skulls is necessary before the observer can tell which hallmarks of sex exist in the skulls and to what degree they are expressed (McWilliams, 1970). No individual in the collection approaches the degree of robusticity of the typical female Arikara, for instance (Bass, 1971). At the same time, an observer familiar only with Fourche Maline skulls would typify most Arikara skulls as exaggerately male. The innominates in both these groups readily identify males and females in the usual way. The conclusion is that the innominate is a consistent indicator of sex regardless of the features of the skull. Often one has only the skull to assess sex from, however, so it is good to learn those features of the skull which indicate sex. Usually estimation of sex based on cranial criteria will be biologically correct. A precautionary note: there is no substitute for familiarity with a typical male and a typical female skull. You should either be shown such a specimen by a qualified person, or if you have a number of skulls to examine, you will find that they are bimodally distributed on the basis of the traits discussed below. Most of the robust group will be male and the gracile ones female. If all the features mentioned are considered there will be few which are intermediate. Beware of skulls from biological supply houses. These skulls are almost always of individuals from India, a region where sexual dimorphism is often very low and the number of intermediate forms high.

### Frontal Bone

A feature of moderate reliability, males usually have paired frontal bosses while females have only a single boss in the midline. This feature is readily observable in the living people around you, and its variability may be seen.

### Orbital Rim Sharpness

This feature is usually reliable. The rim of the orbit in males is rounded and dull to the touch, while that of females usually has a distinct sharp edge. Examine for this characteristic by running a fingertip around the rim just inside the opening.

### Size of the Mastoid Process

The mastoid process of the temporal bone is usually larger in the male than in the female. The variation female to male ideally, is comparable to the terminal segment of the little finger compared to the terminal segment of the thumb. Another way to examine this feature: The mastoid process of the male usually projects below the bottom of the skull while it does not in the female. The reliability of this diagnostic feature is only moderate and varies among different human populations. In general, the more robust the population, the more reliable the dimorphism in the mastoid process.

### Gonial Angle

The gonial angle of the mandible is usually more nearly a right angle in males, more of an obtuse angle in females. In other words, a male mandible has more of a marked "back corner" than a female mandible. This trait can be examined readily by observing the gonial angles of your associates. The reliability is moderate to good.

### Height of Mandibular Body

This feature is best examined at the anterior midline of the mandible. The height of the mandibular body is much greater in males than in females when measured (by eye) from the superior edge of the alveolar process to the inferior border of the mandible. In females, the body contributes about two parts to the height discussed, while the alveolar process contributes one part. In males, the alveolar process only contributes about one part in three or more. Again, this feature can be examined in your long-suffering friends. The reliability of this feature is moderate to very good.

### Shape of the Chin

In females, the lower border of the mandible usually comes to only a single prominence in the chin or mental region, while the male chin more often has two points connected by a more or less straight line. The result is a "square chin" in males. This feature is usually reliable. Once again, examine the chins of your friends.

### Muscular Relief

This is a feature upon which some place great reliance, but others have considerable difficulty in assessing. In general, males have more prominent muscle markings on the skull than do females, especially in the nuchal region, in the region of the external surface of the mandibular angle, and in the relief of the temporal line.

### Other Features

In most cases, males have a more marked nuchal crest than females. The palatal region of males is shallower and broader than that of females. The male skull is, in general, larger than that of the female. The facial area of the skull usually is more nearly square in males, linear in females. These features are of variable reliability, depending upon the population from which the skull is drawn. In the author's opinion and experience, the most reliable features for estimation of sex of a skull are: prominence of the brow ridges, sharpness of the orbital rim, and height of the mandibular body. Another investigator may prefer other criteria.

## Sex Estimation from Post-Cranial Bones Other Then the Pelvis

In general, the characteristics which indicate sex in postcranial bones are the same as those characteristics of the same regions of the living individual which suggest sex. The male limbs are usually longer and more robust, the shoulders broader, the hands and feet larger. The same applies to the bones of these parts. In the living, these criteria are usually reliable, but there is the occasional exception, the unusually gracile and small male or the unusually robust and large female, and the same applies to the bones. Furthermore, the amount of overlap between the sexes depends on the skeletal region examined. Few females have shoulders as broad as most males, which is reflected in the length and robusticity of the clavicle. However, many females have hands or feet as large as those of a large number of males. The number of overlapping cases in these regions is considerable, and the bones reflect this situation.

It is in this area of sex estimation from various postcranial bones that the mental picture held by the investigator of the usual size and shape of the bone appropriate to each sex becomes most important and the opinion of an experienced examiner becomes valuable. The reason for this is that often no quantifiable difference between male and female exists, and statements such as "it is just too massive for a female" begin to count heavily. In other words, it is in this area of sex estimation that art becomes very much as significant as science, and experience and familiarity often count heavily. In most contexts, the problem is in determining the worth of a particular investigator. His/her degree of experience and "track record" are probably the best guides.

### The Clavicle

The clavicle is one of those bones in which sexual differences appear to be fairly well marked, but those differences do not lend themselves to quantification. Thieme (1957) used sexual differences in Negro clavicles as part of a series of measurements used to determine sex in Negro skeletons. Differences found are of the sort which would be expected, in that male clavicles are usually larger and longer with only moderate overlap. Male clavicular mean length is 158.24 mm with a standard deviation of 10.06, while the female mean is 140.28 mm with a standard deviation of 7.99 mm.

Jit and Singh (1966) studied the clavicles of adults from India and found that length alone will determine the sex of only 8 percent of male and 14 percent of female clavicles. Weight of the bone is somewhat more valuable, especially in determining sex of males, but not females. Circumference of the midshaft of the clavicle is found to be the single most diagnostic sexual feature of this bone in males, but again, not in females.

### Humerus

The humerus, like many of the postcranial bones, is more robust in most males than in females.

Dwight (1904/05) has examined the vertical and transverse diameter of the humeral head in Caucasians and found that the diameters in males are greater than those in females.

| | Vertical diameter | Transverse diameter |
|---|---|---|
| male | 48.76 | 44.66 |
| female | 42.67 | 36.98 |

Thieme (1957) stated that biepicondylar breadths below 56.7 mm and above 63.4 mm indicate female and male respectively. Olivier (1969) listed the following data for incompletely macerated humeri:

|  | female if below: | male if above: |
|---|---|---|
| Maximal length | 280 mm | 330 mm |
| Vertical diameter of head with cartilage | 43 mm | 48 mm |
| Transverse diameter of head with cartilage | 40 mm | 44 mm |
| Weight | 98 gm | 136 gm |

Olivier cautioned that the above data applies only to Europeans and notes that any individual falling between the values shown may be of either sex.

### Ulna

Again citing Olivier (1969) :

|  | female if below: | male if above: |
|---|---|---|
| Maximum length | 230 mm | 265 mm |
| Physiological length | 205 mm | 240 mm |
| Weight | 40.5 gm | 54 gm |

The date above applies to French ulnae.

### Radius

|  | female if below: | male if above: |
|---|---|---|
| Physiological length | 215 mm | 250 mm |
| Maximum length | 200 mm | 235 mm |
| Weight | 31 gm | 44 gm |

If the bones are completely defatted and dried, the above figures for weight should be reduced by 25 and 34.5 gm respectively.

### Scapula

Citing Olivier and Pineau (1957) :

|  | female if below: | male if above: |
|---|---|---|
| Breadth of the glenoid fossa | 26.1 mm | 28.6 mm |
| Length of the spine | 127.9 mm | 141.4 mm |
| Infraspinous height of the scapula | 144.4 mm | 157.5 mm |

### Sternum

Often, the body of the sternum in males is more than twice the length of the manubrium, while in the females it is less than twice that length. When the former occurs, the sternum is almost surely from a male skeleton.

### Femur

Pearson (1917/19) supplied the following table for estimating sex from the femur (all measurements in mm) :

|                   | female | female?     | sex?        | male?       | male  |
|-------------------|--------|-------------|-------------|-------------|-------|
| vertical diam head | 41.5   | 41.5- 43.5  | 43.5- 44.5  | 44.5- 45.5  | 45.5  |
| popliteal length  | 106.0  | 106.0-114.5 | 114.5-132.0 | 132.0-145.0 | 145.0 |
| bicondylar width  | 72.0   | 72.0- 74.0  | 74.0- 76.0  | 76.0- 78.0  | 78.0  |
| trochanteric      |        |             |             |             |       |
| oblique length    | 390.0  | 390.0-405.0 | 405.0-430.0 | 430.0-450.0 | 450.0 |

The measurements given above were taken from seventeenth century London. Appropriate adjustments should be made for more recent European bones since average height has increased. Thieme (1957) gave the following data relating to the femur of Negroes:

|               | sex | no. | mean (mm) | S.D.  | S.E.  |
|---------------|-----|-----|-----------|-------|-------|
| Femur length  | m   | 98  | 477.34    | 28.37 | 2.66  |
|               | f   | 100 | 439.10    | 24.55 | 2.456 |
| Head diameter | m   | 98  | 47.17     | 2.75  | 0.278 |
|               | f   | 100 | 41.52     | 2.12  | 0.212 |

Olivier (1969) gave the following values for European femora:

|                                          | female if below: | male if above: |
|------------------------------------------|------------------|----------------|
| "Length in position"                     | 390.0 mm         | 460.0 mm       |
| Vertebral diameter of head with cartilage | 43.5 mm          | 44.5 mm        |
| Bicondylar breadth                       | 74.0 mm          | 76.0 mm        |
| Weight                                   | 270.0 gm         | 375.0 gm       |

In dried and defatted femora the lower and upper weight values must be changed to 209.9 and 291.9 gm respectively.

### Tibia

Olivier (1969) reported:

|                | female if below: | male if above: |
|----------------|------------------|----------------|
| Maximum length | 320.0 mm         | 380.0 mm       |
| Weight         | 156 gm           | 234.0 gm       |

This applies to French tibiae. When dried and defatted the weights should be reduced to 116 and 174 gm respectively.

### Patella, Talus, Calcaneus

We offer a method based on measurement of the volume of the bone. The results are summarized below.

PATELLA

| | male if volume greater than | % error | female if volume less than | % error |
|---|---|---|---|---|
| Caucasian | 15 cc | 4 | 14 cc | 4 |
| Negro | 13 cc | 6 | 11 cc | 8 |
| Unknown | 15 cc | 3 | 11 cc | 3 |

TALUS

| | male if volume greater than | % error | female if volume less than | % error |
|---|---|---|---|---|
| Caucasian | 31 cc | 4 | 26 cc | 4 |
| Negro | 33 cc | 4 | 23 cc | 4 |
| Unknown | 32 cc | 3 | 24 cc | 3 |

CALCANEUS

| | male if volume greater than | % error | female if volume less than | % error |
|---|---|---|---|---|
| Caucasian | 55 cc | 4 | 52 cc | 6 |
| Negro | 58 cc | 6 | 50 cc | 4 |
| Unknown | 58 cc | 3 | 50 cc | 2 |

Several authors have suggested quantitative methods for estimating sex from the skull or post cranial bones (Giles, 1964, 1970a, 1970b; Boulinier, 1968, 1969; Giles and Eliot, 1963; Hanihara, 1958, 1959; Hanihara, Kimura, and Minamidate, 1964). If sex determination in a given skeleton is in doubt, these methods may be useful in lieu of the observational methods described above. Most of the measurements employed are numerical expressions of the subjective assessment of morphological traits already described. Kiszely (1974) has presented a chemical method for assessing sex from fairly fresh bones.

## STATURE RECONSTRUCTION

Reconstruction of the stature of an individual when living from the bones of the skeleton has obvious importance for identification of the recent murder victim who has been allowed to decompose and also for studies of demography, nutrition, growth, and dietary habits in populations long dead. A large number of studies have been made on human skeletons in an effort to devise ways of estimating stature of the living individual from his skeletal remains. Primary attention has been given to the long bones of the skeleton, and regression formulae have been computed which relate the length of one or more of these bones to total stature (Manouvrier, 1892; Pearson, 1899; Telkka, 1950). In other studies, the length of a bone has been reported as a ratio to stature (Nat, 1931). At least one study has taken into account all of the bones which contribute to stature (Fully, 1956). In this section, those methods most useful and/or most commonly used will be presented.

Determination of the stature in subadults is a problem which is all too common in forensic anthropology and is less commonly attempted when dealing with archeological specimens. Still, the student should be aware of the methods for solving this problem.

TABLE XII

TABLE OF SUBADULT STATURE RELATIVE TO THE LENGTH OF THE DIAPHYSIS OF THE FEMUR.*

| Femoral diaphysis (mm) | Stature (cm) | Femoral diaphysis (mm) | Stature (cm) |
|---|---|---|---|
| 80 | 50. | 195 | 111. |
| 85 | 55. | 200 | 114. |
| 90 | 58.5 | 210 | 116. |
| 95 | 61.5 | 220 | 119. |
| 100 | 64.5 | 230 | 122. |
| 105 | 67.5 | 240 | 125. |
| 110 | 70. | 250 | 127.5 |
| 115 | 73. | 260 | 130.25 |
| 120 | 76.5 | 270 | 133.25 |
| 125 | 79. | 280 | 135.75 |
| 130 | 81.5 | 290 | 138.5 |
| 135 | 84.5 | 300 | 141. |
| 140 | 87. | 310 | 143.5 |
| 145 | 89.5 | 320 | 146. |
| 150 | 93. | 330 | 148.75 |
| 155 | 94.5 | 340 | 151. |
| 160 | 96.75 | 350 | 153.75 |
| 165 | 99.25 | 360 | 156. |
| 170 | 101.5 | 370 | 158.75 |
| 175 | 103.5 | 380 | 161.75 |
| 180 | 105.5 | 390 | 165. |
| 185 | 107.5 | 400 | 170. |
| 190 | 109.5 | | |

*From G. Olivier, *Practical Anthoropolgy,* 1969. Courtesy of Charles C Thomas, Publisher, Springfield, Illinois.

For fetal stature, a method of Olivier and Pineau (Olivier, 1969) may be used. The equations are:

$$
\begin{aligned}
\text{Fetal stature (cm)} &= 7.92 \times \text{humeral length} - 0.32 \pm 1.8 \\
&= 13.8 \times \text{radial length} - 2.85 \pm 1.8 \\
&= 8.73 \times \text{ulnar length} - 1.07 \pm 1.59 \\
&= 6.29 \times \text{femoral length} + 4.42 \pm 1.82 \\
&= 7.85 \times \text{fibular length} + 2.78 \pm 1.65 \\
&= 7.39 \times \text{tibial length} + 3.55 \pm 1.92
\end{aligned}
$$

Determination of stature for children is particularly difficult. As a visit to any elementary school will show, children of a given age vary greatly in size. Table XII, extrapolated from a table of normal growth curves, may be useful in some cases. Because of the variability previously mentioned, this table provides only a rough estimate of stature.

The most commonly used method for adult stature reconstruction in the United States are the regression formulae of Trotter and Gleser (1952, 1958)

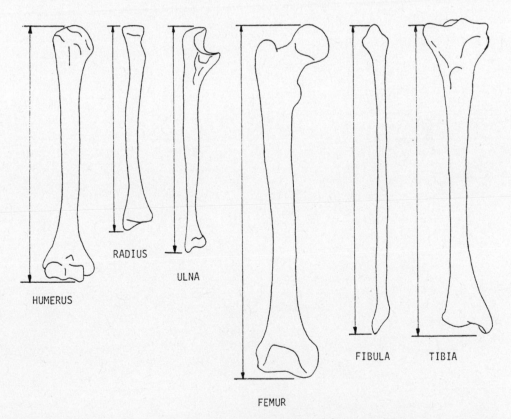

RADIUS

ULNA

HUMERUS

FIBULA  TIBIA

FEMUR

Figure 21: Points of measurement of long bone length for use with Trotter-Gleser equations.

and of Trotter (1970). These formulae have proven to work well on the populations for which they were devised, primarily Caucasian and Negro. In order to use these formulae successfully, it is necessary to know the race of the skeleton and also the sex in order to employ the correct formula. One should also know the age in order to introduce the correction factor for shrinkage in stature with age (Trotter and Gleser, 1951). The formulae are given in Table XIII. Bone length is measured as shown in Figure 21 using an osteometric board.

Mongoloid statures have proven less accurate when estimated by the

TABLE XIII

EQUATIONS TO ESTIMATE LIVING STATURE (CM) WITH STANDARD ERRORS FROM THE LONG BONES OF AMERICAN ETHNIC GROUPS BETWEEN 18 AND 30 YEARS OF AGE.*

| Caucasian Males | | | Negro Males | | |
|---|---|---|---|---|---|
| 3.08 Hum | +70.45 | ±4.05 | 3.26 Hum | +62.10 | ±4.43 |
| 3.78 Rad | +79.01 | ±4.32 | 3.42 Rad | +81.56 | ±4.30 |
| 3.70 Ulna | +74.05 | ±4.32 | 3.26 Ulna | +79.29 | ±4.42 |
| 2.38 Fem | +61.41 | ±3.27 | 2.11 Fem | +70.35 | ±3.94 |
| 2.52 Tib | +78.62 | ±3.37 | 2.10 Tib | +86.20 | ±3.78 |
| 2.68 Fib | +71.78 | ±3.29 | 2.19 Fib | +85.65 | ±4.08 |
| 1.30 (Fem + Tib) +63.29 | | ±2.99 | 1.15 (Fem + Tib) +71.04 | | ±3.53 |

| Caucasian Females | | | Negro Females | | |
|---|---|---|---|---|---|
| 3.36 Hum | +57.97 | ±4.45 | 3.08 Hum | +64.67 | ±4.25 |
| 4.74 Rad | +54.93 | ±4.24 | 2.75 Rad | +94.51 | ±5.05 |
| 4.27 Ulna | +57.76 | ±4.30 | 3.31 Ulna | +75.38 | ±4.83 |
| 2.47 Fem | +54.10 | ±3.72 | 2.28 Fem | +59.76 | ±3.41 |
| 2.90 Tib | +61.53 | ±3.66 | 2.45 Tib | +72.65 | ±3.70 |
| 2.93 Fib | +59.61 | ±3.57 | 2.49 Fib | +70.90 | ±3.80 |
| 1.39 (Fem + Tib) +53.20 | | ±3.55 | 1.26 (Fem + Tib) +59.72 | | ±3.28 |

| Mongoloid Males | | | Mexican Males | | |
|---|---|---|---|---|---|
| 2.68 Hum | +83.19 | ±4.25 | 2.92 Hum | +73.94 | ±4.24 |
| 3.54 Rad | +82.00 | ±4.60 | 3.55 Rad | +80.71 | ±4.04 |
| 3.48 Ulna | +77.45 | ±4.66 | 3.56 Ulna | +74.56 | ±4.05 |
| 2.15 Fem | +72.57 | ±3.80 | 2.44 Fem | +58.67 | ±2.99 |
| 2.39 Tib | +81.45 | ±3.27 | 2.36 Tib | +80.62 | ±3.73 |
| 2.40 Fib | +80.56 | ±3.24 | 2.50 Fib | +75.44 | ±3.52 |
| 1.22 (Fem + Tib) +70.37 | | ±3.24 | | | |

To estimate stature of older individuals subtract 0.06 (age − 30) cm.

To estimate cadaver stature, add 2.5 cm.

*From M. Trotter, Estimation of stature. In T.D. Stewart (ed.), *Personal Identification in Mass Disasters*, 1970. Courtesy of National Museum of Natural History, Washington.

formula of Trotter and Gleser, no doubt due to the fact that their sample of Mongoloids was small and heterogeneous, including American/Japanese, Indian, Filipino, etc. (Genovés, 1967). Genovés (1966), (1967) provided formulae and tables which seem to work more accurately with American Indian skeletons. Indians, of course, form the bulk of the skeletal material with which American physical anthropologists work, so that this is an especially welcome addition. Genovés found that individual long bones are most useful in estimating Mongoloid stature, especially the tibia. His formulae are given in Table XIV. Genovés measured the length of the long bones as the maximum length except the tibia, which is measured excluding the tuberosity. Genovés worked with sixty-nine male and twenty-nine female American Indians, all dissecting room cadavers.

In those rare (it seems) cases where an entire skeleton is available for stature estimation, another method is useful and provides the smallest standard deviation or allowable error. With this method of Fully (1956), it is not necessary to know the sex or race of the skeleton beforehand in order to apply the formula successfully, whereas in the Trotter-Gleser and Genovés formulae these attributes must be predetermined if good results are to be obtained. The Fully method involves measuring the heights of all the bones contributing to stature and adding an amount equivalent to the missing soft tissue. Fully's stature formula may be used if the skeleton is complete or only missing some vertebrae. In instances where a few vertebrae are missing from an otherwise intact skeleton, use Table XV for the average percentage contribution of each vertebra to teh total height of the column. From the table, the heights of the missing segments are calculated. From this, and the measured height of the remaining vertebrae, the

TABLE XIV
CALCULATION OF MONGOLOID STATURE[1] (IN CM) FROM LONG BONES.*

Males:

All bones: Stature $= 2.52$rad $- 0.07$ulna $+ 0.44$hum $+ 2.98$fib $- 0.49$tib $+ 0.68$fem $+ 95.113 \pm 2.614$

Femur: Stature $= 2.26$fem $+ 66.379 \pm 3.417$

Tibia: Stature $= 1.96$tib $+ 93.752 \pm 2.812$

Females:

All bones[2]: Stature $= 8.66$rad $- 7.37$ulna $+ 1.25$tib $- 0.93$fem $+ 96.674 \pm 2.812$

Femur: Stature $= 2.59$fem $+ 49.742 \pm 3.816$

Tibia: Stature $= 2.72$tib $+ 63.781 \pm 3.513$

[1] Substract 2.5 cm to obtain the stature while alive.

[2] In this case, the humerus contributes practically nothing, and therefore is omitted.

*From S. Genovés, Proportionality of the long bones, *Am J Phys Anthropol*, 26:67-77, 1967.

## TABLE XV
### PERCENTAGE CONTRIBUTION OF EACH VERTEBRA TO THE TOTAL HEIGHT OF THE COLUMN.*

| Cervical | | Thoracic | | | | Lumbar | |
|---|---|---|---|---|---|---|---|
| C. 2 | 7.80 | T. 1 | 3.41 | T. 7 | 4.19 | L. 1 | 5.53 |
| C. 3 | 2.80 | T. 2 | 3.61 | T. 8 | 4.24 | L. 2 | 5.62 |
| C. 4 | 2.73 | T. 3 | 3.72 | T. 9 | 4.35 | L. 3 | 5.66 |
| C. 5 | 2.66 | T. 4 | 3.83 | T. 10 | 4.61 | L. 4 | 5.63 |
| C. 6 | 2.67 | T. 5 | 3.98 | T. 11 | 4.96 | L. 5 | 5.76 |
| C. 7 | 2.95 | T. 6 | 4.10 | T. 12 | 5.23 | | |

*From G. Fully, Une nouvelle methode, *Ann Med Legale Crimiol*, 36:266-273, 1956.

total height of the column is derived by a simple proportionality equation. Because of the error introduced by this method, it should not be used when the combined heights of the missing vertebrae exceed 20 percent of the total column.

The following measurements are taken to calculate stature according to Fully's method:

1. *Basion-bregma height*
2. *Total vertebral height:* sum of the heights of the bodies.
3. *First sacral segment height:* anterior corpal height of S1.
4. *Femur oblique length:* with both femoral condyles against the vertical endpiece of the osteometric board, apply the block to the most distant point on the femoral head.
5. *Tibial length:* place the tip of the malleolus against the upright of the osteometric board and align the bone so that the long axis is parallel to the edge of the board. Apply the block to the most prominent part of the lateral half of the lateral condyle.
6. *Tarsal height:* articulate the talus and calcaneus. Place the bones on the osteometric board so that the superior surface of the talus is in contact with the vertical upright. Apply the block to the inferior surface of the calcaneus at a point immediately below which the talus is in contact with the vertical upright.

After you find the values above, sum them to get total skeletal height. This is used in the following regression equation to get antemortem stature:

Stature = 0.98 (total skeletal height) + 14.63 ± 2.05 cm.

Other problems in stature reconstruction are presented by skeletons with only broken and incomplete long bones. The problem of estimation of original length of a long bone from its fragments is considered by Müller (1935), Steele and McKern (1969), and Steele (1970). Müller (1935) divided the humerus, radius, and tibia into sections as follows.

Humerus:  1. the most proximal point of the humerus
2. the most inferior margin of the articular surface of the head
3. the convergence of the muscle lines originating from the greater and lesser tubercles
4. a transverse line passing through the proximal edge of the olecranon fossa
5. a transverse line passing through the distal edge of the olecranon fossa
6. the most distal point of the humerus

Radius:  1. the most proximal point of the radius
2. the inferior margin of the radial head
3. a transverse line passing through the middle of the radial tuberosity
4. the distal epiphyseal line
5. the most distal point of the radius

Tibia:  1. the most proximal point of the tibia
2. the proximal epiphyseal line
3. a transverse line passing through the elevated point of tuberosity
4. a transverse line passing through the proximal end of the anterior crest of the shaft
5. a transverse line passing through the point of smallest circumference of the shaft
6. the inferior epiphyseal line
7. the inferior articular surface of the tibia
8. the most distal point of the medial malleolus of the tibia

Measure the length of whichever one of the above sections is available and find, in Table XVI, what percent the section contributes to the total length of the bone. Use that length to calculate stature from the appropriate stature formula. Müller devised her percentage table based on the bones of Europeans, so a formula for stature designed for use in that population would be appropriate. Müller's data does not discriminate between the bones of males and females, but applies to either.

Steele and McKern (1969) have attempted to refine Müller's (1935) method for application, with greater accuracy, to American Indians. They divide three bones, the femur, humerus, and tibia, into the following segments:

Femur:  1. the most proximal point of the head
2. the midpoint of the lesser trochanter

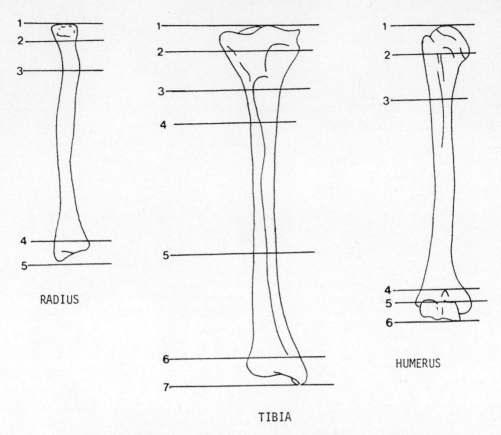

RADIUS

TIBIA

HUMERUS

Figure 22: Diagrams of the longbone segments described by Müller (1935).

3. the most proximal extension of the popliteal surface at point where the medial and lateral supracondylar lines become parallel below the linea aspera
4. the most proximal point of the intercondylar fossa
5. the most distal point of the medial condyle

Humerus:  1. the most proximal point of the head
2. the most distal point of the circumference of the head
3. the point of narrowest diameter anteriorly/posteriorly when measured proximally to the deltoid tuberosity and distally to the greater trochanteric crest
4. the proximal margin of the olecranon fossa
5. the distal margin of the olecranon fossa
6. the most distal point of the trochlea

Tibia:  1. the most proximal point of the intercondylar eminence
2. the most proximal point of the tibial tuberosity

TABLE XVI

MEAN PERCENT TOTAL LENGTH AND PERCENT STANDARD DEVIATION
OF EUROPEAN LONG BONE SEGMENTS.*

| Section | % | S.D. |
|---|---|---|
| | Humerus | |
| 1 | 11.44 ± 1.71 | |
| 2 | 7.60 ± 1.67 | |
| 3 | 69.62 ± 1.74 | |
| 4 | 6.26 ± 0.90 | |
| 5 | 5.47 ± 0.86 | |
| | Radius | |
| 1 | 5.35 ± 1.31 | |
| 2 | 8.96 ± 1.95 | |
| 3 | 78.72 ± 0.25 | |
| 4 | 7.46 ± 1.10 | |
| | Tibia | |
| 1 | 7.88 ± 1.31 | |
| 2 | 4.84 ± 1.31 | |
| 3 | 8.86 ± 0.93 | |
| 4 | 48.54 ± 4.27 | |
| 5 | 22.09 ± 3.35 | |
| 6 | 3.29 ± 0.74 | |
| 7 | 5.03 ± 0.92 | |

*Adapted from G. Müller, Zur bestimmung, *Anthropologischer Anzeiger,* 12:70-72, 1935.

3. the point of confluence of the lines extending from the lower end of the tuberosity

4. the point at which the anterior crest of the tibia crosses over to the medial border of the shaft above the medial malleolus (the measurement is properly taken at the point where the crest crosses the midsection of the shaft)

5. the proximal margin of the inferior articular facet (measured at the point opposite the medial malleolus)

6. the most distal point of the medial malleolus

The points described above from the Steele and McKern method are represented visually in Figure 23.

Once the segment length for a bone is measured, refer to Table XVII to obtain the percent contribution of the segment to the total length of the bone. Note that this table is available for use either when the sex is, or is not, known. Once segment length and percent total length are known, parallel length is calculated using the following formula:

$$\frac{\text{segment length}}{\text{percent total length}} \times 100$$

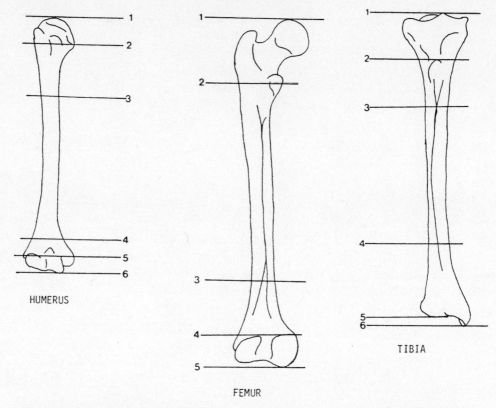

Figure 23: Diagrams of the longbone segments described by Steele and McKern (1969).

The resultant figure, parallel length, is then converted to maximum length using the following conversion factors.

Femur:      male and female maximum length = parallel length + 0.09
Humerus:  male and female maximum length = parallel length.
Tibia:        male maximum length = parallel length − 0.54 cm
                 female maximum length = parallel length − 0.04 cm

The numbering of the landmarks from the proximal end of each bone downwards facilitates the comprehension of the system of numbering the segments: Each segment bears the number of the landmark at its proximal end. Thus, segment one is the part of the bone between landmarks one and two, segment two is that between landmarks two and three, etc.

For greater accuracy (smaller standard deviation) Steele and McKern recommend the use of regression formulae for determination of maximum bone length, rather than the percent total length method. These regression formulae are given in Tables XVIII through XX. All that is needed to enter a table is the measured length of the segment of the bone. Again,

TABLE XVII

PERCENT TOTAL LENGTHS OF SEGMENTS AND COMBINATIONS OF SEGMENTS OF THE LONG BONES OF AMERCIAN INDIANS.*

| .. segment combination | male mean percentage | male mean s.d. | female mean percentage | female mean s.d. | combined percentage | combined s.d. |
|---|---|---|---|---|---|---|
| | | | FEMUR | | | |
| 1 | 16.4 | 1.1 | 15.6 | 1.1 | 16.1 | 1.2 |
| 2 | 56.1 | 2.5 | 56.7 | 2.6 | 56.3 | 2.6 |
| 3 | 19.4 | 2.5 | 19.6 | 2.4 | 19.5 | 2.5 |
| 4 | 7.9 | 0.7 | 7.9 | 0.7 | 7.9 | 0.7 |
| 1-2 | 72.5 | 2.6 | 72.3 | 2.2 | 72.4 | 2.5 |
| 2-3 | 75.5 | 1.3 | 76.3 | 1.2 | 75.8 | 1.3 |
| 3-4 | 27.3 | 2.6 | 27.5 | 2.2 | 27.4 | 2.4 |
| 1-3 | 91.9 | 0.7 | 91.9 | 0.7 | 91.9 | 0.7 |
| 2-4 | 83.5 | 1.1 | 84.1 | 1.1 | 83.6 | 1.1 |
| | | | HUMERUS | | | |
| 1 | 10.5 | 0.8 | 10.1 | 1.0 | 10.3 | 0.9 |
| 2 | 22.6 | 2.2 | 22.0 | 1.7 | 22.4 | 2.1 |
| 3 | 54.6 | 2.4 | 55.1 | 3.0 | 54.7 | 2.6 |
| 4 | 8.1 | 0.7 | 8.3 | 0.8 | 8.1 | 0.8 |
| 5 | 4.3 | 0.5 | 4.5 | 1.0 | 4.4 | 0.7 |
| 1-2 | 33.0 | 2.3 | 32.1 | 2.2 | 32.7 | 2.3 |
| 2-3 | 77.1 | 1.3 | 77.1 | 2.0 | 77.1 | 1.5 |
| 3-4 | 62.6 | 2.4 | 63.4 | 2.7 | 62.9 | 2.5 |
| 4-5 | 12.4 | 0.8 | 12.8 | 1.3 | 12.5 | 1.0 |
| 1-3 | 87.6 | 0.8 | 87.2 | 1.3 | 87.5 | 1.0 |
| 2-4 | 85.2 | 1.0 | 85.4 | 1.6 | 85.3 | 1.2 |
| 3-5 | 67.0 | 2.3 | 67.9 | 2.2 | 67.2 | 2.3 |
| 1-4 | 95.7 | 0.5 | 95.5 | 0.9 | 95.6 | 0.7 |
| 2-5 | 89.5 | 0.8 | 89.9 | 1.0 | 89.6 | 0.9 |
| | | | TIBIA | | | |
| 1 | 6.8 | 1.0 | 6.5 | 1.1 | 6.7 | 1.0 |
| 2 | 17.5 | 2.9 | 16.5 | 2.9 | 17.2 | 3.0 |
| 3 | 47.9 | 3.5 | 49.2 | 4.0 | 48.3 | 3.7 |
| 4 | 25.1 | 2.2 | 24.7 | 2.6 | 24.9 | 2.3 |
| 5 | 4.2 | 0.7 | 4.2 | 0.6 | 4.2 | 0.7 |
| 1-2 | 24.3 | 2.8 | 23.0 | 2.4 | 23.9 | 2.8 |
| 2-3 | 65.4 | 2.4 | 65.8 | 2.0 | 65.5 | 2.3 |
| 3-4 | 73.0 | 2.7 | 73.9 | 2.1 | 73.3 | 2.6 |
| 4-5 | 29.2 | 2.3 | 28.9 | 2.4 | 29.1 | 2.3 |
| 1-3 | 72.2 | 2.1 | 72.3 | 2.3 | 72.3 | 2.2 |
| 2-4 | 90.5 | 1.5 | 90.5 | 1.6 | 90.5 | 1.5 |
| 3-5 | 77.2 | 2.8 | 78.1 | 2.1 | 77.5 | 2.7 |
| 1-4 | 97.3 | 0.9 | 97.0 | 0.9 | 97.2 | 0.9 |
| 2-5 | 94.6 | 1.4 | 94.7 | 1.5 | 94.6 | 1.5 |

*Adapted from D.G. Steele and T.M. McKern. A method for assessment, *Am J Phys Anthropol, 31*:215-227, 1969.

once the length of the bone is estimated, formulae for stature estimation are entered.

Such secondarily derived statural estimates naturally have somewhat larger standard deviations than those derived from intact bones. Still, the estimates are better than ignoring the problem entirely when an estimate is needed.

Steele (1970) has provided data for the estimation of stature from fragmentary long bones of Caucasians and Negroes. The landmarks and segments are the same as those used in the earlier study by Steele and McKern with one exception. Landmark number 3 of the humerus, defined in the

TABLE XVIII

REGRESSION FORMULAE FOR THE AMERICAN INDIAN FEMUR. THE NUMBERS IN PARENTHESES, PRECEDED BY THE LETTER "S", DESIGNATE THE SECTION.*

| Segment | MALE |
|---|---|
| 1. | $32.94 + 0.16(S1) = \text{femur} \pm 1.39\text{cm}$ |
| 2. | $26.20 + 0.07(S2) = \text{femur} \pm 1.31\text{cm}$ |
| 3. | $42.18 + 0.03(S3) = \text{femur} \pm 1.67\text{cm}$ |
| 4. | $37.44 + 0.21(S4) = \text{femur} \pm 1.56\text{cm}$ |
| 1-2. | $20.63 + 0.12(S1) + 0.06(S2) = \text{femur} \pm 1.09\text{cm}$ |
| 2-3. | $5.89 + 0.12(S2) + 0.11(S3) = \text{femur} \pm 0.75\text{cm}$ |
| 3-4. | $34.77 + 0.03(S3) + 0.21(S4) = \text{femur} \pm 1.52\text{cm}$ |
| 1-3. | $1.36 + 0.11(S1) + 0.10(S2) + 0.10(S3) = \text{femur} \pm 0.33\text{cm}$ |
| 2-4. | $2.58 + 0.11(S2) + 0.10(S3) + 0.14(S4) = \text{femur} \pm 0.58\text{cm}$ |

FEMALE

| | |
|---|---|
| 1. | $36.55 + 0.08(S1) = \text{femur} \pm 1.23\text{cm}$ |
| 2. | $28.46 + 0.06(S2) = \text{femur} \pm 1.02\text{cm}$ |
| 3. | $38.90 + 0.03(S3) = \text{femur} \pm 1.23\text{cm}$ |
| 4. | $37.98 + 0.11(S4) = \text{femur} \pm 1.24\text{cm}$ |
| 1-2. | $17.99 + 0.13(S1) + 0.07(S2) = \text{femur} + 0.86\text{cm}$ |
| 2-3. | $10.52 + 0.10(S2) + 0.10(S3) = \text{femur} \pm 0.51\text{cm}$ |
| 3-4. | $32.45 + 0.05(S3) + 0.16(S4) = \text{femur} \pm 1.16\text{cm}$ |
| 1-3. | $3.64 + 0.10(S1) + 0.10(S2) + 0.09(S3) = \text{femur} \pm 0.28\text{cm}$ |
| 2-4. | $7.53 + 0.09(S2) + 0.11(S3) + 0.10(S4) = \text{femur} \pm 0.44\text{cm}$ |

MALE AND FEMALE COMBINED SAMPLE

| | |
|---|---|
| 1. | $27.90 + 0.23(S1) = \text{femur} \pm 1.56\text{cm}$ |
| 2. | $0.19 + 0.10(S2) = \text{femur} \pm 1.53\text{cm}$ |
| 3. | $38.83 + 0.06(S3) = \text{femur} \pm 2.11\text{cm}$ |
| 4. | $32.47 \pm 0.33(S4) = \text{femur} \pm 1.91\text{cm}$ |
| 1-2. | $14.73 + 0.16(S1) + 0.07(S2) = \text{femur} \pm 1.12\text{cm}$ |
| 2-3. | $1.82 + 0.13(S2) + 0.12(S3) = \text{femur} \pm 0.77\text{cm}$ |
| 3-4. | $27.68 + 0.06(S3) + 0.33(S4) = \text{femur} \pm 1.80\text{cm}$ |
| 1-3. | $1.14 + 0.11(S1) + 0.11(S2) + 0.10(S3) = \text{femur} \pm 0.32\text{cm}$ |
| 2-4. | $-0.07 + 0.12(S2) + 0.12(S3) + 0.15(S4) = \text{femur} \pm 0.61\text{cm}$ |

*From D.G. Steele and T.M. McKern, A method for assessment, *Am J Phys Anthropol,* *31*:215-227, 1969.

## TABLE XIX
## REGRESSION FORMULAE FOR THE AMERICAN INDIAN HUMERUS. NUMBERS IN PARENTHESES, PRECEDED BY THE LETTER "S", DESIGNATE THE SECTION.*

Segment                                                          MALE

1. $25.22 + 0.20(S1) = $ humerus $\pm$ 1.18cm
2. $26.70 + 0.07(S2) = $ humerus $\pm$ 1.17cm
3. $17.32 + 0.08(S3) = $ humerus $\pm$ 0.98cm
4. $27.40 + 0.18(S4) = $ humerus $\pm$ 1.23cm
5. $28.66 + 0.24(S5) = $ humerus $\pm$ 1.23cm
1-2. $21.31 + 0.18(S1) + 0.07(S2) = $ humerus $\pm$ 1.06cm
2-3. $5.23 + 0.11(S2) + 0.11(S3) = $ humerus $\pm$ 0.47cm
3-4. $14.25 + 0.08(S3) + 0.14(S4) = $ humerus $\pm$ 0.92cm
4-5. $24.28 + 0.17(S4) + 0.23(S5) = $ humerus $\pm$ 1.16cm
1-3. $1.74 + 0.14(S1) + 0.10(S2) + 0.10(S3) = $ humerus $\pm$ 0.28cm
2-4. $2.37 + 0.11(S2) + 0.10(S3) + 0.14(S4) = $ humerus $\pm$ 0.34cm
3-5. $12.21 + 0.08(S3) + 0.14(S4) + 0.19(S5) = $ humerus $\pm$ 0.85cm
1-4. $0.29 + 0.11(S1) + 0.10(S2) + 0.10(S3) + 0.10(S4) = $ humerus $\pm$ 0.17cm
2-5. $1.55 + 0.11(S2) + 0.10(S3) + 0.14(S4) + 0.12(S5) = $ humerus $\pm$ 0.26cm

FEMALE

1. $25.89 + 0.14(S1) = $ humerus $\pm$ 0.13cm
2. $20.55 + 0.14(S2) = $ humerus $\pm$ 0.84cm
3. $20.73 + 0.16(S3) = $ humerus $\pm$ 1.19cm
4. $25.03 + 0.20(S4) = $ humerus $\pm$ 1.26cm
5. $28.35 + 0.12(S5) = $ humerus $\pm$ 1.26cm
1-2. $21.0 + 0.03(S1) + 0.15(S2) = $ humerus $\pm$ 0.83cm
2-3. $8.25 + 0.15(S2) + 0.07(S3) = $ humerus $\pm$ 0.47cm
3-4. $10.37 + 0.08(S3) + 0.27(S4) = $ humerus $\pm$ 0.92cm
4-5. $24.02 + 0.19(S4) + 0.10(S5) = $ humerus $\pm$ 1.14cm
1-3. $1.88 + 0.15(S1) + 0.13(S2) + 0.09(S3) = $ humerus $\pm$ 0.32cm
2-4. $5.51 + 0.13(S2) + 0.08(S3) + 0.12(S4) = $ humerus $\pm$ 0.37cm
3-5. $4.14 + 0.10(S3) + 0.27(S4) + 0.20(S5) = $ humerus $\pm$ 0.69cm
1-4. $1.34 + 0.12(S1) + 0.12(S2) + 0.09(S3) + 0.08(S4) = $ humerus $\pm$ 0.26cm
2-5. $2.91 + 0.11(S2) + 0.09(S3) + 0.13(S4) + 0.11(S5) = $ humerus $\pm$ 0.22cm

MALE AND FEMALE COMBINED SAMPLE

1. $22.60 + 0.27(S1) = $ humerus $\pm$ 1.32cm
2. $23.12 + 0.12(S2) = $ humerus $\pm$ 1.26cm
3. $14.79 + 0.10(S3) = $ humerus $\pm$ 1.18cm
4. $25.46 + 0.23(S4) = $ humerus $\pm$ 1.47cm
5. $28.64 + 0.20(S5) = $ humerus $\pm$ 1.52cm
1-2. $18.82 + 0.19(S1) + 0.09(S2) = $ humerus $\pm$ 1.12cm
2-3. $4.67 + 0.13(S2) + 0.10(S3) = $ humerus $\pm$ 0.55cm
3-4. $9.55 + 0.10(S3) + 0.22(S4) = $ humerus $\pm$ 1.03cm
4-5. $23.33 + 0.22(S4) + 0.18(S5) = $ humerus $\pm$ 1.41cm
1-3. $20.86 + 0.15(S1) + 0.11(S2) + 0.10(S3) = $ humerus $\pm$ 0.31cm
2-4. $17.25 + 0.12(S2) + 0.10(S3) + 0.15(S4) = $ humerus $\pm$ 0.39cm
3-5. $6.68 + 0.10(S3) + 0.20(S4) + 0.21(S5) = $ humerus $\pm$ 0.92cm
1-4. $7.52 + 0.12(S1) + 0.11(S2) + 0.10(S3) + 0.10(S4) = $ humerus $\pm$ 0.21cm
2-5. $0.49 + 0.11(S2) + 0.10(S3) + 0.15(S4) + 0.12(S5) = $ humerus $\pm$ 0.28cm

*From D.G. Steele and T.M. McKern, A method for assessment, *Am J Phys Anthropol,* *31*:215-227, 1969.

## TABLE XX
REGRESSION FORMULAE FOR SEGMENTS OF THE AMERICAN INDIAN TIBIA. NUMBERS IN PARENTHESES, PRECEDED BY THE LETTER "S", DESIGNATE THE SECTION.*

*Segment*          MALE

1. $34.85 + 0.08(S1) = \text{tibia} \pm 1.64\text{cm}$
2. $34.14 + 0.04(S2) = \text{tibia} \pm 1.60\text{cm}$
3. $26.73 + 0.06(S3) = \text{tibia} \pm 1.38\text{cm}$
4. $31.40 + 0.06(S4) = \text{tibia} \pm 1.58\text{cm}$
5. $35.26 + 0.11(S5) = \text{tibia} \pm 1.64\text{cm}$
1-2. $30.67 + 0.12(S1) + 0.05(S2) = \text{tibia} \pm 1.53\text{cm}$
2-3. $15.48 + 0.10(S2) + 0.09(S3) = \text{tibia} \pm 0.96\text{cm}$
3-4. $13.56 + 0.08(S3) + 0.11(S4) = \text{tibia} \pm 1.07\text{cm}$
4-5. $29.30 + 0.06(S4) + 0.12(S5) = \text{tibia} \pm 1.55\text{cm}$
1-3. $11.35 + 0.13(S1) + 0.10(S2) + 0.09(S3) = \text{tibia} \pm 0.82\text{cm}$
2-4. $4.24 + 0.09(S2) + 0.10(S3) + 0.10(S4) = \text{tibia} \pm 0.54\text{cm}$
3-5. $12.62 + 0.08(S3) + 0.11(S4) + 0.08(S5) = \text{tibia} \pm 1.05\text{cm}$
1-4. $0.60 + 0.12(S1) + 0.10(S2) + 0.10(S3) + 0.10(S4) = \text{tibia} \pm 0.30\text{cm}$
2-5. $3.49 + 0.09(S2) + 0.10(S3) + 0.10(S4) + 0.07(S5) = \text{tibia} \pm 0.51\text{cm}$

FEMALE

1. $30.93 + 0.14(S1) = \text{tibia} \pm 0.98\text{cm}$
2. $37.26 + 0.06(S2) = \text{tibia} \pm 1.02\text{cm}$
3. $25.73 + 0.05(S3) = \text{tibia} \pm 0.74\text{cm}$
4. $36.41 - 0.03(S4) = \text{tibia} \pm 1.13\text{ cm}$
5. $31.50 + 0.17(S5) = \text{tibia} \pm 1.09\text{cm}$
1-2. $33.23 + 0.10(S1) - 0.03(S2) = \text{tibia} \pm 0.97\text{cm}$
2-3. $16.08 + 0.08(S2) + 0.08(S3) = \text{tibia} \pm 0.64\text{cm}$
3-4. $12.88 + 0.08(S3) + 0.09(S4) = \text{tibia} \pm 0.51\text{cm}$
4-5. $32.96 - 0.01(S4) + 0.15(S5) = \text{tibia} \pm 1.09\text{cm}$
1-3. $13.07 + 0.09(S1) + 0.10(S2) + 0.08(S3) = \text{tibia} \pm 0.57\text{cm}$
2-4. $6.58 + 0.06(S2) + 0.10(S3) + 0.08(S4) = \text{tibia} \pm 0.43\text{cm}$
3-5. $11.05 + 0.08(S3) + 0.10(S4) + 0.10(S5) = \text{tibia} \pm 0.48\text{cm}$
1-4. $24.68 + 0.10(S1) + 0.09(S2) + 0.10(S3) + 0.09(S4) = \text{tibia} \pm 0.26\text{cm}$
2-5. $5.31 + 0.06(S2) + 0.10(S3) + 0.09(S4) + 0.08(S5) = \text{tibia} \pm 0.40\text{cm}$

MALE AND FEMALE COMBINED SAMPLE

1. $31.15 + 0.20(S1) = \text{tibia} \pm 1.88\text{cm}$
2. $32.02 + 0.07(S2) = \text{tibia} \pm 1.91\text{cm}$
3. $23.67 + 0.07(S3) = \text{tibia} \pm 1.66\text{cm}$
4. $27.71 + 0.09(S4) = \text{tibia} \pm 1.86\text{cm}$
5. $32.51 + 0.24(S5) = \text{tibia} \pm 1.97\text{cm}$
1-2. $25.47 + 0.24(S1) + 0.08(S2) = \text{tibia} \pm 1.65\text{cm}$
2-3. $10.62 + 0.12(S2) + 0.10(S3) = \text{tibia} \pm 1.01\text{cm}$
3-4. $7.32 + 0.09(S3) + 0.14(S4) = \text{tibia} \pm 1.07\text{cm}$
4-5. $23.80 + 0.10(S4) + 0.25(S5) = \text{tibia} \pm 1.75\text{cm}$
1-3. $8.63 + 0.14(S1) + 0.12(S2) + 0.09(S3) = \text{tibia} \pm 0.84\text{cm}$
2-4. $2.10 + 0.09(S2) + 0.11(S3) + 0.10(S4) = \text{tibia} \pm 0.54\text{cm}$
3-5. $6.37 + 0.09(S3) + 0.14(S4) + 0.12(S5) = \text{tibia} \pm 1.03\text{cm}$
1-4. $1.07 + 0.12(S1) + 0.10(S2) + 0.10(S3) + 0.09(S4) = \text{tibia} \pm 0.29\text{cm}$
2-5. $1.59 + 0.09(S2) + 0.11(S3) + 0.10(S4) + 0.08(S5) = \text{tibia} \pm 0.51\text{cm}$

*From D.G. Steele and T.M. McKern, A method for assessment, *Am J Phys Anthropol*, *31*:215-227, 1969.

first study, was eliminated in the second. This landmark, the point of greatest narrowing at the middle of the humeral shaft, was found to be too vague to locate with sufficient constancy to give useful results. Therefore, for Caucasians and Negroes, landmark 4 becomes landmark 3, etc., making a total of 5 landmarks rather than 6 on the humerus.

Tables XXI through XXIII give the regressions of segment length to maximum bone length. Given maximum bone length, the tables of Trotter and Gleser may be used to estimate stature.

TABLE XXI

REGRESSION FORMULAE FOR CALCULATING LIVING STATURE AND STANDARD ERROR (IN CM) FROM AN INCOMPLETE FEMUR.*

CAUCASIAN MALES          *MEAN AGE* = 52.97

2.71(Fem.2) + 3.06(Fem.3) + 73.00 = stature ± 4.41cm
2.89(Fem.1) + 2.31(Fem.2) + 2.62(Fem.3) + 63.88 = stature ± 3.93cm
2.35(Fem.2) + 2.65(Fem.3) + 7.92(Fem.4) + 54.97 = stature ± 3.95cm

NEGRO MALES          *MEAN AGE* = 43.25

2.59(Fem.2) + 2.91(Fem.3) + 75.74 = stature ± 3.72cm
1.20(Fem.1) + 2.48(Fem.2) + 2.78(Fem.3) + 69.94 = stature ± 3.71cm
2.53(Fem.2) + 2.84(Fem.3) + 2.40(Fem.4) + 68.32 = stature ± 3.72cm

CAUCASIAN FEMALES          *MEAN AGE* = 63.35

2.80(Fem.2) + 1.46(Fem.3) + 76.67 = stature ± 4.91cm
2.16(Fem.1) + 2.50(Fem.2) + 1.45(Fem.3) + 68.86 = stature ± 4.81cm
2.57(Fem.2) + 1.21(Fem.3) + 5.03(Fem.4) + 66.05 = stature ± 4.77cm

NEGRO FEMALES          *MEAN AGE* = 39.58

2.12(Fem.2) + 1.68(Fem.3) + 93.29 = stature ± 6.17cm
3.63(Fem.1) + 1.86(Fem.2) + 1.27(Fem.3) + 77.15 = stature ± 5.80cm
2.00(Fem.2) + 1.08(Fem.3) + 6.32(Fem.4) + 77.71 = stature ± 6.01cm

*From D.G. Steele, Estimation of stature. In T.D. Stewart (ed.): *Personal Identification in Mass Disasters*, 1970. Courtesy of National Museum of Natural History, Washingington.

TABLE XXII
REGRESSION FORMULAE FOR CALCULATING LIVING STATURE AND
STANDARD ERROR (IN CM) FROM AN INCOMPLETE TIBIA.*

CAUCASIAN MALES         *MEAN AGE* = 52.97

$3.52(Tib.2) + 2.89(Tib.3) + 2.23(Tib.4) + 74.55 = $ stature $\pm$ 4.56cm
$2.87(Tib.3) + 2.69(Tib.4) - 0.96(Tib.5) + 92.36 = $ stature $\pm$ 5.45cm
$4.19(Tib.1) + 3.63(Tib.2) + 2.96(Tib.3) + 2.10(Tib.4) + 64.95 = $ stature $\pm$ 4.22cm
$3.54(Tib.2) + 2.96(Tib.3) + 2.18(Tib.4) - 1.56(Tib.5) + 75.98 = $ stature $\pm$ 4.60cm

NEGRO MALES         *MEAN AGE* = 43.25

$2.26(Tib.2) + 2.22(Tib.3) + 3.17(Tib.4) + 5.86 = $ stature $\pm$ 3.88cm
$2.23(Tib.3) + 3.51(Tib.4) + 0.51(Tib.5) + 91.70 = $ stature $\pm$ 4.49cm
$1.79(Tib.1) + 2.18(Tib.2) + 2.25(Tib.3) + 3.10(Tib.4) + 75.87 = $ stature $\pm$ 3.88cm
$2.32(Tib.2) + 2.23(Tib.3) + 3.19(Tib.4) - 1.60(Tib.5) + 82.50 = $ stature $\pm$ 3.92cm

CAUCASIAN FEMALES         *MEAN AGE* = 63.35

$4.17(Tib.2) + 2.96(Tib.3) + 2.16(Tib.4) + 66.09 = $ stature $\pm$ 4.69cm
$2.75(Tib.3) + 3.65(Tib.4) + 1.17(Tib.5) + 79.92 = $ stature $\pm$ 5.69cm
$1.51(Tib.1) + 4.03(Tib.2) + 2.97(Tib.3) + 2.12(Tib.4) + 62.89 = $ stature $\pm$ 4.71cm
$4.31(Tib.2) + 3.05(Tib.3) + 2.20(Tib.4) - 2.34(Tib.5) + 66.60 = $ stature $\pm$ 4.72cm

NEGRO FEMALES         *MEAN AGE* = 39.58

$2.56(Tib.2) + 2.21(Tib.3) + 1.56(Tib.4) + 91.91 = $ stature $\pm$ 4.59cm
$2.11(Tib.3) + 2.61(Tib.4) + 3.58(Tib.5) + 94.57 = $ stature $\pm$ 5.04cm
$3.60(Tib.1) + 2.15(Tib.2) + 2.26(Tib.3) + 1.84(Tib.4) + 81.11 = $ stature $\pm$ 4.46cm
$2.58(Tib.2) + 2.17(Tib.3) + 1.63(Tib.4) + 3.80(Tib.5) + 86.64 = $ stature $\pm$ 4.59cm

*From D.G. Steele, Estimation of stature. In T.D. Stewart (ed.): *Personal Identification in Mass Disasters*, 1970. Courtesy of National Museum of Natural History, Washington.

TABLE XXIII
REGRESSION FORMULAE FOR CALCULATING LIVING STATURE AND
STANDARD ERROR (IN CM) FROM AN INCOMPLETE HUMERUS.*

CAUCASIAN MALES          *MEAN AGE* = 52.97

3.42(Hum.2) + 80.94 = stature ± 5.31cm
7.17(Hum.1) + 3.04(Hum.2) + 63.94 = stature ± 5.05cm
3.19(Hum.2) + 5.97(Hum.3) + 74.82 = stature ± 5.15cm
7.84(Hum.1) + 2.73(Hum.2) + 6.74(Hum.3) + 55.45 = stature ± 4.80cm
2.94(Hum.2) + 6.34(Hum.3) + 4.60(Hum.4) + 72.54 = stature ± 5.14cm

NEGRO MALES          *MEAN AGE* = 43.25

3.80(Hum.2) + 70.68 = stature ± 4.94cm
8.13(Hum.1) + 3.34(Hum.2) + 51.98 = stature ± 4.56cm
3.79(Hum.2) + 0.69(Hum.3) + 69.53 = stature ± 5.00cm
8.12(Hum.1) + 3.33(Hum.2) + 0.56(Hum.3) + 51.08 = stature ± 4.62cm
3.76(Hum.2) + 1.19(Hum.3) + 4.54(Hum.4) + 61.58 = stature ± 5.00cm

CAUCASIAN FEMALES          *MEAN AGE* = 63.35

3.87(Hum.2) + 66.14 = stature ± 5.40cm
8.84(Hum.1) + 3.65(Hum.2) + 42.43 = stature ± 5.14cm
3.77(Hum.2) + 3.35(Hum.3) + 62.59 = stature ± 5.42cm
8.55(Hum.1) + 3.60(Hum.2) + 1.93(Hum.3) + 41.16 = stature ± 5.18cm
3.44(Hum.2) + 2.92(Hum.3) + 10.84(Hum.4) + 54.91 = stature ± 5.16cm

NEGRO FEMALES          *MEAN AGE* = 39.58

2.95(Hum.2) + 89.15 = stature ± 4.88cm
5.05(Hum.1) + 2.64(Hum.2) + 80.13 = stature ± 4.83cm
2.75(Hum.2) + 3.76(Hum.3) + 87.08 = stature ± 4.85cm
4.54(Hum.1) + 2.50(Hum.2) + 3.19(Hum.3) + 79.29 = stature ± 4.82cm
2.66(Hum.2) + 4.03(Hum.3) + 2.83(Hum.4) + 84.25 = stature ± 4.87cm

*From D.G. Steele, Estimation of stature. In T.D. Stewart( ed.): *Personal Identification in Mass Disasters,* 1970. Courtesy of National Museum of Natural History, Washington.

# CHAPTER V

# ANTHROPOMETRY

WHILE MOST TECHNIQUES USED by physical anthropologists are borrowed from anatomy, biochemistry, genetics, medicine, pathology, and statistics, there are two which are uniquely the contribution of anthropology: anthroposcopy and anthropometry. Anthroposcopy is the visual observation and description of biological characteristics whether living or dead which cannot be measured. In the living these include color of hair, skin, and eyes, form of lip and nose, and in archeologically derived skeletal material the recording of nonmetric traits. (epigenetic or discrete variables such as the presence of sutural bones, foramina, etc.). Anthropometry is divided into three categories by Ashley Montague (1960) : Somatometry, the measurement of the body in the living and in the cadaver; Osteometry, the measurement of the skeleton and its parts; Craniometry, the measurement of the skull, included in osteometry.

## DEFINITIONS

Before continuing this discussion on anthropometry, it is helpful to be acquainted with various terms and types of measurements used in anthropometry.

Skull—the skeleton of the braincase, face, and mandible.

Cranium—the skull minus facial portion and mandible, i.e. the braincase.

Calva or Calotte—the skull cap or the top of the braincase.

Calvarium—the braincase minus the facial bones and mandible.

### Cranial Landmarks

(Modified after Hrdlička, 1947; Montague, 1960; Brothwell, 1972)

ASTERION: The point at which the temporoparietal, temporooccipital, and lambdoid sutures meet.

BASION: The median point of the anterior border of the foramen magnum in the midsagittal plane.

BREGMA: The intersection point of the coronal and sagittal sutures.

DACRYON: The point on the medial wall of the orbit at which the frontal, lacrimal, and maxillary bones meet.

ECTOCONCHION: The point on the lateral margin of the orbit marking the maximum width, taken roughly parallel to its axis as well as to the superior border of the orbit.

106

ECTOMOLARE: The most lateral point on the inner surface of the lingual margins of the alveolar process, usually opposite the middle of the lingual surfaces of the second molar teeth.

EURYON: The points marking maximum biparietal breadth of the skull.

GLABELLA: The most prominent point midway between the two supraorbital ridges just above the nasofrontal suture.

GONION: The most lateral external point on the lower borders of the ascending ramii.

INFRADENTALE: The most anterior-superior point on the alveolar margin between the lower incisors on the lower jaw.

INION: The most prominent point on the external occipital protuberance. In some cases the protuberance may be absent, doubled with the depression between, or in instances may be completely replaced with a depression.

LAMBDA: The junction of the sagittal and lambdoid sutures. This point is often obliterated by the Inca and/or wormian bones.

MAXILLOFRONTALLE: Where the prolongation of the anterior lacrimal crest crosses the maxillofrontal suture.

MENTON (GNATHION): The most inferior (lower) point on the midsagittal plane on the lower border of the mandible.

NASION: The median point of the nasofrontal suture.

NASOSPINALE: The point at which a line tangent to the lower margins of the nasal aperture is intersected at the midsagittal plane.

OBELION: A point on the sagittal suture on a line connecting the right and left parietal foramina. When foramina are absent, the point may be estimated by comparison with other skulls.

OPHRYON: The central point of the smallest transverse diameter of the forehead. Measured from one temporal line to the other.

OPISTHION: The median point of the posterior margin of the foramen magnum at the transition from the external occipital protuberance, or inion.

ORALE: The point in the bony palate where the midsagittal plane bisects a line drawn tangentially to the point of maximum of the lingual margins of the alveoli for the two central incisor teeth.

ORBITALIA: The lowermost point on the margin of either orbit.

PORION: The highest middle point on the margin of the external auditory meatus.

PROSTHION (ALVEOLAR POINT): The most anterior-inferior point on the maxilla between the upper central incisor teeth.

PTERION: The region on the side of the cranial vault where the frontal, parietal, temporal, and sphenoid bones meet.

RHINION: The inferior extremity of the internasal suture.

STAPHYLION: Where a line tangent to the most anterior border of the posterior margins of the palatine bones cross the midline.

STEPHANION: The point where the coronal suture crosses the temporal lines.

SUBNASAL POINTS: The lowest points, on each side, on the lower border of the nasal aperture, i.e. the lowest points anteriorly of the two nasal fossae.

VERTEX: The summit or most superior point on the midsagittal plane on the external cranial vault.

## Cranial Measurements

(Modified after Hrdlička, 1947; Montague, 1960; Brothwell, 1972)

BASION-BREGMA HEIGHT (SKULL HEIGHT): From basion to bregma.

BASION-NASION LENGTH: From basion to nasion.

BIORBITAL BREADTH: From the middle of the one lateral orbital border (ectoconchion) to the other.

FORAMEN MAGNUM BREADTH: Points of maximum separation in transverse lines of the lateral borders of the foramen.

FORAMEN MAGNUM LENGTH: Between basion and opisthion.

INTERORBITAL BREADTH: Bilaterally between the two points where the posterior lacrymal crests meet the inferior border of the frontal, i.e. the distance between the right and left dacryon points.

LOWEST NASAL BREADTH: The distance between the points at which the nasomaxillary suture terminates at the nasal aperture on the left and right sides.

MAXILLO-ALVEOLAR BREADTH: Maximum breadth between the buccal surfaces of the second molars.

MAXILLO-ALVEOLAR LENGTH: Between the anterior surfaces of the alveolar border between the central incisors and the middle of the transverse line connecting the posterior extremities of the alveolar border.

MAXIMUM CRANIAL LENGTH: The greatest anterio-posterior diameter from glabella to the most posterior point in the mid-sagittal plane on the occipital bone, the opisthocranian.

MAXIMUM CRANIAL BREADTH: The greatest horizontal and transverse diameter of the skull. This can usually be taken above the auditory meatus or the supramastoid crest.

MINIMUM FRONTAL BREADTH: Minimum distance between the temporal crests on the frontal bone. This is the shortest distance between the origins of the zygomatic processes of the frontal bones.

MAXIMUM BIZYGOMATIC BREADTH: Maximum distance between the zygomae.

NASAL BREADTH: The maximum distance between the points of intersection of the nasofrontal and the nasomaxillary sutures on the right and left side.

NASAL HEIGHT: From the nasion to the lowest tip of the nasal spine on the lower border of the nasal aperture (subnasale or nasospinale).

ORBITAL BREADTH: From dacryon to the middle of the lateral orbital border (ectoconchion).

ORBITAL HEIGHT: The maximum distance between the upper and lower margins of the orbital cavity, taken at right angle to the orbital breadth.

PALATE BREADTH: The distance between the internal alveolar borders between the second molars.

PALATE LENGTH: Anteriorly, the median point of a line tangent to the posterior alveolar border of the median incisors; posteriorly, the median point of a transverse line connecting the most anterior points of the notches in the posterior border of the palate. From staphylion to orale.

TOTAL FACIAL HEIGHT: The distance from nasion to menton with the lower jaw in place and the teeth in apposition. Dental wear must be accounted for in taking this measurement.

UPPER FACIAL HEIGHT: From nasion to prosthion (aleolare).

## The Lower Jaw

BICONDYLAR WIDTH: The distance between the most external points on each condyle. The separation between these points constitutes the measurement.

BIGONIAL BREADTH: The distance between the gonia on the lower most margins.

CRANIAL CAPACITY DETERMINATIONS The most frequently used method is to fill the cranial cavity with mustard seeds or small shot. The contents are then poured into a cubic centimeter glass and the reading taken directly.

THE FRANKFURT HORIZONTAL LINE: The horizontal plane of the skull determined by the right and left porion and the lowest point on the inferior margin of the left orbit. The skull is normally oriented in the plane when measurements taken in a constant plane are to be made or when craniograms or photographs are to be made for comparative or illustrative purposes.

HEIGHT OF THE ASCENDING RAMUS: Between gonion and the uppermost point of the condyle.

MANDIBULAR LENGTH: From menton to a line perpendicular to the most posterior point on the condyles.

MAXIMUM BREADTH OF THE RAMUS: Anteriorly, the most prominent point on the anterior border of the coronoid process; posteriorly, the farthest point on the posterior border of the bone.

MAXIMUM CRANIAL CIRCUMFERENCE: From glabella around the maximum projection of the occiput (opisthocranion) to glabella.

MINIMUM BREADTH OF THE ASCENDING RAMUS: The minimum distance between the anterior and posterior edge of the ramus perpendicular to its height.

SYMPHYSEAL HEIGHT: Distance between the inferior border of the symphysis and the highest point on the alveolar border, i.e. between gnathion and infradentale.

TRANSVERSE CRANIAL ARC: From left porion across bregma to the right porion.

## Craniometric Indices

1. Cranial Index $\quad\quad\quad$ $\dfrac{\text{Max. Cranial Br.} \times 100}{\text{Max. Cranial Len.}}$

    Dolichocranic $\quad\quad\quad\quad$ X — 74.9
    Mesocranic $\quad\quad\quad\quad\quad$ 75.0 — 79.9
    Brachycranic $\quad\quad\quad\quad\;$ 80.0 — 84.9
    Hyperbrachycranic $\quad\quad$ 85.0 — 89.9

2. Cranial Length-Height Index $\quad$ $\dfrac{\text{Basion-Bregma Height} \times 100}{\text{Max. Cranial Len.}}$

    Chamaecranic $\quad\quad\quad\quad$ X — 69.9
    Orthocranic $\quad\quad\quad\quad\;$ 70.0 — 74.9
    Hypsicranic $\quad\quad\quad\quad\;$ 75.0 — X

3. Cranial Breadth-Height Index $\quad$ $\dfrac{\text{Basion-Bregma Height} \times 100}{\text{Max. Cranial Br.}}$

    Tapeinocranic $\quad\quad\quad\quad$ X — 91.9
    Metriocranic $\quad\quad\quad\quad\;$ 92.0 — 97.9
    Acrocranic $\quad\quad\quad\quad\quad$ 98.0 — X

4. Total Facial Index $\quad\quad\quad$ $\dfrac{\text{Nasion-Gnathion Height} \times 100}{\text{Bizygomatic Br.}}$

    Hypereuryprosopic $\quad\quad$ X — 79.9
    Euryprosopic $\quad\quad\quad\quad\;$ 80.0 — 84.9
    Mesoprosopic $\quad\quad\quad\quad$ 85.0 — 89.9
    Leptoprosopic $\quad\quad\quad\quad$ 90.0 — 94.9
    Hyperleptoprosopic $\quad\quad$ 95.0 — X

5. Upper Facial Index $\quad\quad\quad$ $\dfrac{\text{Nasion-Prosthion Height} \times 100}{\text{Bizygomatic Br.}}$

    Hypereuryene $\quad\quad\quad\quad$ X — 44.9
    Euryene $\quad\quad\quad\quad\quad\quad$ 45.0 — 49.9
    Mesene $\quad\quad\quad\quad\quad\quad$ 50.0 — 54.9

| | |
|---|---|
| Leptene | 55.0 — 59.9 |
| Hyperleptene | 60.0 — X |

6. Nasal Index
$$\frac{\text{Max. Nasal Br. of Nasal Aperture} \times 100}{\text{Nasion-Nasospinale Height}}$$

| | |
|---|---|
| Leptorrhine | X — 46.9 |
| Mesorrhine | 47.0 — 50.9 |
| Chamaerrhine | 51.0 — 57.9 |
| Hyperchamaerrhine | 58.0 — X |

7. Orbital Index
$$\frac{\text{Max. Orbital Breadth} \times 100}{\text{Max. Orbital Length}}$$

| | |
|---|---|
| Chamaeconch | X — 75.9 |
| Mesoconch | 76.0 — 84.9 |
| Hypsiconch | 85.0 — X |

8. Palatal Index
$$\frac{\text{Max. Palatal Breadth} \times 100}{\text{Max. Palatal Length}}$$

| | |
|---|---|
| Leptostaphyline | X — 79.9 |
| Mesostaphyline | 80.0 — 84.9 |
| Brachystaphyline | 85.0 — X |

9. Maxillo-Alveolar Index
$$\frac{\text{Bi-Ectomolare Breadth} \times 100}{\text{Maxillo-Alveolar Length}}$$

| | |
|---|---|
| Dolichouranic | X — 109.9 |
| Mesuranic | 110.0 — 114.9 |
| Brachyuranic | 115.0 — X |

## Postcranial Measurements and Indices

### Upper Extremity—Humerus

ANTERIOPOSTERIOR MIDDLE SHAFT DIAMETERS (sliding compass)

MAXIMUM DIAMETER OF THE HEAD: (sliding compass)

MAXIMUM LENGTH (OSTEOMETRIC BOARD): Between the most proximal and most distal points, the bone being held parallel to the long axis of the board.

MAXIMUM MEDIOLATERAL DISTAL DIAMETER: (sliding compass) Taken at the epiphyseal end of the bone immediately above its associated process.

MEDIOLATERAL MIDDLE SHAFT DIAMETER: (sliding compass)

RADIO-HUMERAL INDEX:
$$\frac{\text{Maximum Length Radius} \times 100}{\text{Maximum Length Humerus}}$$

### Lower Extremity—Femur

BICONDYLAR LENGTH: The two condyles rest up against the fixed upright and the moveable upright is brought against the femoral head, so that the whole femur rests naturally between the two uprights.

MAXIMUM DIAMETER OF THE HEAD:   (sliding compass)

MAXIMUM LENGTH:   (osteometric board) Between the internal condyle and the head.

| PLATYMERIC INDEX: | Anteroposterior diameter $\times$ 100 |
|---|---|
| | Mediolateral diameter |
| Hyperplatymeric | X — 74.9 |
| Platymeric | 75.0 — 84.9 |
| Eurymeric | 85.0 — 99.9 |
| Stenomeric | 100.0 — X |

SUBTROCHANTERIC ANTEROPOSTERIOR DIAMETER:   (sliding compass) Immediately below the lesser trochanter in the sagittal plane.

SUBTROCHANTERIC MEDIOLATERAL DIAMETER:   (sliding compass) From the medial to the lateral surfaces of the level of the preceding measurements.

### Lower Extremity—Tibia

ANTEROPOSTERIOR DIAMETER MIDDLE OF SHAFT:   (sliding compass)

ANTEROPOSTERIOR NUTRIENT FORAMEN DIAMETER:   (sliding compass) Diameter of the shaft at the level of the nutrient foramen.

MAXIMUM LENGTH:   (osteometric board) Taken with the bone resting on its dorsal surface with the medial malleolus resting against the upright.

MEDIOLATERAL DIAMETER OF MIDDLE OF SHAFT:   (sliding compass)

MEDIOLATERAL NUTRIENT FORAMEN DIAMETER:   (sliding compass)

| PLATYCNEMIC INDEX: | Medio-lateral nutrient diameter $\times$ 100 |
|---|---|
| | Anterio-posterior nutrient diameter |
| Hyperplatycnemic | X — 54.9 |
| Platycnemic | 55.0 — 62.9 |
| Mesocnemic | 63.0 — 69.9 |
| Eurycnemic | 70.0 — X |

## METRIC TRAITS

Metric traits are continuous morphological variables dealing with the size and dimensions of the skull and postcranial skeleton. The inheritance of these traits depends on the combined influence of many genes (Hanna, 1962; Boyd and Li, 1963). Their utility in biological distance studies is limited by several factors. These include low phenotypic specificity, plasticity, unknown mode of inheritance, age progressive and age regressive tendencies, and other environmental determinants which influence them during the lifetime of the individual. In spite of this, physical anthropologists have, for centuries, accumulated metric data on human groups and used them to hypothesize biological relationships and to trace certain historical events. This is because only skeletal material can provide information on the physical characteristics, behavior, and adaptation of past human groups; serological data did not live up to expectations in providing a more adequate explanation of genetic relationships or for historical reconstruction; and several lines of evidence (discussed below) show that biological relationships based on anthropometric differences correspond positively with linguisitic, geographic, and historic relationships.

Traditional anthropometry has come under severe criticism, e.g. Boyd (1950), as a useful tool in biological distance studies. Boyd advocated the use of blood group genes for such studies since their mode of inheritance is known, but there are several cases in which blood data failed to correspond to the known cultural history, linguistic affinity, and geographic entities of peoples of East Africa (De Villiers, 1968), New Guinea (Livingstone, 1969), and North America (Merbs, 1965). On the other hand, studies show that metric traits correspond positively when compared with linguistic, geographical, and historical relationships (Sanghvi, 1953; Jantz, 1970; Friedlaender, et al., 1971; Spielman, 1973). For example, Spuhler (1954) used metric data to measure relationships between several Pueblo groups that lack written historical documentation. The relationships were found to parallel the linguistic similarities and differences as determined by Spier (1936). Utilizing metric data from seven living Southwestern tribes, Hanna shows a positive correlation between the above data and linguistic affiliations of these groups. Hanna concludes that, "The analysis of morphological (metric) traits which, being polygenic in origin respond more slowly to gene transfer, may reveal patterns of relationships which more nearly represent the true historical picture" (Hanna, 1962).

Little attention has been given by physical anthropologists to studies of the genetic nature of metric traits. Studies of living subjects show, however, that many traditional metric variables, e.g. facial height and arm and chest breadths, do have high heritability indices (Clark, 1956; Osborne and De George, 1969).

According to Birdsell (1951, 1952) and Bielicki (1962), polygenic traits are relatively less sensitive to the action of selection than monogenic traits. Bielicki further indicated that polygenic traits with multiple loci are more stable through time, and hence far better markers in historical reconstruction of population affinities than single gene traits. Birdsell (1951) showed that genetic drift acting on small groups would more quickly cause extinction or fixation of extreme phenotypes when these types are determined by genes acting at one or a few loci, than when a large number of loci are involved. Hiernaux (1962) and Workman and Niswander (1970) suggested that polygenic traits are less sensitive to selection. Mourant (1962) noted that, where a population has been markedly reduced, single gene characters may show considerable change in frequency or disappear as a result of random fluctuation. Mourant indicated that polygenic characters are much more likely to remain stable, even though the frequency of some individual genes has probably been greatly affected. In relation to selection, Mourant suggested that polygenic traits will be selected for or against by environmental conditions, and thus all genes involved are likely to change in frequency to an extent comparable with that shown by a single gene character. Bielicki (1962), on the other hand, found the frequency of a selectively disadvantageous polygenic trait will decrease more slowly in a population than the frequency of a trait equally disadvantageous in terms of reproductive fitness but controlled by a single locus. According to Bielicki, this follows from the fact that segregation and recombination produces a lower percentage of individuals homozygous for many loci than those monozygous for a single locus. Consequently, in polygenic inheritance the extreme phenotypes segregate out more rarely, which means that a smaller portion is exposed to the full impact of selection than in the case of single factor inheritance.

Curt Stern (1960) discussed some simple examples, such as the efficiency of complete selection against a single factor homozygote and against a double homozygote, and concluded that "The speed with which selection permanently accomplishes specific results decreases with increasing number of loci" (Stern, 1960). Another genetic mechanism which tends to reduce the efficiency of selection upon polygenic traits is provided by linkage. Sheppard (1960) pointed out that polygenes which affect a particular character tend to form a balanced system, i.e. to be linked in such a way that in each chromosome involved there occurs a combination of allelomorphs which produce the optimum expression of the trait in the given environment. Consequently, if the environment changes and the expression of the trait is no longer at its optimum, there is in the population no inherited variability on which selection could operate and evolution would be impossible as long as variability is not released by crossing-over, which would take some time. Sheppard summarized the effects of such a situation as follows: "Integrated polygenic systems result in an inertia which has to be overcome by large and prolonged environmental changes before there will be any evolutionary change in the population despite the fact that selection is often intense, evolution is usually very slow" Sheppard 1960: 111).

The basic problem inherent in the analysis of distance statistics, utilizing archeological specimens, lies in their interpretation. Since the genetics of metric and nonmetric traits are still inadequately understood, conclusions must be viewed with caution. The nature of skeletal material and the problems encountered in using such material must be taken into consideration.

The degree of similarities or differences between archeological populations is at best descriptive and does not imply genetic affinity. Selection, gene flow, and genetic drift may have acted singly or in combination at the same time or at different time levels to produce the observed similarities or differences in the skeletal material. Similar diets and environmental conditions under which the groups lived may have also been responsible for the observed similarities or differences in their skulls.

# CHAPTER VI

# SKELETAL NONMETRIC TRAITS

Minor variants of the human skeleton have attracted the attention of students of anatomy for more than two millennia. For instance, Hippocrates, the father of medicine (460-377? BC), described wormian bones in human cranial sutures (LeDouble, 1903), although 2400 years passed before a serious attempt was made to compare human populations in terms of such traits. In 1900, Russell examined approximately 2000 skulls for nine variants generally believed to be potential criteria for racial differentiation. He attempted to use them to distinguish between North and South American Indians by examination of their frequencies in samples drawn from the two continents. LeDouble (1903, 1907) examined each bone of the vault and the face and described most of the known anomalies, often illustrating them with drawings, and considered etiology and possible causative factors. A good deal of attention was given to the relationship between the bony anomalies and related soft tissue variation. LeDouble reported group frequencies for some of his traits and compared frequencies in various human populations. Sullivan (1922) attempted characterization of American Indians using the incidence of variants in his study entitled "The Frequency and Distribution of Some Anatomical Variation in American Crainia." For this work, he utilized the collection of approximately 2500 American Indian skulls at the American Museum of Natural History. Like Russell and LeDouble, Sullivan reported frequencies but attempted no statistical analysis since the appropriate techniques did not yet exist. He was the first to discuss the criteria used in scoring the seven variants he considered and mentioned the problem of lack of standards for scoring which make the work of different men incomparable. Sullivan anticipated the current use of nonmetric traits when he said, "I am led to believe that when proper study is made of these anatomical characteristics considerable progress can be made towards indicating both racial and local affinities, but more particularly local affinities" (Sullivan, 1922).

The next major study of group incidence of cranial variants was Oetteking's (1930) monograph on the skulls of Northwest Coast Indians. He concentrated on nonmetric traits since the majority of the crania he studied are distorted by artificial deformation and therefore, not appropriate for a standard metric study. Oetteking compared his series of 526 crania with Old World Mongoloids and Caucasoids and also attempted to characterize Indians of the North Pacific Coast in terms of traits.

In the first large work concerning Southwestern Indian physical anthropology, Hooten (1930) explored both metric and nonmetric characteristics of a population sample from this region. His use of nonmetric traits to define subsamples was a pioneering effort in this regard.

In a series of papers (Wood-Jones, 1931, 1934, 1934b) generally entitled "The Non-metrical Morphological Characters of the Skull as Criteria for Racial Diagnosis," Frederick Wood-Jones discussed the evolutionary background and variation in expression of twenty-six traits which are commonly used today in differentiating between populations. Akabori's (1933) monograph on Japanese skulls is a model for the analysis of traits in a single population. He tested for significant differences by sex, age, and side of body of eighty-five traits in about four hundred crania of modern Japanese cadavers and found little or no influence of age or sex although there were several important exceptions in commonly used traits such as wormian bones, mandibular torus, and dehiscences of the tympanic plate. He noted that his bilateral frequencies, like Russell's, are reported on a "per head" rather than a "per occurrence" basis, methodological note often omitted by others.

A number of studies have focused on individual traits of the human skull, usually attempting to elucidate the cause of the anomalous variation. A majority of the older studies report these anomalies simply as curiosities, sometimes offering some explanation for their occurrence. More recently, a number of these traits have been recognized as being due to underlying genetic causes, and attention has focused on intensive studies of one or a few traits in efforts to determine the genetic mechanism involved. Examples of such studies include Anderson (1962) on dehiscences; Moorrees, Osborne, and Wilde (1952), Klatsky (1956), Suzuki and Sakai (1960), and Johnson, Gorlin, and Anderson (1965) on mandibular torus; Torgerson (1951a, 1951b), Urison (1959), Borian, Attwood, and Jaconette (1964), and Bennett (1965) on variation in facial foramina. Unfortunately, none of these studies have definitely established the mode of inheritance for any of the traits.

Animal studies have provided most of what little knowledge there is concerning the genetics of minor skeletal variants since animals are obviously more amenable to the necessary experimental studies in familial strains than are humans. Deol, Gruneberg, Searle, and Truslove (1957) describe skeletal traits in an inbred strain of mice, some of which are morphologically similar to traits found in man. They examined the range of incidence of twenty-seven nonmetric traits in seven sublines of an inbred strain of mice, all seven derived from siblings of the same mating. They found that after forty generations, fourteen of the traits diverged in incidence in the sublines, while all sublines showed a similar incidence for the remaining thirteen traits. The differences were attributed to a high rate of mutation although it was suggested that maternal nutrition also affected the expression of the traits. Grewal (1962) reported the relative incidences of twenty-seven traits in eleven sublines of an inbred mouse strain with known times of separation and, using this information, was able to devise a measure of the rate of divergence of the sublines. Gruneberg (1965) investigated third molar agenesis in the house mouse and suggested the trait may occur as a pleiotropic consequence of the action of any of three "major genes" on at least two different chromosomes, all of which act to reduce the size of all the molars as well as having other effects throughout the body. Earlier, Gruneberg (1951) showed third molar agenesis to have a characteristic incidence over many generations in three inbred strains and hence to serve to characterize these strains. He also demonstrated that the genetic substrate only determines tooth size, and that unidentified factors of maternal physiology determine whether or not a tooth falls below the critical size to permit it to develop. He noted, however, that tooth loss is more common in first litters and in large litters, both cases where total body size of the offspring is usually reduced. While the tendency is toward small teeth, actual molar agenesis, a discontinuous manifestation, is determined by other factors. Such a trait is termed by Gruneberg "quasi-continuous."

A similar situation in man was demonstrated by Carter and Wilkinson (1964). Congenital hip dislocation has been shown to have a familial incidence, with girls more prone to dislocation than boys, suggesting a genetic factor, but only 40 percent of monzygotic twin pairs are concordant for dislocation, indicating an environmental component to be operating. Apparently there is a genetic predisposition to acetabular dysplasia in certain families, augmented by general joint laxity induced by estrogen secreted by the female fetus. Dislocation itself may result from a number of environmental factors such as breech birth or tight swaddling. As in mouse molar agenesis, the factors leading to the presence of this anomalous variant are complex and environmentally influenced, but still basically genetic. This may be the case with many of the traits usually examined in skeletal studies in man.

R. J. Berry (1968) reported "applied" studies using nonmetric variants in mice. An island population of mice off the English Coast was introduced after 1881 according to anecdotal evidence. This population is believed locally to be derived from an adjacent coast while resembling those from a more distant village. It was found that the island population was indeed introduced from the distant region by a shepherd who commuted by boat between his home there and his flock on the island, thus confirming the unexpected results of the trait study and demonstrating the utility of such investigations in tracing population movements. Both Berry (1968) and

Petras (1967), who found variation in trait incidence in mice trapped at different locations on a single farm, attributed the observed frequency difference to genetic drift and found effect in inbred isolates.

In summary, the mouse data indicates that minor nonmetric traits of the skeleton apparently do indirectly reflect part of the underlying genotype of the population and that biological comparison of related groups is legitimate and accurate using population incidence of these traits. A similar study carried out with deer (Rees, 1969a, 1969b) indicates the reliability of the technique with animals other than mice, which suggests that it may also be applicable to man.

Laughlin and Jorgensen (1956) used trait analysis successfully to demonstrate the presumed prehistoric movement of contiguous groups of Eskimo around the coastal periphery of Greenland, but Brothwell (1959) achieved somewhat equivocal results comparing populations from scattered points on the globe, although the expected relationships (as among various Mongoloid populations versus Caucasoids) are broadly acceptable.

Berry and Berry (1967) also compared widely scattered populations and achieved expected similarity within demonstrably related groups such as two American Indian populations and within a series of Egyptian skeletons, but very unlikely results when the groups are totally unrelated. For example, their results show close affinity between American Indians and the Ashanti of Nigeria.

Bennett (1967) uses trait analysis as part of his description of the Point of Pines skeletons and finds that population to be more similar to those of Casas Grandes and Mesa Verde than to Pecos Pueblo, a not unexpected result based on probable contacts among the three more westerly groups. Yamaguchi (1967) examined eighteen traits in Ainu, Japanese, and two groups of aboriginal skulls and found that the closest resemblance was between two groups of aborigines as expected. J. E. Anderson (1968), working with skeletons from mound and premound groups from the same sites, found that he was often able to place individual skeletons in their correct population by comparing the skeletal traits of the individuals with the trait profiles of the populations. DeVilliers (1968), in her extensive morphology and metric study of the skull of South African Negroes, employed trait distance as a measure of relationship among South African groups. Her profusely illustrated work is especially valuable for defining her method of scoring traits. Nancy S. Ossenberg (1969) examined more than 1200 skulls of American Indians and Eskimo/Aleuts for a number of traits. Her contribution adds to the body of knowledge concerning trait studies, primarily in the area of trait classification. Kellock and Parsons (1970a) found differences of the sort to be expected among Australian aborigines from different parts of the continent and, in a later paper (1970b), found that the subdivisions of aborigines were more similar to one another than to either Melanesians or Polynesians.

It may be concluded from trait analyses in human groups that the method has most validity when applied to groups believed to be fairly closely related on linguistic or other grounds, but to be less reliable in comparing widely disparate groups such as American Indians to Nigerians.

As previously noted, the mode of inheritance has not yet been stabilized for any of these nonmetric traits. What is needed are familial studies of the traits in the bones, a task which presents almost insuperable problems since it requires collection of skeletal evidence from individuals of known consanguinty spanning several generations. A possible solution to this problem may lie in examination of X rays. Meschan (1973) illustrated many traits in radiographs, which suggest that a familial study may be possible using films now stored in hospitals and other repositories.

A list is offered here of some of the nonmetric skeletal traits that have been used in studies of human skeletal populations. For various reasons, not all of these traits are equally appropriate to every study and some reason must be used in their selection. Some of the theoretical and impirical reasons for selecting a certain number of these traits include: frequency of a given trait in the skeletal sample, condition of the skeletal material at hand, durability of the traits in "mishandled" material, etc. For instance, if a trait has a very low or a very high frequency in the material examined, the likelihood of miscounting the trait increases. If the skeletal sample is fairly small relative to the percent frequency of the trait, a true count of its presence or absence may be missed by chance alone. A trait with a frequency in man of about 5 percent may not be present at all in a sample of fifty skeletons, or it may occur in 20 percent of the cases. Either way the results are biased. It is better to use traits whose frequency falls between perhaps 20 percent and 80 percent.

## CRANIAL NONMETRIC TRAITS

### Supraorbital Foramen

The supraorbital foramen or notch (see Figure 24) is located on the medial one third of the superior margin of the orbit. It permits passage of fibers of the corrugator supercilius nerve exiting from the roof of the orbit to the external surface of the frontal bone. The passage may take the form of a broad shallow notch, a narrow deep notch approaching a closed foramen, or a foramen. The foramen is formed by ossification of a "supraorbital ligament" crossing the notch (Breathnach, 1965). Variations include a notch, a foramen plus a notch, or multiple notches plus a foramen. The complex occurring above one eye is often different from that found above the other.

A notch may be as much as 5 mm wide and less than 1 mm in depth or it may be very narrow, as little as 2 mm in width. Depth ranges up to 5 mm. A foramen is counted only if completely encircled by bone. Foramina, if single, usually tend to be approximately 1.5 mm in diameter but may be as large as 3 mm. If multiple, they tend to be 1 mm or less in diameter. In number, there may be from one foramen to three or more. Rarely, there is no evidence on the frontal bone of the passage of the supraorbital vessels at

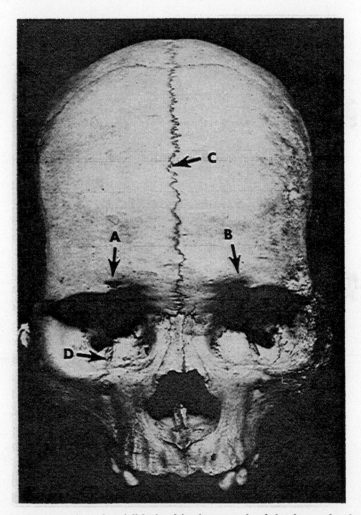

Figure 24: Nonmetric traits visible in this photograph of the front of a skull are:

A — Supraorbital foramen
B — Supraorbital notch
C — Metopic suture
D — Sulcus infraorbitalis

all. A notch, a foramen, or combinations of both may be found in infant skulls.

A foramen is scored present only if completely surrounded by bone creating a discrete hole or opening. If the border is incomplete in any degree at any point it is counted as a notch. Scoring only foramen versus notch, no sex difference was seen by Oetteking (1930), Akabori (1934), Berry and Berry (1967), or Ossenberg (1969). Oetteking (1930) found the foramen the more common expression among Northwest Coast crania. Wood-Jones (1931) reported notches to be more common in male than in female Hawaiians. DeVilliers (1968) reported a tendency for a notch to occur more often than a foramen in South African Negro crania, and for a foramen, if present unilaterally, to occur slightly more frequently on the right side than on the left. Ossenberg (1969) reported a trend toward increase in the presence of the foramen form among males and an opposite trend among females. Sublett (1970) reported no difference by size or sex in Seneca skulls.

### Metopic Suture

The frontal bone at birth is divided into two halves bilaterally by a metopic suture (see Figure 24). The metopic suture in infancy extends from the nasofrontal suture superiorly along the midline to bregma. This suture usually closes between the first and second years of life, with persistence of the suture beyond the second year considered to be anomalous (Breathnach, 1965). While a metopic suture may rarely persist throughout life as a discrete suture separating the frontal bone, it more commonly manifests itself as a partially obliterated suture persisting only as a remnant extending 2 or 3 cm above the nasofrontal suture. The remnant suture seldom penetrates deeper than the outer table of the frontal bone, or it may not penetrate the outer table at all. Often it is so indistinct as to be very difficult to detect. This remnant, as with the inferior portion of a complete metopic suture, is very tortured in its path. Only this torturous portion tends to persist as a remnant supranasal suture, the more nearly straight part being the portion which is obliterated in almost all skulls.

The metopic suture has received considerable attention (LeDouble, 1903; Bryce and Young, 1916; Bolk, 1917; Sullivan, 1922; Maslovskie, 1927; Augier, 1928; Schultz, 1929; Akabori, 1934; Montagu, 1937; Comas, 1942; Hess, 1946b; Woo, 1949a; Urison, 1959; and Ossenberg, 1969). Limson (1924), studying Filipino skulls, reported a higher male incidence. Hess (1946b) defined a "metopic syndrome" of correlated cranial and finger anomalies, probably genetically determined. Montagu (1937), based on a survey of the literature concerning metopism in man and other primates, came to the same conclusion. Torgersen (1951b) studied the trait radiographically in the living and concluded that the presence of the suture is due to a dominant gene with varying penetrance. Ossenberg (1969) concluded that the trait is present slightly more often in females than in males, a condition also found by Akabori (1934).

### Parietal Foramina

The parietal foramina are located on each parietal bone beside the posterior half of the sagittal suture. The foramina transmit emissary veins from the superior sagittal sinus and sometimes a small branch of the occipital artery (Breathnach 1965). The foramina may be absent, present unilaterally, or present in varying numbers on each side.

Akabori (1934) reported a tendency for the right foramen to be larger than the left, but that no sex difference in frequency was seen in Japanese crania. Other authors (LeDouble 1903; Oetteking 1930; Berry and Berry 1967; Ossenberg 1969) report only the presence or absence of the foramen. Bass (1964) reported the foramen absent in more than half the central Plains Indian skulls he examined, with a single foramen most often present on the right side. Hooten (1930) reported missing foramina were more common in Pecos females. Sublett (1970) found the foramina absent more commonly on the left in Seneca skulls and absent slightly more often in females.

### Epipteric Bone

A wormian bone may occur at pterion and is termed an epipteric bone (see Figure 25). When it occurs, it ordinarily separates the frontal bone from the temporal bone. It may take any of a number of shapes, separating the two bones completely, separating all four of the bones which meet at this junction, or it may occur only as a bone "chip."

The occurrence of an epipteric bone has been reported by Oetteking (1930), DeVilliers (1969), Ossenberg (1969), Sublett (1970), and many others, although most authors report only presence/absence data. Ossenberg (1969) reported a decrease in frequency of the epipteric bone with age and a somewhat higher frequency in females. She found epipteric bones to be generally more common on the left side of the skull. Oetteking (1930) reported a slightly higher incidence of epipteric bone in male skulls and a common occurrence bilaterally. His data included no information on age change in the frequency of the bone. Sublett (1970) found these bones more common on the left side of the skull and in females.

### Pterion Shape

The junction of the great wing of the sphenoid, the frontal, parietal, and temporal bones is known as pterion. It is a region of considerable variety

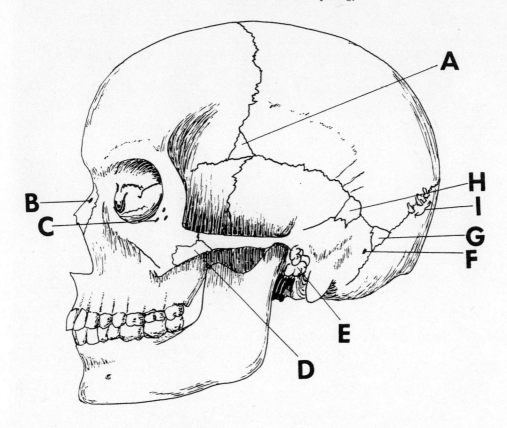

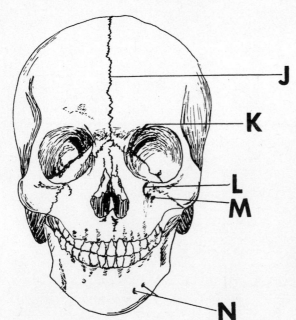

**FIGURE 25:** Key to traits visible on the front and side of the skull.

A – Epipteric bone and configuration of pterion.
B – Nasal foramen
C – Zygomatic foramen
D – Os japonicum
E – Auditory exostosis
F – Location of mastoid foramen
G – Asterionic bone
H – Parietal notch (with wormian bone)
I – Lambdoid wormian bones
J – Metopic suture
K – Supraorbital foramen/notch
L – Infraorbital suture
M – (Multiple) infraorbital foramina
N – (Multiple) mental foramina

Drawing courtesy of Sally Heald.

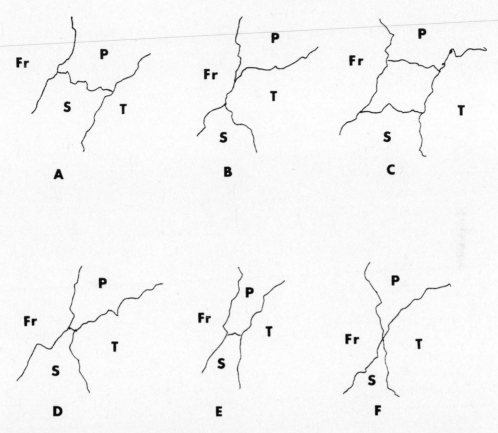

Figure 26: Various configurations of the suture pattern at pterion. Fr = frontal bone, P = parietal, T = temporal, and S = sphenoid.

since the area of contact between the sphenoid and parietal is not constant. The usual contact occupies about 1 cm, but may be reduced to only a few millimeters. In rare cases the four bones (frontal, parietal, sphenoid, and temporal) may meet at one point. In some cases pterion may be reversed by the meeting of the temporal and frontal bones to the exclusion of the parietal and sphenoid.

Bass (1964) reported the wide H pattern to be by far the most common one in central Plains Indians. He found no side difference. Hooten (1930) also found the wide H most common, but in females the narrow H and K forms are more frequent than in males. Murphy (1956) reported no influence of age, sex, or side in the Australian aboriginal skull. Collins (1926; 1930) reported no sex difference in pterion configuration in a large, worldwide sample of skulls.

### Asterionic Bone

The junction of the temporoparietal suture and the lambdoid suture is known as asterion (see Figure 25). A wormian bone may occur at this juncture separating the lambdoid suture from the temporoparietal suture. The bone may vary in size but is normally triangular in shape and approximately 1 cm on a side.

Sublett (1970) and Akabori (1934) reported an asterionic bone present slightly more often on the right side than the left. Akabori found no age or sex influence on the trait. Sublett (1970) found the trait more commonly in Seneca females.

### Parietal Notch

In the fetus the temporal bone is composed of two parts, the petrous portion and the squamous portion or fanlike superior part of the bone. The two parts are separated by the squamosal suture of the temporal bone. Where the squamosal suture meets the temporoparietal suture a notch may be formed (see Figure 25). This notch apparently represents advancement of the parietal bone into the temporosquamosal suture before the union of the two parts of the temporal at approximately the sixth month in utero (Breathnach 1965). The notch may be absent or it may persist in varying depths. It may also contain a wormian bone.

Observations of this trait are reported by Ossenberg (1969), Oetteking (1930), Akabori (1934), Laughlin and Jorgensen (1956), Brothwell (1959), Anderson and Merbs (1962), Bass (1964), and Berry and Berry (1967). All of the above reported only the presence of a wormian bone in the notch. Ossenberg (1969) reported a higher male incidence of the notch bone, while Berry and Berry (1967) found no significant sex difference. Sublett (1970) reported no sex difference in Seneca skulls. Bass (1964) found notch bones to be rare in central Plains Indian skulls (2 to 13%) with no marked side preference.

Scoring of this trait may be done by measuring depth of the notch in 2 mm increments. Depth is measured from a line drawn across the notch representing a continuation of the superior margin of the temporal bone. The depth of the intrusion of the parietal bone into the temporal bone is measured in 2 mm increments up to 10 mm.

### Supramastoid Crest

The supramastoid crest serves as an attachment for the temporal fascia. The size of the supramastoid crest varies from complete absence of any manifestation of a crest, to a barely perceptible line, to a considerable moundlike linear structure.

Supramastoid crest is scored by DeVilliers (1968), Hooten (1930), Oetteking (1930), Washburn (1947), and Scott (1957). Oetteking (1930) observed that the supramastoid crest is often large and projects posteriorly in deformed Northwest Coast crania more than in undeformed skulls. However, the same situation is frequently encountered in undeformed skulls. His conclusion was that the trait is not solely dependent on size or form of function of the skull. DeVilliers (1968) found a marked supramastoid crest more frequently in South African males than in females while a slight crest is more typical of females than of males. Washburn removed the temporal muscles in a series of day-old rats and examined the development of the crest in the fully grown specimens. He reported that the supramastoid crest fails to develop in these animals. Scott, however, noted that Eskimos and Lapps, living under similar environmental conditions, do not have the same sort of supramastoid crest. Eskimos have massive craniofacial skeletons while those of the Lapps are rather delicate. He concluded "that the ability of the craniofacial skeleton to respond to functional demands of increased masticatory activity is to a large extent determined by the genetically controlled plasticity of the bone" (Scott 1957). Hooten (1930) found the crest rarely at Pecos. He reported the crest present more often in males.

### Lambdoid Bone

A lambdoid bone may form at the junction of the lambdoid and sagittal sutures at the time of initial closure of the lambdoid fontanel. It is usually small and approximately triangular or diamond shaped. It may occur as a single wormian bone, or it may be divided horizontally into two parts or by a vertical suture into left and right halves.

Akabori (1934) reported that the frequency of the lambdoid bone is independent of age and shows a slightly greater frequency in Japanese males although the latter difference is not significant. Berry and Berry (1967) found no significant difference in the expression of the trait by sex. Sublett (1970) reported it present more often in Seneca females.

### Inca Bone

In the fetus, the formation of the Inca bone (see Figures 28 and 29) takes place from inferior and superior squama of the occipital. These are separated by a suture which runs from asterion to asterion. This suture, if it persists into adult life, creates the Inca bone. Closure of the suture normally occurs before birth. The superior squama may be divided into as many as four parts, two paired central portions and two lateral portions (Oetteking, 1930). Failure of any of the fetal sutures of the superior squama of the occipital bone to close may produce Inca bones which are bipartite, tri-

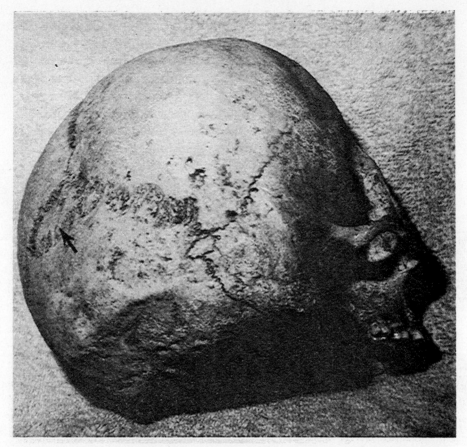

Figure 27: A lamboid bone (arrow).

partite, or four separate elements.  The latter case is the least common.  It is also possible for any single element described to be present alone; i.e. a left or right half, third, or fourth of the Inca bone may be present.

The Inca bone has been discussed by Oetteking (1930), LeDouble (1907).  Torgersen (1951a) reported pedigree studies suggesting that Inca bones are inherited as a dominant trait with a penetrance of around 50 percent and varying expression depending on modifiers influencing head shape in general.  Many other authors have reported frequencies for this variant in various cranial series.  However, the usefulness of the trait for comparisons is limited because different criteria have been used in assessing the presence or absence of this trait.  That is, certain authors combine lambdoid and Inca bone as one trait and do not clearly differentiate between the two.  In the mouse (Deol and Truslove 1957), the analogous trait shows a wide range in incidence among inbred strains sug-

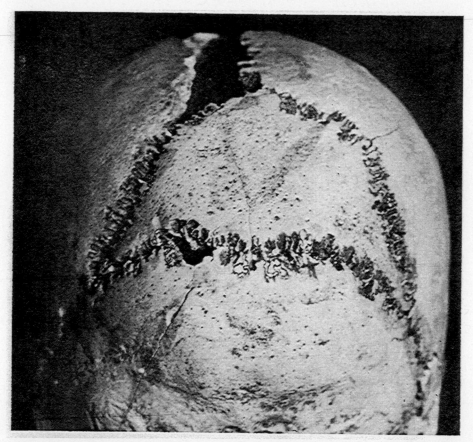

Figure 28: A true Inca Bone. Note the suture passing approximately from asterion to asterion. This feature is not to be confused with the lambdoid bone, as shown in figure 27.

gesting the trait to be genetically determined. Hooten (1930) reported only one Inca bone in Pecos Pueblo males and one in females, both from the late (Glaze V and VI) period. Both Hooten and Matthews (1889) denied the influence of cranial deformation in the production of the Inca bone.

### Lambdoid Suture Wormian Bones

Wormian bones may occur in the lambdoid suture at any point from asterion to asterion, but bones which occur at lambda or asterion are considered separately elsewhere since they occur at sutural junctions rather than in the course of a single suture. The bones themselves may be small or large, single or multiple. The presence of wormian bones in the lambdoid suture has been attributed to stress brought about by cranial deformation (Bennett, 1965). However, these wormian bones are often found in

Figure 29: A tripartite Inca bone.

undeformed crania and may be absent in the crania which are artificially deformed.   This would suggest that there is a predisposition to lambdoid suture wormian bones which is certainly influenced by the presence of artificial deformation.

Torgerson (1951a) and Hess (1946a) attributed the presence of these ossicles to developmental malfunctions possibly having a genetic component. It is also noteworthy that hydrocephalic crania almost always exhibit numerous lambdoid as well as other wormian bones.   Stress is no doubt a contributing component in the formation of this feature.   El-Najjar and Dawson (1977a) studied a sample of Southwestern skulls giving attention to the number of bones "per side."   They reported the number of bones to be higher on the "affected" side in cases of asymmetric deformation, but to be present in skulls lacking any evidence of deformation.   Dorsey (1897) noted the connection between the pressure of deformation and an increase in the num-

Figure 30: Elaborate wormian bones in the lambdoid suture. In this case, the skull was that of a child whose skull had been artificially deformed.

ber of lambdoid wormian bones. Ossenberg (1969) noted a higher incidence of lambdoid sutural bones in male skulls, although the difference is not statistically significant. She found no side difference in undeformed crania. Sublett (1970) found them more commonly in Seneca males than females. This trait was attributed entirely to pressure by Bennett (1965), an interpretation which seems unlikely in light of the above.

Lambdoid suture wormian bones are counted "per side." By this it is meant that bones to the observer's left of lambda are counted as left side bones. Bones to the right of lambda are counted as right side bones.

### Postcondylar Foramen

A foramen may usually be found on the posterior portion of the occipital condyle which transmits an emissary vein from the sigmoid sinus to the

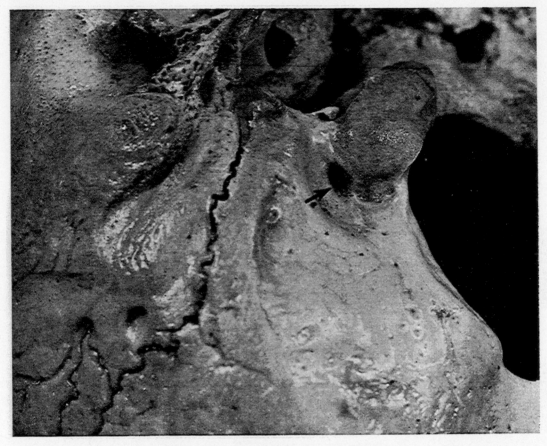

Figure 31: A postcondylar foramen (arrow).

vertebral plexus of the spine (Breathnach, 1965). This foramen may be present or absent, although the former is by far the most common. To be counted as a sealed or absent foramen, the aperture has to be entirely sealed so that a straw cannot be passed through the usual site of the opening.

Presence or absence of this foramen is scored or reported by Wood-Jones (1931, 1934), Berry and Berry (1967), Akabori (1934), Oetteking (1930), and Ossenberg (1969). Oetteking reported no difference in frequency of "foramen absent" in adult Northwest Coast Indians of all ages as did Ossenberg for Sioux and Akabori for Japanese. Sublett found no side difference for this trait in Seneca skulls, nor any sex difference (Sublett, 1970).

### Pharyngeal Fossa

The pharnygeal fossa is a depression resulting from incomplete closure of the two sides of the basilar portion of the occipital bone (LeDouble, 1903).

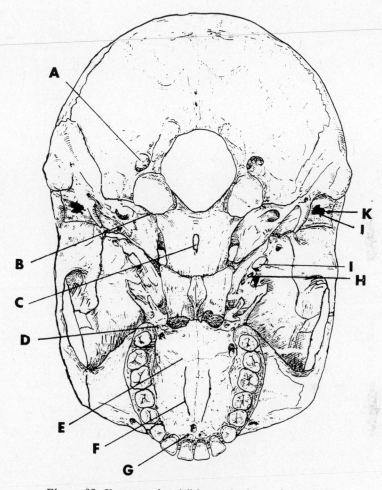

Figure 32: Key to traits visible on the base of the skull.
A — Postcondylar foramen
B — Hypoglossal canal
C — Pharyngeal fossa
D — Accessory lesser palatine foramen
E — Transverse palatine suture
F — Palatine torus
G — Anterior palatine alveolar foramen
H — Pyterygospinous bridge
I — Foramen ovale configuration
J — Tympanic dehiscence
K — Tympanic marginal foramen
Courtesy of Carolina Biological Supply Company, Burlington, North Carolina.

If present, the fossa is located in the midline of the basilar part of the occipital bone 5 to 10 mm in front of the anterior rim of the foramen magnum.

Figure 33: A shows a hypoglossal canal; B shows a tympanic dehiscence.

The width of the fossa usually varies from 2 to 4 mm. Its depth may vary from less than 1 mm to as much as 7 mm.

In addition to LeDouble (1903), frequency of occurrence of the fossa was reported by Sullivan (1922), Collins (1926), Oetteking (1930), Ossenberg (1969), Bass (1964), and many others. Collins (1926) found a higher female incidence for the trait but no age influence. LeDouble (1903) found a decrease in the percentage of fossae with advancing age, as did Ossenberg. Ossenberg (1969) also noted a slightly higher female incidence for the trait. No variation in frequency by either sex or age was recorded by Oetteking (1930). Other studies of this trait have been made by Romiti (1891), Rizzo (1901), and Sullivan (1920).

The pharyngeal fossa is scored by measuring the depth below the apparent normal surface of the basilar portion of the occipital bone. No fossa apparent and a fossa depth of 2 mm or less are combined into a single grade for measurement. The reason for this is that irregularity normally occurs on the surface of the bone at this point and it cannot be determined whether a depression of less than 2 mm is actually an incident pharyngeal fossa or only the normal rugosity of the bone.

## Hypoglossal Canal

The hypoglossal canal, located anterior to and beneath the occipital condyle bilaterally, is the emissary foramen of the hypoglossal nerve. The canal may be a single foramen, or it may be bifurcated either by a tongue of bone overgrowing it externally or by a bar dividing it internally.

Oetteking (1930) reported bifid canals in embryonic human crania. Ossenberg (1969) found a slight increase in the incidence of bifid hypoglossal canals with age in Aleut-Eskimo and Sioux skulls. A similar situation was found in Northwest Pacific Coast Indian crania by Oetteking (1930). However, Japanese crania show a slight decrease from youth to older adults (Akabori, 1934). Ossenberg (1969) found no sex difference in this trait. Sublett (1970) found a higher incidence of bifidity in male Seneca skulls. Ossenberg also found a slightly higher incidence of bifidity on the left side of the skull. Many other workers reported the population incidence of the trait, including LeDouble (1903) and Berry and Berry (1967).

## Occipital Condyles

The occipital condyles are located lateral to the foramen magnum on the occipital bone and support the skull on the first cervical vertebrae. They vary in size from one individual to another.

This size of the occipital condyle was considered by DeVilliers (1968), Oetteking (1930), and many others. DeVilliers reported no significant sex differences in the distribution of the size categories of this trait. No comparable data is found for this size study in other reports.

## Jugular Foramen

The jugular foramina are located bilaterally on the margins of the occipital and temporal bone of the base of the skull, lateral to the occipital condyles. These are the emissary foramina of the jugular vein from the internal skull. They may be quite variable in relative size. The left foramen may be larger than the right, the right foramen may be larger, or they may be equal in size.

Akabori (1934) and Oetteking (1930) both found the right jugular foramen to be commonly larger than the left, but found no sex difference in the expression of this size difference.

### Pterygo-Spinous Bridge or Spur

The pterygoid plate of the sphenoid bone may have a highly irregular posterior surface. Jagged excrescences may occur on the posterior margin of the plate which may arch back to form a bridge over a vessel passing behind the plate along the base of the skull. More often, a spur of bone may form a tongue or an arc which is an incipient bridge (see Figure 32).

The literature concerning this trait has been reviewed by LeDouble (1903) and more recently by Chouké (1946; 1947). Other studies of large cranial series have been made by Oetteking (1930) and Akabori (1934). Chouké found no significant difference in the occurrence of this trait between sexes nor did he find any significant variation with age. Ossenberg (1969) also reported no significant change according to age in her series of North American Indians, but did find the trait to be more common in males than in females. She also found it to be slightly more common on the left side than on the right. Hooten (1930) reported the foramen or spur to be fairly common at Pecos Pueblo and most common in males. Sublett (1970) found spurs slightly more commonly on the left side in Seneca skulls and in males.

### Foramen Ovale Configuration

The foramen ovale is located in the sphenoid bone on the base of the skull. It permits exit from the skull of the mandibular division of the fifth cranial nerve, its motor root, and the accessory meningeal artery (Breathnach, 1965).

Variations in the configuration of the foramen ovale have been noted by various authors (LeDouble, 1907; Akabori, 1934). Akabori (1934) found no appreciable age or sex difference in expression of this trait, but did find anomalous foramina to be more common on the right side than the left.

### Superior Sagittal Sulcus Direction

The superior sagittal sulcus is found in the midline of the skull on the internal surface. On the occipital bone it changes direction normally to the right side of the skull. However, it may turn to the left, it may continue down the occipital, or it may terminate indistinctly.

In Seneca skulls, Sublett (1970) found a left deflection of the sinus in approximately 22 percent of the 130 skulls examined. There was no sex difference. LeDouble (1903) reviewed the studies of this trait made up to the turn of the century. He did not report incidence of direction by sex, but did find that the sinus usually turns to the right.

### Tympanic Plate Thickness

This trait has been studied by Anderson (1962), DeVilliers (1968), and others. Stewart studied the tympanic plate in Eskimos and Northern and California Indians and reported distinct differences. The Eskimo exhibited comparatively massive development of bone below and anterior to the external auditory meatus. The same occurred to a somewhat lesser degree in Northern Indians, but the California Indians showed a thin tympanic plate. Stewart concluded that the thickened plate of Eskimo is a hereditary trait as is the development of this trait in oher groups, although possibly secondarily influenced by irregular ossification resulting from diet or disease. DeVilliers (1968) found the tympanic plate to be usually moderately developed in the South African Negro. A massive plate occurs slightly more frequently in males than in females, whereas a delicate plate is more common in females than in males. Sublett (1970) found no meaningful side or sex difference for this trait in Seneca skulls.

Tympanic plate thickness is graded by measuring the thickest part of the tympanic plate of the temporal bone with small sliding calipers.

### Tympanic Marginal Foramen

A small foramen may sometimes occur 1 to 5 mm from the lateral margin of the tympanic plate (see Figure 32). Its etiology is uncertain, but in location and form this trait resembles a true foramen rather than any expression of tympanic dehiscence. It is not known what vessel(s) pass through this foramen when present.

Ossenberg (1969) is the only person to date to report the incidence of this trait in a cranial series, although Laughlin (1963) mentioned it in conjunction with the dehiscence of the tympanic plate in the third skull from the upper levels of Chou Kou Tien. Ossenberg (1969) reported a rapid increase in the frequency of the trait through childhood with stability occurring after adolescence. She found a very slightly higher frequency of the trait in females and a slightly higher frequency in occurrence on the left side than on the right.

### Tympanic Dehiscence

Perforations of the floor of the anterior wall of the auditory meatus are found in varying sizes and frequencies in the immature as well as the mature skull. According to Anderson (1962), in the former they are a normal feature of the growth of the tympanic wall and the perforation closes about the fifth year of life. If they persist in the adult, however, such perforations are considered anomalous. They may occur as a single irregular-edged perforation, as a number of small perforations, or there may be a complete absence of ossification of the anterior wall of the tympanic plate. It is said to be difficult at times to determine whether a perforation is antimortem or postmortem. However, careful inspection of the margins will usually indicate whether they have been broken, or whether they have the rounded edge typical of normal growth leading to the anomaly.

Tympanic dehiscence (foramen of Hushke) has been recognized as a defect in the floor of the tympanic plate (LeDouble, 1903; Oetteking, 1930; Anderson, 1962), although LeDouble suggested that the imperfection may actually be the result of rarefaction of the bone. Anderson (1962) noted that the imperfection is almost universally present before the age of eight years. He reported a decrease in the incidence to the age of approximately twenty, beyond which those skulls which are to retain perforated tympanic plates do not change much in frequency. Ossenberg reported a similar situation in Hopewellian and Aleutian skulls and concluded (1969) that "there is a rapid decline in the frequency of the trait during childhood after which its incidence remains stable." Ossenberg (1969) found a slightly higher incidence of perforated tympanic plate in females and believes that this difference is found in most populations. She found no consistent tendency toward occurrence of the trait on one side over the other. Hooten (1963) reported the trait more commonly in males than in females at Pecos Pueblo and noted that "this sex difference is usual" (1930). Sublett (1970) found no side difference for this trait in Seneca skulls, but a slightly higher frequency in females. Anderson (1962) noted that dehiscence appears to be more common in females and on the left side.

### Auditory Exostoses

Auditory exostoses (see Figure 25) are hyperostoses lying within the auditory canal and visible through the auditory meatus. They usually arise from the posterior wall of the tube and may be exposed as small ridges or "pearls" or may be so large as to nearly occlude the lumen of the meatus.

This trait has received the attention of many workers (Turner, 1879; Russell, 1900; Oetteking, 1930; Hrdlička, 1935); Oetteking (1930) suggested that the trait is correlated with cranial deformation. However, in his series of Northwest Coast crania, a number of undeformed skulls showed evidence of this trait, while many which were deformed lacked it. He concluded that there is likely a population tendency toward the presence of exostoses regardless of cranial deformation.

Hrdlička (1935) attributed the first description of the variant to J. H. F. Autenrieth in 1809. An extensive annotated review of the earlier literature on auditory exostoses may be found in Hrdlička's work. His final conclusion concerning the etiology of the growth was that it is caused by neurovascular derangement rather than disease and falls properly into the category of abnormality rather than pathology, probably having a hereditary predisposition aggravated by mechanical or chemical irritation (1935). The exostoses are found more commonly in males than in females according to Hrdlička.

### Suprameatal Pit

Superior to the auditory meatus on the temporal bone and just outside the margin of the meatus may occur a shallow pit. This pit most typically has a thin shelflike floor while the upper margin blends into the temporal bone. It possibly serves as a point of attachment for some of the cartilagenous ear.

Akabori (1934) found the pit absent more often in females than in males, and in the young more often than in the old. He found no side difference. Turner and Laughlin (1963) reported the pit present from birth in Sadlermiut Eskimo skulls more frequent in adult males than females.

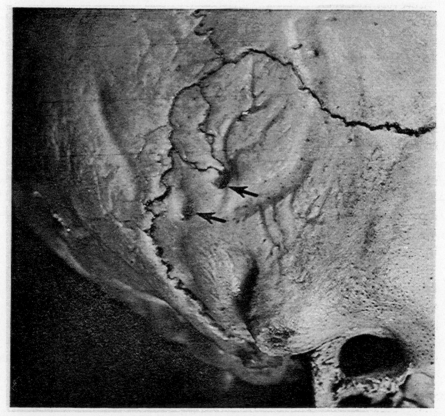

Figure 34: Mastoid foramen (arrows). In this case one of the foramina is extrasutural.

### Mastoid Foramen Locus

The mastoid foramen (see Figure 34) is typically located in the occipito-mastoid suture, but may be found in the mastoid portion of the temporal bone or on the occipital. It may also be absent altogether.

Oetteking (1930) observed the size and number of this foramen, but gave no summary. Boyd (1931) reported no age or sex differences in 1500 crania examined. Akabori (1934) however, found the frequency of the foramen increases to age thirty in Japanese and remains stable after that age. He found the foramen absent slightly more often in females. Berry and Berry (1967) found no association with sex.

### Multiple Infraorbital Foramina

The infraorbital foramen (see Figure 25) occurs bilaterally beneath the inferior orbital margin on the maxillary bone. It permits the passage of the infraorbital nerve and vessels. This foramen is usually single. On either side, however, it may be internally divided by a bar of bone, or it may occur as two or more separate foramina existing on the external surface of the maxilla.

DeVilliers (1968) found this trait to be very rare in South African Negro crania. She found a slightly greater incidence of multiple foramina on the left side, but the difference was not significant. Riesenfeld (1956) found occasional significant differences in the frequency of multiple foramina between different neighboring localities but could determine nothing about the kinship relations between these groups. Schultz (1954) described crania from Tierra del Fuego belonging to a single family all showing multiple foramina. He suggested, therefore, that a genetic factor may be involved in the feature. DeVilliers noted that in the South African Negro, multiple foramina show a slight preference for the left side. Sublett (1970) finds a well-marked preference for occurrence of this trait on the left side in Seneca skulls (19% right versus 29% left) and for occurrence in males.

### Infraorbital Suture

A small suture (see Figure 25) may occur on the maxillary bone extending from the inferior margin of the orbit into the infraorbital foramen. The suture may be entirely absent, it may be complete, or it may be present only in part. If partial, the superior third is the portion ordinarily present.

Oetteking (1930) noted that the presence of an infraorbital suture is generally assumed to be an Eskimo characteristic but that high frequencies have also been observed in other groups. The suture persists in roughly 20 to 40 percent of European crania (Oetteking, 1930). Ossenberg (1969) noted that the incidence of the suture decreases with age. The same was noted in Japanese crania (Oetteking, 1930; Akabori, 1934). The same authors noted a slightly higher female incidence for the trait. No significant side difference in the expression of the trait was seen by Ossenberg. Bass (1964) found a higher frequency of the suture on the left side in Plains Village Indians.

### Sulcus Infraorbitalis

The sulcus infraorbitalis (see Figure 24) occurs on the floor of the bony orbit as the groove for the passage of the infraorbital nerves and vessels within the orbital cavity. It disappears anteriorly in the floor of the orbit while the vessels exit again at the infraorbital suture on the facial surface of the bone. This groove may be a narrow and deep trench, or it may be a broad and shallow furrow. In addition, it may be partially or completely bridged. No discussion of this trait by other authors is found.

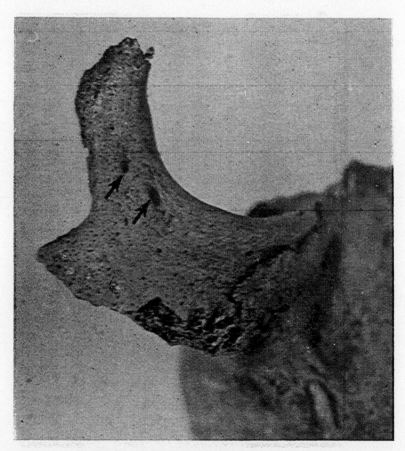

Figure 35: Multiple zygomatic foramina (arrows).

## Os Japonicum

The zygomatic bone is normally single. However, it may be divided into superior and inferior portions by the transversozygomatic suture due to incomplete fusion of two primary growth centers. The inferior bone thus separated is termed os japonicum (see Figure 25). The occurrence of a complete os japonicum is very rare, but the transversozygomatic suture may be present partially. It occurs in partial form as a faint remnant on the lateral surface of the zygoma extending anteriorly approximately 1 cm from the zygomaticotemporal suture and obliterated or fused beyond that point. The result may be termed an incomplete os japonicum and is not infrequent in American Indian skulls.

Oetteking (1930) found no case of a complete os japonicum in his Northwest Coast Indian cranial series. Examination of his raw data indicates no meaningful sex or side differences in the occurrence of the partial os. DeVilliers (1968) reported the complete os japonicum in only three of 714 South African Negro crania examined. Birdsell (1949) believed the os japonicum to be of simple genetic determination. He added, however, that the mode of inheritance would be difficult to establish since the character is affected by age changes. Torgersen (1951a) believed that the os japonicum may be partly determined by a gene which delays suture closure.

## Zygomatic Foramen Number

On the external surface of the lateral portion of the zygomatic bone usually occurs an emissary foramen for the zygomaticofacial branch of the zygomatic nerve (Breathnach 1965). The foramen may be absent, single, or multiple. On occasion it is difficult to separate multiple foramina from the normal porosity of the bone. However, one or more of the foramina are usually distinctly larger than the pores and can therefore be detected as being emissary foramen. Berry and Berry (1967) found no difference in expression of the trait between the sexes.

## Nasal Bone Shape

Martin and Saller (1959) classify eight shapes of nasal bones. DeVilliers (1968) reported grade 2 nasal bones to be characteristic of South African Negroes with no difference in frequency by sex. Sublett (1970) found "hourglass-shaped" nasal bones most common in Seneca males, and "triangular" bones in females.

## Nasal Foramen

An emissary foramen (see Figure 25) normally occurs near the center of each nasal bone. This foramen may be absent, single, or multiple.

Akabori (1934) found this trait not to be age dependent but absence of

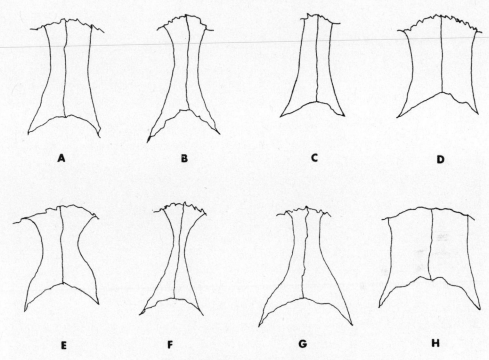

Figure 36: Shapes of nasal bones.

one foramen to be slightly more frequent in males. Also, absence was more frequent on the left side than the right.

### Palatine Torus

The palatine torus is a bone elevation or benign exotosis occurring along the intermaxillary suture on the roof of the mouth. In form and size the torus may vary considerably. It usually begins near the incisive foramen and may extend posteriorly on the surface of the palatine bone to its posterior margin. In width it may extend approximately 1 cm for most of its length, tapering at the ends. It may be uniform and smooth or it may exist as irregular rounded globules. It may also occur as a sharp edged but small bony ridge following the margins of the suture closely.

Classification schemes for the palatine torus have been introduced by Campbell (1925), Miller and Roth (1940), Hooten (1918), and Woo (1950). DeVilliers (1968) showed a slightly higher incidence of the torus in females and a slightly higher incidence of the ridge form than of the mound form. She found no examples of the lump form. She reported the sex difference to be statistically insignificant. DeVilliers (1968) also found the torus to be slightly more frequent in younger than older individuals, although it occurs in all age groups. By manipulating the age interval re-

Figure 37: Palatine torus (arrow).

ported by Miller and Roth (1940), Woo showed that the age difference demonstrated by them is no longer apparent. Miller and Roth (1940) and Woo (1950) found the torus slightly more common in living females. These sex differences are not significant. The development of the torus has been ascribed to the following: pathology of the palate (Thoma, 1937); functional stress (Hooten, 1918; Matthews, 1933; Hrdlička, 1940); genetic factors by Lasker (1947, 1950) who attributed the torus to autosomal dominant inheritance in at least some instances. Scott (1957) believed there is a genetic component involved as well as masticatory stress. Hooten (1930) found a small palatine torus in about 12 percent of Pecos crania of both sexes. Sublett (1970) found a torus more common in Seneca female skulls.

### Transverse Palatine Suture

The transverse palatine suture (see Figure 32) separates the palatine bone from the paired maxillae anterior to it. The suture may be a straight line, it may be irregular, or it may be deflected anteriorly or posteriorly (Stieda, 1894, cited in Akabori, 1934).

Akabori (1934) found no significant sex difference in the expression of this trait in Japanese crania. Sublett (1970) reported anterior curvature to be 58 percent in Seneca females versus 32 percent in males. The suture is straight in 16 percent of females and 29 percent of males.

### Torus Maxillaris

A bony hyperostosis may occur on the surface of the maxillae just lateral to the molar teeth. This exostosis varies in size and is usually globular and irregular in shape.

Hooten (1918) believed torus maxillaris to result from irritation of the bony tissue. Hrdlička (1940) believed, however, that the torus is functional in origin and is caused by excessive masticatory stress. Woo (1950) demonstrated a high percentage of both torus maxillaris and torus mandibularis for both Caucasian and Negro crania and concluded that correlation exists between these structures. DeVilliers (1968) found a slight correlation between torus palatinus and maxillaris in South African crania.

### Anterior Palatine Alveolar Foramen

The anterior palatine alveolar foramina (see Figure 32) occur bilaterally on the lingual surface of the maxillae usually 2 to 4 mm superior to the inferior margin of the bones directly above the central incisor teeth. They may be absent, single bilaterally, or multiple, although single bilateral occurrence is apparently most typical. No reference to this trait is found by other authors.

### Accessory Lesser Palatine Foramen

Posterior to the maxillary third molar teeth and internal to the alveolar process occurs a foramen in the maxilla termed the lesser palatine foramen. Frequently an accessory foramen (see Figure 38) is also present in the same region. Berry and Berry (1967) detected no difference in occurrence between the sexes.

### Three-Rooted Mandibular Permanent First Molar

The first permanent mandibular molar, in common with other mandibular molars, is normally a double-rooted tooth. However, in certain cases, a relatively diminutive third root may arise on the lingual side of the distal root below the cervical border. Tratman (1951) suggested that this third root is a true root. Turner (1971) however, believed the feature to be a lingually displaced portion of the distal root.

Figure 38:   Accessory lesser palatine foramen (arrow).

A. E. Taylor (1899) is apparently the first to calculate frequencies for three-rooted mandibular first permanent molars. Tratman (1938) suggested that this trait might be a Mongoloid population marker. Pederson (1949) and Gabriel (1948) have also studied this trait. Turner (1969; 1971) has given the most attention to 3RM1. He noted that the frequency of the trait does not differ significantly between the sexes except in Aleut-Eskimos. He noted the bilateral asymmetry of 3RM1 is frequent in both sexes and in all groups studied. He has also shown a slightly higher male frequency for this trait in American Indian crania and a significant difference between the sexes in Aleut-Eskimo crania. He has suggested a simple recessive X-linked mode of inheritance for the trait for the Aleut-Eskimo population data but notes that it does not fit any other population.

### Mandibular Torus

Mandibular torus (see Figure 39), named by Furst (1908), is a hyper-ostosis occurring on the lingual surface of the mandible above the mylohyoid line and below the alveolar process. It may extend anteroposteriorly from the vicinity of the first premolar roots to approach the third molar roots. It may vary in size from a faint irregularity confined to the region of the

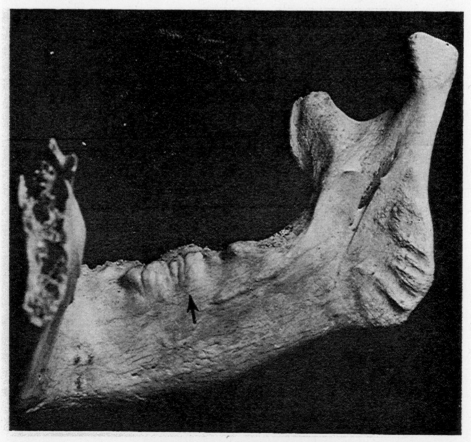

Figure 39: Mandibular torus (arrow).

premolar roots to massive billowing bilateral hyperostoses which may nearly
meet in the midline.  It is composed of normal bone.  Usually, the trait is
approximately symmetrical bilaterally although Lasker and Lee (1957) reported frequent exceptions in Caucasian twins.

Presence of the torus was attributed to functional stress by Hooten
(1918), Campbell (1925), and Hrdlička (1940).  Many other investigators
attribute the growth to genetic factors, probably modified by environment
(Furst and Hansen, 1915; Drennan, 1937; Moorrees, Osborne, and Wilde,
1952; Suzuki and Sakai, 1960; Johnson, Gorlin, and Anderson, 1965).  As
observed in studies by Moorrees (1957), Suzuki and Sakai (1960), Sublett
(1970), and others, the expression of the trait in certain populations appears
to be sex influenced, although other studies do not find this to be the case.

## Mylohyoid Bridge

The mylohyoid groove runs approximately vertically on the internal
surface of the ramus of the mandible.  This groove permits passage of the
mylohyoid nerve and artery (Breathnach 1965).  The groove formed in the
mandible may be partially or completely bridged.

Frequency of this trait has been reported by LeDouble (1907), Laughlin
and Jorgensen (1956), Anderson (1962), Bass (1964), Ossenberg (1969), and
Sublett (1970), among others.  Ossenberg reported an increase in the incidence of the trait from 0 percent in the first decade of life to a peak of approximately the age of twenty years, with stability in frequency thereafter.
She found no significant sex difference, but a possible tendency toward a
higher incidence in males.  She found no consistent side difference, although
Bass (1964) found a higher incidence on the left side than on the right in a
Plains Indian series.  Sublett (1970) found a left side preference for this
trait in Seneca skulls and a more common occurrence in males.

In addition to an unmodified mylohyoid groove, varying degrees of incipient bridge may occur, or there may be a complete bridge.

## Everted Gonial Angle

The gonial angle, which occurs at the inferoposterior corners of the
mandible, may be a straight line continuation of the inferior border of the
mandible or it may be deflected medially or laterally (inverted or everted).
In scoring this trait attention must be given to the inferoposterior margin
of the angle primarily as the indicator of its deflection or lack of deflection,
although the deviation, if any, usually extends a centimeter or more onto the
body of the mandible.

Horowitz and Shapiro (1955) showed that the angular process of the
mandible may be modified by the removal of the masseter muscle.  Wash-

Figure 40: Photograph of the internal aspect of a plaster cast of a mandible exhibiting a bridged mylohyoid groove (arrow).

burn (1947) and Avis (1959) also demonstrated that the muscles of mastication have to do with the formation of the angular process of the mandible. Moss and Simon (1968) discussed the angular process of the human mandible and noted that it alters its inclination with age, changing from a medial to a lateral flair during the transition from the neonatal to the adult stage. They attributed this change to a change in orientation of the masseter muscle. In the Gran Quivira skeletal series (McWilliams, 1974), everted gonial angles are found in mandibles of individuals as young as three to six years of age. No doubt muscle function can alter mandibular architecture, but other factors seem to be operating as well.

### Multiple Mental Foramen

The mental foramen is located externally on the anterior portion of the body of the mandible, usually just below the root apex of the first premolar.

*Forensic Anthropology*

It permits the exit of the mandibular branch of the trigeminal nerve and accompanying vessels from the interior of the body of the mandible to the external surface where it serves the fascia of the lower lip (Breathnach 1965). The mental foramen is usually single but may be multiple, usually two. The accessory foramina are of two types. One type commonly lies on or just within the rim of the principle or larger foramen and is separated from it by a small spicule of bone which is usually easily distinguished. In some cases, however, it may not be readily observed. In other cases two discrete foramina may be present, one of which is usually larger than the other. The accessory foramin may occur in any direction from the primary foramen but is most commonly posterior to it and usually no more than 3 to 5 mm distant.

This trait has been examined by LeDouble (1907), Oetteking (1930), Montagu (1954), Riesenfeld (1956), Murphy (1957), and Ossenberg (1969), among others. Montagu (1954) noted a higher frequency on the right side, and in females. Ossenberg (1969) reported an increase in fre-

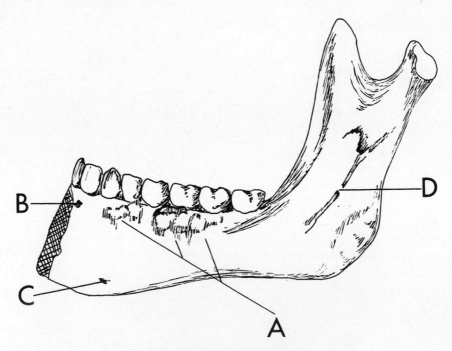

Figure 41: Key to traits visible on the mandible.
  A — Mandibular torus
  B — Mental alveolar foramen
  C — Internal mental foramen
  D — Mylohyoid bridge

Drawing courtesy of Sally Heald.

quency through the adolescent years until the age of approximately twenty, after which stability occurs. Akabori (1934) found no age difference in Japanese crania. Ossenberg found no significant difference between sexes or sides. Sublett (1970) found no side preference or sex difference in Seneca skulls.

Mental foramina are scored as single, barred internally, or occurring as two separate foramina.

### Mental Alveolar Foramen

The mental alveolar foramina (see Figure 41) occur bilaterally on the lingual surface of the mandible just inferior to its superior margin and immediately below the central incisors. These foramina may be absent, single or multiple.

DeVilliers (1968) reported that when these foramina occur in unequal numbers on the two sides, they tend to be more numerous on the right side. She found no significant sex difference in the expression of the trait.

### Lateral Infracondylar Tubercle

On the lateral portion of the ramus of the mandible, just inferior to the mandibular condyle, a knoblike eminence of bone may occur, to which attaches the lateral temporomandibular ligament (Breathnach, 1965). This eminence, when present, varies in size. It may rise no more than 1 mm from the surface of the bone or may be as much as 4 mm in height. Its surface dimensions vary from approximately 1 mm to 1 cm vertically and from 4 to 7 mm horizontally. No description of this trait has been found in the literature concerning anatomy or physical anthropology.

Variation in the shape of the mandibular coronoid process is described by LeDouble, who found several classifications for the shapes (LeDouble 1907).

Grade 1. (LeDouble grade d). The coronoid process is pointed and tends to lean anteriorly.

Grade 2. (LeDouble grade f). The coronoid process is pointed and essentially vertical.

Grade 3. (LeDouble grade a). The coronoid process is pointed and curves posteriorly "en forme de lame sabre" (LeDouble 1907).

Grade 4. (LeDouble grade c). The process is blunt and approximately vertical in orientation.

LeDouble's grades e (bicuspid) and b (truncated pyramid) are uncommon.

According to LeDouble (1907), the trait is age influenced, becoming progressively more elongated and posteriorly recurved with advancing years. Avis (1959) presented evidence which suggests that the process becomes recurved posteriorly under the influence of tension from the temporal muscle.

# CHAPTER VII

# CONGENITAL VARIATIONS, ANOMALIES, AND MALFORMATIONS

FAMILIARITY WITH THE normal variations, anomalies, and deformities of the human skeleton is important in order to differentiate such conditions from those due to local and systemic manifestations of disease. In this chapter, skeletal anomalies and malformations that are easily diagnosed with fairly good accuracy are examined. Most of these are congenital and/or developmental in nature. Congenital defects are those anomalies or deformities existing at the time of birth. They can be inherited or acquired as a birth injury. In general, our knowledge of the range of congenital abnormalities in prehistoric and historic human groups is slim. The incidence, distribution, pathogenesis, and probable etiology of those lesions that leave recognizable marks on archeologically derived human skeletal remains are discussed. In diagnosing these defects students should be aware that there is no sharp line of distinction between normal skeletal variants and congenital variations which border on the abnormal or show a wide range of expression. Often, many of these defects are associated with otherwise normal cranial and postcranial skeletons and thus go unnoticed by many students.

The first part of this chapter deals with the various types of cranial defects resulting in abnormal size and shapes due to premature closure of the sutures (craniostenosis). The second part examines both cranial and postcranial defects that are due to growth or developmental problems at the embryological or postnatal stages. Also, due to its importance in prehistoric and living groups, a discussion is presented dealing with trephination.

## CRANIOSTENOSIS

Craniostenosis is a relatively rare anomaly in which the sutures of the skull close prematurely causing compression of the intracranial contents and consequent cessation of growth. The condition has been known for centuries. Homer, in the *Iliad,* talks of a man who came to Ilium complaining that his head was pointed at the top, or towerlike. The term "craniostenosis" was introduced by Virchow in 1851 to describe skull changes due to a premature synostosis of the cranial sutures. Under this term, several different types of deformity resulting from generalized and/or localized premature suture closure are included.

In addition to the term craniostenosis, premature closure of skull sutures is known as: premature synostosis, synostosis cranii, oxycephaly, pyrago-cephaly, turricephaly, "steeple-skull", "sugar-loaf skull", plagiocephaly, clinocephaly, trigonocephaly, leptocephaly, acrocephaly, craniofacial dyso-stoses of Crouzon, and acrocephalosyndactylism.

Simmons and Peyron (1947) suggested the following classification for the various types of skull deformities resulting from premature closure of the sutures:

A. Complete, early, premature synostosis of the cranial sutures:
    1. oxycephaly without facial deformity,
    2. craniofacial dysostosis of Crouzon,
    3. acrocephalosyndactylism, and
    4. delayed oxycephaly (onset after birth).
B. Incomplete early synostosis of the cranial sutures:
    1. scaphocephaly,
    2. brachycephaly,
    3. plagiocephaly, and
    4. mixed.
C. Late (normal) synostosis of the cranial sutures occurs after the skull has reached adult size so that no deformities and no symptoms result.

All cases of premature synostosis have abnormally shaped skulls. The nature and degree of deformity depends on the number of sutures involved, the order in which they close, the age at which synostosis begins, and the underlying mechanisms producing such deformities. Severe degrees of skull deformity occur only if the sutures close early in life. If the sagittal suture closes, the skull is dolichocranic (long), but if the coronal suture closes, the skull becomes brachycranic (round). The limitation of growth is compen-sated for by excessive growth in other directions, resulting in peculiar and anomalous shapes of the skull. For example, closure of the sutures on one side of the skull will cause asymmetry, and closure of all the sutures will cause the skull to be tower-shaped as a result of pressure upward against the open anterior fontanelle by the growing brain. Sutures may become com-pletely obliterated in skulls at a much earlier age than that considered normal. Bolk (1915) examined 1,820 human skulls varying in age from three to twenty years and found synostosis in one or more sutures in 343 of the skulls.

Normal growth and obliteration of skull sutures are directly dependent upon normal brain growth. The rate of the growth of the skull parallels that of the brain. Within the first three years of life, approximately 80 per-cent of the entire growth of the brain is completed (Hope, Spitze, and Slade,

1955). After three years of age, there is only a slight increase in intra-cranial capacity. Any increase in skull size is due largely to thickening of the skull bones and growth of accessory sinuses and bones of the face. The base of the skull is not usually affected in craniostenosis. Rieping (1919) produced postmortem evidence to prove that the base of the skull is not involved. Moss (1957a), on the other hand, shows that abnormalities in the cranial base are positively correlated with premature closure of the metopic suture in the skulls of cleft palate individuals. Moss (1957b) states ". . . we postulate that a correlation exists between malformations of the skull base and premature cranial synostosis which is mediated by an altera-tion of the fibrous organization of the dura matter."

Various hypotheses have been suggested to explain the nature and possi-ble causes of this condition. According to Virchow (1851), when sutures close prematurely normal growth is inhibited in the direction perpendicular to the suture undergoing synostosis and compensatory growth takes place in other directions. Inflammation of the meninges is suggested by Virchow as causing premature suture closure.

In 1907, Thoma advanced the hypothesis that pressure produced all pathologic closure of sutures during fetal life. Park and Powers (1920) in-sisted that the margins of the cranial bones are kept apart by interstitial normal growth of mesenchymal tissue. Greig (1926) defined synostosis of a suture as fusion of contiguous bones so that movement or growth is no longer possible. Sear and Sydney (1937) considered craniostenosis to be essentially a dystrophy of the membranous bones.

The most reasonable explanation for premature suture closure was put forth by Morselli (1875) who suggested that synostosis occurs as a result of premature closure of adjoining bones caused by too close a proximity to their ossific centers. This theory was later modified by Rieping (1919). Rieping's theory was stated with special reference to oxycephaly as a defect in the germ plasm resulting in a dislocation of the primary ossific centers of the frontal and parietal bones causing synostosis of the coronal suture. Rieping thought that there was, in addition, some fault in the blastodermal matrix separating the bone. Giblin and Alley (1942) showed in experi-mental animals that synostosis of the cranial sutures is influenced by the mobility of the bones when they demonstrated that synostosis of a suture will occur if the bones are immobilized by a bony bridge across the suture. Recently, Moss (1959) suggested that etiological factors of premature suture closure include meningeal inflammation, rickets, birth trauma, atavism, hyper- and hypovascularization, and disturbances of growth correla-tion between the brain and vault.

Using pedigree analysis, several authors have shown that craniostenosis

is inherited. Young (1922) believed the abnormality to be the result of
some inherent defect in the germ plasm rather than any mechanical factor.
More recently, Bennett, in his review of the literature as well as his own
analysis of several cases, concluded "The available evidence strongly supports the viewpoint that sutural fusion, whether normal or pathological,
may be added to the list of secondary morphological skeletal characteristics.
This of course does not detract from possible genetic explanations; it simply
eliminates sutural fusion as the primary event." (Bennett, 1967).

## Scaphocephaly (sagittal synostosis)

Scaphocephaly (boat- or keel-shaped skull) is a condition in which the
skull is long and narrow as a result of premature closure of the sagittal
suture. Widening and elevation of the frontal region and medial ridging
(keeling) may also be present. This form of craniostenosis is characterized
by an excess of growth in anteroposterior direction while the width of the
skull is relatively smaller. The cephalic index is usually well below seventy.
The base of the skull and the upper jaw are narrow and the parietal bones
are flatter than usual.

Scaphocephaly has been used interchangeably with the term "dolicho-
cephaly" (Hope et al., 1955). Anthropologists have reserved this term to
describe people with long heads, e.g. the skulls of the ancient Basketmakers
of the American Southwest as compared to the Puebloans who had
brachyranic or more rounded skulls. According to Bernat and Bernat
(1973), scaphocephaly is not usually accompanied by additional congenital
defects in the cranial or postcranial skeleton. The pattern of inheritence
seems to be autosomal dominant with variable penetrance (French and
Suechting, 1955; Anderson and Geiger, 1965).

## Turricephaly

Turricephaly is the most common type of craniostenosis. The skull is
increased in height and often in width. As a result of interference in development due to early synostosis of the transverse sutures, marked bulging
occurs in either the frontal or parietal region of the skull (Pendergrass,
Schaeffer, and Hodes, 1956). There are a number of different types of
turricephaly. Two, oxycephaly (broad vertex) and microcephaly (small
rounded skull) are discussed in detail.

### *Oxycephaly*

Oxycephaly refers to premature closure of the coronal and saggital
sutures which prevents normal expansion both in the transverse and anteroposterior direction. According to Greig (1926), the term "oxycephalides"

was used in 1830 by the great naturalist H. Milne Edwards to designate a variety of crustaceans in which the head is more or less moulded like a rostrum. This condition is also known as acrocephaly, dysostosis cranio-facialis (Crouzon), and tower or "steeple skull" (Cohn, 1945; Fairman and Horrax, 1949; Hope et al., (1955). Because of the frequent association of this condition with syndactylism of the extremities, it is also known as acrocephalosyndactylia (Cohn, 1945). This term was first introduced by Apert in 1907. Oxycephaly is not always associated with syndactylism and the association varies in degree and extent.

In oxycephaly, the shape of the skull is variable, depending on the extent of suture involvement. In general, the oxycephalic skull is shortened anterioposteriorly and is highest at or near bregma, resembling a tower. The orbital cavities are shallow leading to forward protrusion of the eyeballs in living individuals, disproportion of the maxilla and mandible, narrow, highly arched palate, poor development of maxillary and zygomatic bones, and a parrotlike nose (Cohn, 1945). Oxycephaly does not occur at all ages, but occurs most often during the period of brain growth.

Greig (1926) divided oxycephaly into three types: (a) true oxycephaly which is congenital and often associated with syndactylism or other deformities of the extremities; (b) delayed oxycephaly which may appear at any time during childhood and never presents other deformities; and (c) false oxycephaly which is localized synostosis, not congenital, and often of definite origin. Cohn (1945) later suggested that in false oxycephaly the synostosis is limited to one or a few of the cranial sutures, the facial bones are never involved, and associated deformities of the skull are not present. Furthermore, in true oxycephaly the apex of the head is at or near bregma while in false oxycephaly the maximum head height shows a wide range of variability, in many cases being located at the posterior part of the skull (Cohn, 1945).

Greig (1926) found the condition to be transmitted from the first to the next generation but not to the third. Torgerson (1951a), on the basis of family studies, concluded that there appear to be two groups of genes influencing the sutural patterns of the skull, one determining the ossification centers and sutures and the other determining the rate of obliteration. Brothwell (1972) believed the disorder is dictated by abnormal growth at the coronal suture, but that other sutures may be involved. The normal anterioposterior growth is prevented by the premature closure of the coronal suture leading to compensatory growth upwards.

### Microcephaly (small headedness)

Microcephaly refers to partial agenesis of the brain accompanied by irregularities in the thickness of the cranial bones resulting in a lacunar or fenestrated skull.  Microcephaly has been classified by Schuller (1918) as: congenital underdevelopment of the brain or "microcephalus vera," often weighing but one-fourth as much as the average normal brain; and, an arrest in the development of the brain tissue following primary brain disease or "pseudomicrocephalus".

In general, the circumference of the microcephalic skull is two or three standard deviations below the mean for the appropriate age and sex (Martin, 1970).  The abnormally small head is often associated with and results from a primary developmental defect in the brain.  Microcephaly may be detectable at birth or go unnoticed until the skull bones are found to be growing at a different rate than facial bones.

According to Brushfield and Wyatt (1926) the characteristic features of the true microcephalic skull include: marked recession of the frontal and parietal regions; flattening of the occipital; large prominent nose and receding chin; cranial capacity less than 1000 cc; cranial measurements all below normal; often thick bones of the skull; early closure of the bregmatic fontenalle and all the sutures; a face that is large in comparison to the head; and large and long hands and feet.  All microcephalics show some evidence of mental retardation from near normal to profound idiot.  Their physical stamina is below normal and their susceptibility to minor illnesses and infection is marked.

Various hypotheses have been advanced to explain the mechanisms responsible for microcephaly.  Zappert (1926) suggested that irradiation of the uterus during the early months of gestation will cause microcephaly in 50 percent of the subsequent births.  Murphy (1928), and recently Dudgeon (1967), reported similar findings.  Rubella, Herpes virus 2, and cytomegalovirus have also been implicated as causative agents in microcephaly (Baron, Youngblood, Siewars, and Medearis, 1969; Reisman and Matheny, 1968; South, Tomkins, Morris, and Rawls, 1969).

According to Whitney (1932), microcephaly is produced by arrested development occurring at about the fourth or fifth month of gestation and that hereditary factors are without a doubt a factor, since the microcephalics almost invariably come from either mentally deficient or markedly neuropathic individuals.  This has been supported by several family studies (Zappert, 1926; Brunshfield and Wyatt, 1926).  Genetic forms of microcephaly include the autosomal recessive type and others that are associated with assorted chromosomal anomalies (Reisman and Matheny, 1968; Baron et al., 1969; South et al., 1969; Daniel, 1971).  Other studies (Dyggve and Mikelson, 1965; Insley, 1967; McKusick, Mahlouji, Abbot, Lindenberg, and Kepas, 1967) have described various anomalies ranging from mosiacism for a C chromosome to the deletion of the short or long arms of chromosomes 5 and 18, respectively.  The recessive form is usually uncomplicated, with the exception of mental retardation, although microcephalics with normal intelligence have been observed (Martin, 1970). Daniel (1971) found chromosomal abnormalities in three microcephalic children and suggested that microcephalics have a higher risk for cytogenic and biochemical anomalies than other retarded children.

## Plagiocephaly (lop-sided head)

Plagiocephaly is the result of unilateral premature synostosis of one or more of the sutures, with the temporoparietal being most often involved. The skull appears to be normally developed on the one side and underdeveloped on the other, or one side more anteriorly and the other side more posteriorly (Morse, 1969). Unilateral temporomandibular joint dysfunction, developing in childhood, may produce asymmetrical changes as the result of unequal tension of muscles of mastication upon the skull (Pittard and Baicoyano, 1928-1929). In the American Southwest, skull deformation of the vertical occipital type, due to the usage of cradleboards, may produce changes similar to plagiocephaly. These skulls, however, show no evidence of premature closure of any of the skull sutures. The etiology of plagiocephaly is not known. Most probably, the condition is due to differential growth rates of various cranial bones.

## OTHER CRANIOFACIAL DEFORMITIES AND ANOMALIES
### Anencephaly

Anencephaly is a lethal congenital malformation in which the brain is amorphous and the vault of the skull is absent (Nakano, 1973). About three fourths of the anencephalics are stillborn and those surviving die within a week after birth. The incidence of anencephaly in human populations varies from 0.29 to 5.93 per 1,000 births. In both American and African Negroes the incidence is low (Casady, 1969). In Asians, except for the Sikh Indians, the incidence is also low (Searle, 1959). Anencephaly occurs six times more frequently in Caucasians than in Negroes (Casady, 1969). In general, there is a high rate of occurrence among the Irish, born both in Ireland and in the U.S. (Elwood and MacKenzie, 1971). Rates for children of Irish ancestry are three times greater than for their neighbors studied in Boston by Naggan and MacMahon in 1967, but were still considerably lower than those reported in Ireland itself.

### Arachnodactly (Marfan's Syndrome)

Arachnodactly was first described by Marfan in 1896 in a child with extreme length and slenderness of the bones of the hands and feet. Marfan considered the anomaly to be congenital or familial in origin and suggested the name "dolichostenomelia". Individuals with arachnodactly have long extremities, depressed sternum, a skull that tends to be dolichocephalic in contour, pronounced supraorbital ridges, frontal bossing, pointed chin, kyphosis, and a broad and somewhat flattened nose.

The etiology of arachnodactly is not known but is thought to be hereditary (Piper and Irving-Jones, 1926; Parker and Hare, 1945). Hereditary and congenital embryonic derangement in the mesodermal elements in the body tissue during the early weeks of life has also been suggested (Parker and Hare, 1945).

## Hydrocephaly

Hydrocephaly is a condition characterized by abnormal accumulation of fluid in the ventricular and subarachnoid spaces associated with a large, globular skull and frontal bossing. By definition, it is the quantity of fluid within the cranium and the size of the ventricular system, and not the size of the skull, that determines whether or not the term hydrocephaly is applicable. In archeological specimens the following features are usually present: enlargement of the head; the fetal skull may show an increased circumference in contrast to the relatively small mass of the facial bones; thinning of the skull bones; bulging fontanelles; widely separated sutures often filled with sutural (wormian) bones; atrophy of the supraorbital ridges; and a flattened cranial base.

Hydrocephaly appears to be the result of intracranial pressure caused by infection, tumor, or injury. According to Laurence (1960), the symptoms are evident in the first six months of life and the death rate is highest in the first eighteen months. Trevor (1950b) reported a case of a Romano-British male from Norton, Yorkshire, with a cranial capacity of about 2,600 cc, some 1,000 cc more than the average adult male skull.

## Hypertelorism

Hypertelorism is a rare congenital craniofacial deformity. The orbits are unusually widely separated, circular in configuration, directed laterally, and of considerable depth. The skull has a low forehead and a pronounced vertex; the nasal bones are short and the binasal width is increased; the mastoid processes are comparatively massive; the hypophyseal fossae is large; the smaller wings of the sphenoid are well developed and the great wings retarded in their development. According to Pendergrass et al. (1956), the disturbance of growth is in the prechordal part of the skull and, therefore, affects the nose and eyes in particular.

## Trigonocephaly

Trigonocephaly is a condition in which the skull is triangular in shape with the frontal bone pointed anteriorally. This happens when the metopic suture, usually fused at about two years of age, undergoes very slow fusion. The frontal bone does not attain its normal growth pattern, but is very narrow above the orbits and expands toward the coronal suture. Whether the synostosis of the metopic suture is a primary anomaly of the calvarium or secondary to a deficit in growth of the underlying brain is not yet known.

## DEVELOPMENTAL ANOMALIES OF THE SKULL AND POSTCRANIAL SKELETON

### Achondroplasia

Achondroplasia or chondrodystrophia foetalis is the name given to the most common form of dwarfism. It is a condition resulting from a disturbance along the osseoscartilaginous growth zones involving the preparatory stage of calcification and the position of the columns (Schmorl and Junghanns, 1971). Abnormal bone growth, deformities, and malformation of the skull and post cranial skeleton are usually present. Most achondroplastic infants are stillborn or die soon after birth. Those who survive have normal intelligence and can lead a normal life. Dwarfs are usually less than four feet in height as a result of short lower limbs. The skull is large with a prominent frontal region; the bridge of the nose depressed and flattened; and the facial bones are small. In the postcranial skeleton the long bones are thick; the legs bowed; and the phalanges are short and broad. The vertebral bodies are thinned, the sacrum is narrow and articulates low on the iliac bones. According to Epstein (1968), about 30 percent of achondroplastic dwarfs have a thoracolumbar kyphosis. According to Luck (1950), the etiology is not known but is assumed to be inherited. According to Epstein (1968), the condition is transmitted by a dominant mutant gene.

### Absence of the Odontoid Process

Congenital absence of the odontoid process of the second cervical vertebra is a rare anomaly. According to Gillman (1959) only twenty-one cases of congenital malformation of the dens have been reported in the medical literature. The odontoid process is ossified from three centers, two lateral appearing during the fifth month and one apical which occurs from the second to the fifth year. In the third or fourth year the odontoid process and the axis coossify. The cause of this defect appears to be the failure of the three centers to develop.

## Fusion of the Vertebral Bodies

Congenital fusion of the cervical vertebral bodies is fairly common. According to Evans (1932), fusion occurs most frequently at the cervical level and occasionally at the thoracic. Shank and Kerley (1950), on the other hand, suggest that fusion may occur in any part of the spine. Trial and Rescanieres (1944/45) and Stanislavjevic and St. John (1958) report three cases of lumbar vertebral body fusion. These authors believe that fusion is due to congenital absence of the vertebral discs, which should appear in the first month of fetal life. Consequently, when ossification takes place the vertebrae are fused into a so-called congenital block vertebrae consisting of two or more of the primary segments (Schmorl and Junghanns, 1971). Associated skeletal changes include fusion of the neural arches, and the spinous processes may be partially or completely fused and represented by a solid block of bone.

## Klippel-Feil Syndrome

Klippel-Feil syndrome is congenital nonsegmentation of various cervical segments. It was first described by Klippel and Feil in 1912 (Schmorl and Junghanns, 1971) who found a combination of congenital malformations involving the lower cervical vertebrae and consisting of extensive fusion of vertebral bodies. According to Hadley (1956) and Epstein (1968), the defect arises within the first month of intrauterine life. The fused elements unite into a solid block with a single spinous process, neural arch, and vertebral body. Other skeletal changes associated with this syndrome include malformation of the occiput, scoliosis, and spina bifida (Feller and Sternberg, 1929; Hadley, 1956). The hereditary nature of Klippel-Feil syndrome has been described in several families by Sicard and Lermoyez (1923) and by Demeter (1933). Recent studies by Schmorl and Junghanns (1971) attribute the syndrome to inflammation or fusion.

## Congenital Absence of the Pedicles

Congenital absence of the pedicles is probably the result of an abberation of segmentation arising in the first eight weeks of fetal life (Epstein, 1968). If the deformity is more advanced, changes in the adjacent neural arch such as absence of the laminae or articular processes in the transverse processes may be present. Several pedicles may be missing in the same arch. In examining three cases of congenital absence of pedicles of the cervical vertebrae, Hadley (1946) found enlarged intervertebral foramen, defective transverse processes, and denser neural arches to be common features associated with this condition. Steinbach, Boldrey, and Sooy (1952) suggested that the absence of pedicles and related bony structures is due to defects of varying degrees in the cartilaginous neural arch.

## Hereditary Multiple Exostosis (diaphysial aclasis)

According to Epstein (1968), hereditary multiple exostoses (diaphysial aclasis) is a hereditary disturbance in the nature of a mesodermal dysplasia. The growing ends of bones are usually the parts most often affected. The exostoses may be unilateral or bilateral and occur as single lesions or in multitudes. The bones most frequently involved are the femora or tibiae, the upper portions of the humeri, the fibulae, radii, and ulnae. Exostoses projecting from the middle of the bone shaft are uncommon. Pelvic bones, clavicles, sternum, mandible, ribs, and the vertebral neural arches may also be affected to a lesser degree.

## Congenital Absence of the Sacrum and Coccyx

Sacrococcygeal agenesis is a rare anomaly with less than one hundred cases reported. The defect develops early in fetal life (Epstein, 1968). Skeletal changes associated with this defect include prominence in the lumbar area, dislocated hip, clubfeet, vertebral anomalies such as wedged or hemivertebrae, narrowing of the pelvis, and congenital subluxation of the knees (Del Ducca, Davis and Barroway, 1951; Epstein, 1968). The etiology of this condition is not known. Hereditary factors have been suggested by Del Ducca and his associates.

## Cleidocranial Dysostosis

Cleidocranial dysostosis (Cleidocranial dystogenesis, congenital cleidal dysostosis) is a relatively rare congenital defect of the skeleton. Characteristic features include complete or incomplete aplasia of one or both clavicles, incomplete ossification of the skull, widening of the suture lines which are usually filled with sutural (wormian) bones, delayed ossification of the fontanelles with defective closure of the suture, and frontal bossing. In comparison with the size of the calvaria, the bones of the face show considerable disproportion and are much smaller than usual (Salmon, 1944). In severe cases the shoulders may meet in front. In the postcranial skeleton, scoliosis and other deformities in the vertebrae may be present. Malformation of the finger joints, shortness of the phalanges, deficient ossification and separation of the pubic symphysis, shortening of the femoral neck, and blunting of the femoral head have also been reported (Salmon, 1944; Holt and Hodges, 1945). The development of the teeth is usually delayed with faulty implantation, defective enamel coating, deficiency in the development of roots, impaction, and supernumerary tooth buds noted (Salmon, 1944).

The etiology of cleidocranial dysostosis is not precisely known. That it is preosseous and predental in origin has been suggested (Salmon, 1944). The presence of amniotic bands with hypertension, amniotic fluid, abnormalities of the germ plasm, injury to the embryo, arrested development, the absence of certain chemical constituents necessary for the calcification of the membranous bones have all been suggested as responsible for this defect.

### Kyphoscoliosis and Kyphosis

This congenital defect is often mistaken for tuberculosis. It is characterized by angular or curvilinear deformity of the spine in which convexity is directed dorsally or dorsolaterally and occurs most frequently in the thoracic region. According to Bingold (1953) there are two types of congenital kyphosis: one is associated with a widespread disturbance of ossification and is seen in chondro-osteodystrophy, gargoylism, cretinism, and achondroplasia; the other is due to localized malformation of the spine and the rest of the skeleton is usually normal. The term kyphoscoliosis has often been used to describe an effect due to rib rotation without knowing whether a kyphosis is present. According to James (1954), one type of kyphoscoliosis (congenital kyphoscoliosis) is the result of congenital skeletal abnormalities. Examples of such a defect include congenital wedging, vertebral fusion, hemivertebrae, absent vertebral bodies, and spina bifida (James, 1954, 1955).

According to Bingold (1953), kyphosis has been observed between the fourth thoracic and the fourth lumbar vertebrae but is often found between the tenth thoracic and the second lumbar. Bingold suggested that the defect may consist of: (1) absence of the body of the vertebra; (2) absence of the body of the vertebra associated with microspondyly of a neighboring vertebra; (3) microspondyly of one or two vertebrae; (4) incomplete segmentation of two neighboring vertebrae; (5) absence of a corner of a vertebra; and (6) wedging of a vertebra in the lateral view which is associated with a butterfly appearance in the anteroposterior view.

The etiology of kyphosis is not known. The presence of lumbosacral kyphosis in two brothers suggested to Assen (1930) that the condition may be inherited. According to Epstein (1968), kyphosis may be due to faulty posture, generalized weakness, poliomyelitis, congenital deformities, neurofibromatosis and occupational diseases, various forms of arthritis, osteoporosis, rickets, Paget's disease, acromegaly, hyperparathyroidism, syphilis, congenital anomalies of the vertebral column, and compression fracture. Tuberculosis has also been suggested (Gulledge and Brav, 1950). In his experimental studies in which animals were inflicted with various degrees of injury to the epiphyseal cartilaginous plates, Haas (1939) concluded that growth of the body of the vertebra depends upon the integrity of these plates and that injury to a part of the plate will cause an asymmetrical growth of the body, manifested by an irregularity in the shape of the vertebra and the development of scoliosis.  If the anterior part of the plate is injured, a kyphosis will occur, because of the greater growth on the posterior aspect of the body.

### Scoliosis

Scoliosis refers to lateral deviation in the normally straight line of the vertebral column.  Classification of scoliosis takes into account curvatures of known and unknown etiologies (Epstein, 1968).  Accordingly, they are designated as due to congenital abnormalities, such as osteocondrodystrophy, and vertebral malformations, such as hemivertebrae or neurofibramatosis. Aside from those caused by obvious destructive lesions and developmental anomalies, the mechanism by which scoliosis is produced is still unknown. Several forms or types of scoliosis are known to exist.

### *Idiopathic Scoliosis*

This defect consists of lateral deviation of the vertebral column with rotation of the vertebrae (Epstein, 1968).  According to Epstein, idiopathic scoliosis may involve the lumbar vertebrae alone beginning at about ten years of age and continuing to adolescence.  Involvement of the thoracolumbar region is not common.  The structural change in the vertebrae responsible for this change in alignment is primarily the development of a wedgelike deformity of the vertebral body.  Arkin (1949a) believed wedging to be the result of unilateral epiphyseal arrest.  This suggestion has been supported by several experimental studies (Epstein, 1968).

### *Physiological Scoliosis*

The existence of physiological scoliosis was first described in 1777 by Sabatier.  According to this author, in the lumbar and cervicothoracic segments, the convexity is usually to the left side, and in the thoracic is on the right side.  Sabatier's initial findings have been confirmed by Farkas (1941). According to Farkas, every true scoliotic spine is composed of three types of vertebrae: wedge-shaped, rhombic, and neutral.  In the wedge-shaped vertebrae the most striking feature is the diminishing height of the vertebral body on one side as though the vertebra had collapsed on that side, leaving the impression of a wedge.  Rhombic vertebrae are those which have a conspicuous rhombic shape, but show little or no difference in their height between the right and left side.  Neutral vertebrae are those with obvious signs of deformation but normal in shape.  According to Farkas, wedging plays a chief role in the production of the lateral curve and is regarded by many authors as the principle feature of this deformation. The most striking feature of physiological scoliosis is a dorsoventral elongation of the vertebral bodies and deformities of the pedicles. Farkas (1941) attributed the cause of physiologic scoliosis to the human gait, which forces the spine into a threefold curve changing alternately every step.

## Paralytic Scoliosis

This type of scoliosis results from weakening of spinal muscles by poliomyelitis and produces structural and postural imbalances causing a wide variety of spinal curvatures (Farkas, 1943). According to Farkas, three types of rotation may be present in paralytic scoliosis: (1) unilateral vertebral rotation in which one or two of the vertebrae are rotated; (2) segmented vertebral rotation in which most of the vertebrae of the same segment are rotated in the same direction; and (3) alternating vertebral rotation in which most of the vertebrae of the same segments are rotated in alternate directions.

Rotation of the spinous process occurs in one of the following ways: (a) all or most of the spinous processes point in one direction; (b) the spinous processes of the first seven to nine thoracic vertebrae point to one side, and the spinous processes from the tenth, eleventh, or twelfth thoracic vertebrae to the fourth or fifth lumbar point to the opposite side; and (c) the spinous processes of the first to the fourth or fifth thoracic vertebrae point to one side, while the rest of the spinous processes remain in the midline.

The cause of rotation appears to be a pathological imbalance between the two sides of the body in carrying out rotary motions of different degrees during the performance of daily routines, especially during locomotion. Paralytic scoliosis can be differentiated from scoliosis of any other etiology by the uniform density of the spine, by excessive and early rotation of the vertebrae, and by the temporary concave rotation.

## Osteogenesis Imperfecta

Osteogenesis imperfecta (idiopathic fragilitas ossium, osteopathyrosis, brittle bones with blue sclerae, osteosclerosis, osteitis parynchymatosa chronica, dystrophia, periostalsis, periosteal aplasia, and periosteal dysplasia) is a fairly common hereditary disturbance of normal mesenchymal development which produces a marked alteration in skeletal structures characterized by softening and brittleness in varying proportions (Epstein, 1968). Brailsford (1943) suggested that all these terms be dropped and that the term osteogenesis imperfecta be extended to include fetal, infantile, adolescent, and adult forms. Caniggia, Stuart, and Guideri (1958) were of the opinion that the term fragilitas ossium hereditaria, typus Vrolick, or osteogenesis imperfecta Vrolick type be used to describe the congenital fetal form of the disease while the adult form should be called osteogenesis imperfecta Ekman-Lobstein type.

According to Schmorl and Junghanns (1971), the early form is generally a severe hereditary disease with nonviable children. The late forms have a common anatomicopathologic base with a considerably diminished firmness of the bones. According to Hellner and Poppe (1956), the disease is most likely a congenital, functional deficiency of the osteoblasts resulting from a deficient protein matrix. Since the vertebral bodies contain only a few osseous trabeculae in the region of the spongiosa (Schmorl and Junghanns, 1971), they collapse similarly to the frequent osseous fracture of the extremities and result in various types of skeletal deformities. The pelvis is deformed becoming "heart-shaped". The skeletons of individuals with this condition are usually of short stature and display many bony deformities and multiple fractures. The skull is usually triangular in shape and dental development is retarded (Epstein, 1968). The pathologic changes associated with osteogenesis imperfecta are abnormal formation and calcification of the bony trabeculae. The outer cortex portion of the bone is replaced by imperfectly calcified osteoid trabeculae. When normal bone is present it is discontinuous and fragmentary. Angular deformities of the femora and tibiae, ribs and vertebrae are also known to occur.

## Osteopetrosis

Osteopetrosis (stony bone) is an abnormality of the osseous development, first described by the German roentgenologist, Albers-Schonberg, in 1904. It was given the name of osteopetrosis, or "marble-bone", by Karshner in 1926. This condition is also known as Albers-Schonberg's disease, osteosclerosis fragilis generalisata, and congenital osteosclerosis. According to Seigman and Kilby (1950), characteristic features of osteopetrosis are increased density of the cortical and medullary portions of the entire osseous system. The trabecular structure of the bone is partially or completely destroyed and the medullary canal is reduced in size or absent. Clubbing of the ends of the long bones, especially the proximal humerus and distal femur, and transverse bands in the metaphyses of the long bones may also be present. Usually, the bones are of normal length, but changes may occur in contour. The vertebrae, pelvis, skull, proximal end of the femur, and the distal ends of the tibiae and fibulae are most severely affected. In the skull, suture lines are often wider than normal, the posterior clinoid processes are clubbed, the sella turcica is shallow and the base of the skull is narrowed in an anteroposterior diameter and is very dense. Enticknap (1954) reported a case in which the calvarium was enormously thickened (mean thickness 1.7 cm) and showed no differentiation between the inner and outer tables. Similar skeletal changes have been reported by Callender and Miyakawa (1953). Multiple fractures are also common in individuals with this condition (Seigman and Kilby, 1950). Fairbank (1951) stated that although there is a tendency toward an excessive number of fractures, the fragility of the bones has been much exaggerated.

Osteopetrosis has been observed in utero and in elderly individuals, but is most often diagnosed before the age of ten. According to Seigman and Kilby (1950), familial occurrence of osteopetrosis is so striking that most authors believe the defect to be inherited.

## Spina Bifida

Spina bifida occulta is a developmental anomaly in which incomplete fusion of the posterior neural arch is present. The term is used (Dittrich, 1938) to indicate any congenital defect of the laminae of the upper sacral vertebrae. The more advanced form of spina bifida, characterized by the absence of laminae and pedicles, is known as "rachischisis". Spina bifida is considered a developmental defect due to failure of fusion of the dorsal walls of the primitive ectodermal neural canal (Epstein, 1968). The most common site of this defect is the fifth lumbar and the first and second sacral vertebrae (Epstein, 1968).

According to Dittrich (1938), the application of the term spina bifida occulta should not be limited to the presence of an incomplete fusion or cleft of the neural arches, but to defects which in their morphological and developmental characteristics are identical with spinal clefts and are, therefore, true cases of spina bifida occulta.

Dittrich (1931) stated that spinal clefts appear to be hereditary in nature. The familial tendency of this defect was also suggested by Alpers and Waggoner (1929) who found the defect present in seven of nine members of one family. Mixter (1945) gave an excellent description of "spina bifida occulta" and considered it to be a congenital malformation consisting of a defect in the closure of the vertebral arch, usually with an associated defect of the meninges and nerve tissue.

## Spondylolysis

Spondylolysis (spondylosschsis, prespondylolisthesis) is a developmental anomaly of the lumbar vertebrae which results from a failure in the ossification of the laminae between the superior and inferior articular processes. This separation divides the vertebra into the body and the superior articular facet, and the neural arch and the inferior articular process (Lester and Shapiro, 1968). Mechanically, this permits the defective vertebra to slide or slip forward because the anchoring effect of the inferior articular facet is lost, thus, producing spondylolisthesis. Strictly speaking, the term spondylolisthesis refers to the displacement of the vertebral body, transverse process, pedicles, superior articular process, and adjacent vertral portions of the laminae (Garland and Thomas, 1946).

Spondylolysis can be regarded as an acquired defect in the nature of a stress fracture which may affect a single or several pars interarticularis (Epstein, 1968). Epstein suggested that it may appear after multiple small traumata of a recurrent nature, as for example, in ballet dancers or athletes. Spondylolysis is usually bilateral (Morse, 1969) and occurs most often at the fourth and fifth lumbar articulations (Epstein, 1968). Moreton (1966), in reviewing 32,600 cases, found the defect to be bilateral in 72 to 88 percent and to involve the fifth lumbar in 91.2 percent.

Spondylolysis is known to occur in all human groups studied. Stewart (1931), in examining 350 Alaskan Eskimos, found the overall incidence of separate neural arches to be present in 27.4 percent. In examining a large skeletal sample of 4,200 specimens, Rowe and Roche (1953) found the highest incidence of spondylolysis in Caucasian males (6.4 percent) and the lowest in Negro females (1.1 percent). Stewart (1953) reported spondylolysis in 26.3 percent of the 786 Alaskan Eskimo skeletons he examined at the Smithsonian Institution, Washington, D.C. Lester and Shapiro (1968) found an incidence of 21.0 percent (10/47) in the prehistoric Ipiutak Eskimos and 45.0 percent (111/248) in the Tigara. Morse (1969) reported an incidence of 31.0 percent in the Morse Red Ochre Site. No significant sex differences were found between males and females by Lester and Shapiro (1968), but they did find the incidence of spondylolysis to increase significantly with age.

Spondylolysis is not known to exist at birth (Morse, 1969). Batts (1939) found no defective neural arches in the 200 fetuses he examined with separate neural arches, and Rowe and Roche (1953) found none in over 500 stillborn and neonatal cadavers. In reviewing the published literature in the past century, evidence suggests that spondylolysis is an acquired defect in the nature of stress fracture rather than failure of fusion of the two centers of ossification (Epstein, 1968). Stewart (1953) believed that the sitting position in kayaks may impose strain on the lumbar region. Garland and Thomas (1946) suggested the defect to be the result of the normal stress of body weight combined with occupational strains, trauma, weakening of muscles or ligaments from age or diseases, and softening of some of these tissues from pregnancy. Wiltse (1962), on the other hand, found the defect in the pars interarticularis to be hereditary dysplasia characterized by a lack of normal ability of the bone to repair itself.

## TREPHINING OR TREPANNING

Trephination refers to the process by which one or more small bones are removed from the skull. According to Browthwell (1972), trephining is known to have been present from early days in Europe, the Pacific area, South America, North America, Africa, and Asia. In some parts of the world trephining is still being practiced in its simple form by native medicine men. According to Moodie (1923), the earliest European trephination reported is from the end of the Paleolithic period. Ruffer (1918/19) suggested a later date, sometime during the Neolithic period.

Different motives for trephination have been suggested. Broca (1876) believes that trephination was performed for the relief of certain intracranial maladies. Moodie (1923), Stewart (1958a), and Russo and Bologa (1961) suggested that the majority of the operations were performed as a surgical treatment, either to repair a fracture of the skull or to alleviate headaches.

The reason for postmortem trephination is to obtain roundels of human skull bone (Brothwell, 1972). This type of trephination was undertaken in prehistoric Europe and is still practiced in parts of Africa (Oakley, Brooke, Akester, and Brothwell, 1959). These roundels are usually circular in shape and often perforated and polished to be worn as a necklace.

Several methods of performing the operation have been described. They include (1) scraping, by which the bone is scraped away gradually; (2) grooving, in which a series of curved grooves are drawn and redrawn with a sharp tool until the bone between the grooves becomes loose and can be removed; (3) boring-and-cutting, where the bone is perforated by a circle of closely adjoining holes, the perforation connected by cuts, and the bone removed; and (4) straight incisions intersecting at right angles and the fragment between removed. The most common site for trephining is the frontal bone, followed by the parietals, and occasionally the occipital. The number of perforations may vary, and as many as seven healed trephination holes have been reported (Oakley et al., 1959).

Other perforations may be mistaken for these operations. These include: holes made by picks during excavation; the continued pressure of a sharp instrument; erosion; postmortem skull injuries due to earth pressure; falling rocks; deposition of new material; antemortem pathologies such as syphilitic lesions in the skull; and inflammation and bone rarefication (Brothwell, 1972).

# REFERENCES

1. Akabori, E.: The non-metric variations in the Japanese skull. *Jap J Med Sci, 1, Anatomy, 4*:61-318, 1934.
2. Albers-Schonberg, H.: Roentgenbilder einer seltenen Knochenerkrankung. *Munch Med Wochenschr, 51*:365, 1904.
3. Alpers, B.J. and Waggoner, R.W.: Extraneural and neural anomalies in Friedreich's ataxia; occurrence of spina bifida occulta in several members of one family with Friedreich's disease. *Arch Neurol Psych, 21*:47-60, 1929.
4. Anderson, F.M. and Geiger, L.: Craniosynostosis: A survey of 206 cases. *J Neurosurg, 22*:229-240, 1965.
5. Anderson, J.E.: *The Human Skeleton.* National Museum of Canada, 1962.
6. Anderson, J.E.: The Serpent Mounds Site physical anthropology. Royal Ontario Museum of Art and Archeology, occasional papers no. II, Toronto, Canada, 1968.
7. Anderson, J.E. and Merbs, C.F.: A contribution to the human osteology of the Canadian Arctic. Royal Ontario Museum of Art and Archeology, occasional papers no. IV, Toronto, Canada, 1962.
8. Angel, J.L.: The bases of paleodemography. *Am J Phys Anthropol, 30*:427-437, 1969.
9. Apert, E.: Traité des maladies familiales et des maladies congénitales. Paris, 1907.
10. Arkin, A.M.: Mechanisms of structural changes in scoliosis. *NY State J Med, 49*: 495-499, 1949a.
11. Arkin, A.M.: The mechanisms of structural changes in scoliosis. *J Bone Joint Surg, 31A*:519-528, 1949b.
12. Assen, J. Van: Angeborne Kyphose. *Acta Chir Scand, 67*:14, 1930.
13. Augier, M.: Sur les origines du métopisme. *L'anthropologie, 38*:505-522, 1928.
14. Avis, V.: The relation of the temporal muscle to the form of the coronoid process. *Am J Phys Anthropol, 17*:99-104, 1959.
15. Baron, J., Youngblood, L., Siewars, C.M.F., and Medearis, D.N.: The incidence of cytomegalovirus, herpes simplex, rubella and toxoplasma antibodies in microcephalic, mentally retarded, and normocephalic children. *Pediatrics, 44*:932-939, 1969.
16. Bass, W.M.: The variation in physical types of the prehistoric Plains Indians. *Plains Anthropol, 9*:65-145, 1964.
17. Bass, W.M.: *Human Osteology.* Columbia, Missouri Archeological Society, 1971.
18. Batts, M.: Etiology of spondylolisthesis. *J Bone Joint Surg, 21*:879-884, 1939.
19. Batujeff, W.: Carabelli's Hockerchen und andre unbestamdige Hocker der obern Mahlzahne beim Menschen und Affen. *Bull L'acad Imp Sci St. Petersbourg, 5*: 93-109, 1896.
20. Bennett, K.A.: The etiology and genetics of wormian bones. *Am J Phys Anthropol, 23*:255-260, 1965.
21. Bennett, K.A.: Craniostenosis: A review of the etiology and a report of a new case. *Am J Phys Anthropol, 27*:1-10, 1967.

22. Bennett, K.A.: *The Indians of Point of Pines.* Ann Arbor, Michigan, University Microfilms 68-792, 1967.

23. Bernat, M. and Bernat, N.: Radioulnar synostosis and craniosynostosis in one family. *J Pediatr, 83:*88-89, 1973.

24. Berndt, H.: Entwickelung einer roengenolagischen Alterbestimmung am proximalen Humerusende. *Z Gesamte Inn Med, 2:*122, 1947.

25. Berry, A.C. and Berry, R.J.: Epigenetic variation in the human cranium. *J Anat, 101:*361-379, 1967.

26. Berry, R.J.: The biology of non-metrical variation in mice and men. *Symp Soc Study Hum Biol, 8:*103-133, 1968.

27. Bielicki, T.: Some possibilities for estimating interpopulation relationships on the basis of continuous traits. *Curr Anthropol, 3:*3-8, 1962.

28. Bingold, A.C.: Congenital kyphosis. *J Bone Joint Surg, 35b:*579-583, 1953.

29. Birdsell, J.B.: The problem of the early peopling of the Americas as viewed from Asia. In Laughlin, W.S. (Ed.): *Physical Anthropology of the American Indian.* New York, The Viking Fund, 1949.

30. Birdsell, J.B.: Some implications of the genetical concept of race in terms of spatial analysis. *Cold Spring Harbor Symp Quant Biol, 15:*259-314, 1951.

31. Birdsell, J.B.: On the various levels of objectivity in genetical anthropology. *Am J Phys Anthropol, 10:*355-362, 1952.

32. Birkby, W.H.: An evaluation of race and sex identification from cranial measurements. *Am J Phys Anthropol, 24:*21-28, 1966.

33. Black, J.V.: Descriptive anatomy of the human teeth. Philadelphia, S.S. White Dental Manufacturing Co., 1902.

34. Bohart, W.H.: Anatomic variations and anomalies of the spine: relation to prognosis and length of disability. *JAMA, 29:*698-701, 1929.

35. Bolk, L.: On the premature suture obliteration of sutures in the human skull. *Am J Anat, 17:*495-523, 1915.

36. Bolk, L.: Problems of human dentition. *Am J Anat, 19:*91-148, 1916.

37. Bolk, L.: On metopism. *Am J Anat, 22:*27-48, 1917.

38. Borian, T.V., Attwood, C.R., and Jaconette, J.R.: Anterior fontanelle bone in siblings. *Am J Dis Child, 108:*625-626, 1964.

39. Boucher, B.J.: Sex differences in the fetal sciatic notch. *J Forensic Med, 2:*51-54, 1955.

40. Boucher, B.J.: Sex differences in the fetal pelvis. *Am J Phys Anthropol, 15:*581-600, 1957.

41. Boulinier, G.: La détermination du sexe des crânes humaines à l'aide des fonctions discriminantes. *Bull Mem Soc d'Anthropol Paris,* 12th series, *3:*301-316, 1968.

42. Boulinier, G.: Variations avec l'âge du dimorphisme sexuel des crânes humains adultes: Influence sur les possibilités de discrimination statistique des sujets. *Bull Mem Soc d'Anthropol Paris,* 12th series, *4:*127-138, 1969.

43. Bourne, G.H.: *The Biochemistry and Physiology of Bone.* New York, Acad Pr, 1972.

44. Boyd, G.I.: The emissary foramina in man and the anthropoids. *J Anat, 65:*108-121, 1931.

45. Boyd, W.C.: *Genetics and the Races of Man, An Introduction to Physical Anthropology.* Boston, Little, 1950.

46. Boyd, W.C. and Li, C.C.: Rates of selective action on unifactorial and multifac-

torial traits. *Am J Phys Anthropol, 21*:521-526, 1963.

47. Boyle, P.E.: Manifestations of vitamin A deficiency in a human tooth germ. *J Dent Res, 13*:39-50, 1933.

48. Brailsford, J.F.: Osteogenesis imperfecta. *Br J Radiol, 16*:129-136, 1943.

49. Braur, J.D. and Blackstone, C.H.: Congenital syphillis association with enamel hypoplasia. *J Am Dent Assoc, 28*:1633, 1924.

50. Breathnach, A.S.: *Frazer's Anatomy of the Human Skeleton,* 6th ed. London, J and A Churchill, Ltd, 1965.

51. Broca, P.: *Sur la Trépanation du Crâne et les Amulettes Cârnienne a L'époque Néolitique.* Paris, Ernest Leroux, 1876.

52. Brooks, S.T.: Skeletal age at death: The reliability of cranial and public age indicators. *Am J Phys Anthropol, 13*:567-597, 1955.

53. Brooks, S.T.: Human or not? A problem in skeletal identification. *J Forensic Sci, 20*:149-153, 1975.

54. Brothwell, D.R.: The use of non-metrical characters of the skull in differentiating populations. *Dtsch Ges Anthropol, Bericht u.d. Tagung, Gott, 6*:103-109, 1959.

55. Brothwell, D.R.: *Digging Up Bones,* 2nd ed. London, The British Museum of Natural History, 1972.

56. Bruno, G.: Uber senil Strukurveranderungen der proximalen Humerussepiphyse. *Fortschr Roentgenstr, 50*:287, 1934.

57. Brushfield, T. and Wyatt, W.: Microcephalic children. *Br J Child Dis, 23*:265-270, 1926.

58. Bryce, F. and Young, M.: Observations on metopism. *J Anat, 11*:153-163, 1916.

59. Butting, R.W.: *Textbook of Oral Pathology.* Philadelphia, Lea & Febiger, 1929.

60. Callender, G.R. and Miyakawa, G.: Osteopetrosis in an adult, a case report. *J Bone Joint Surg, 35A*:204-210, 1953.

61. Campbell, T.D.: *Dentition and Palate of the Australian Aborigines.* Adelaide, Australia, Haswell Press, 1925.

62. Caniggia, A., Stuart, C., and Guideri, R.: Fragilitas ossium heredetaria tara, Ekman-Lobstein disease. *Acta Med Scand* (Suppl 340), Stockholm, 1958.

63. Carter, C.O. and Wilkinson, J.A.: Genetic and environmental factors in the etiology of congenital dislocation of the hip, *Clin Orthop, 33*:119-128, 1964.

64. Casady, G.: Anencephaly. *Am J Obstet Gynecol, 103*:1154-1159, 1969.

65. Chouke, K.S.: On the incidence of foramen civinni and porus crotaphitico-buccinatorius in American Whites and Negroes. II. Observations on 1,544 skulls. *Am J Phys Anthropol, 5*:59-86, 1946.

66. Chouké, K.S.: On the incidence of foramen Civinni and porus crotaphitico-buccinatorius in American Whites and Negroes. II. Observations on 2,745 additional skulls. *Am J Phys Anthropol, 5*:87-94, 1947.

67. Clark, P.J.: The heretability of certain anthropometric characters as ascertained for measurements of twins. *Am J Hum Genet, 8*:49-54, 1956.

68. Cohn, B.N.E.: True oxycephaly with syndactylism. *Am J Surg, 68*:93-99, 1945.

69. Collins, H.B.: The temporo-frontal articulation in man. *Am J Phys Anthropol, 9*:343-348, 1926.

70. Collins, H.B.: Notes on the pterion. *Am J Phys Anthropol, 14*:41-44,1930.

71. Comas, J.: *Contributions à l'étude du métopisme.* Geneva, Kundig, 1942.

72. Crouzon, M.O.: Dysostose cranio-faciale héréditaire. *Bull Mem Soc Med Hop Paris, 33*:545-555, 1912.

73. Crouzon, M.O.: *Etudes sur les maladies familiales nerveuses et dystrophiques.* Paris,

Masson & Cie., 1929.

74. Dahlberg, A.A.: The changing dentiton of man. *JAMA, 32*:676-690, 1945.

75. Dahlberg, A.A.: The dentition of the American Indian. In Laughlin, W.S. Ed.): *Papers of the Physical Anthropology of the American Indian.* New York, the Viking Fund Inc., 1949.

76. Dahlberg, A.A.: The evolutionary significance of the protostylid. *Am J Phys Anthropol, 8*:15-25, 1950.

77. Daniel, W.L.: A genetic and biochemical investigation of primary microcephaly. *Am J Ment Defic, 75*:653-662, 1971.

78. Del Ducca, V., Davis, E.V., and Barroway, J.N.: Congenital absence of the sacrum and coccyx, report of two cases. *J Bone Joint Surg, 33A*:248-252, 1951.

79. Demeter, W.: *Ueber familiare Missbildungen der Wirbelsarle.* Munster, Inaug Diss, 1933.

80. Deol, M.S., Gruneberg, H., Searle, A.G., and Truslove, G.M. Genetical differentiation involving morphological characters in an inbred strain of mice. *J Morphol, 100*:345-375, 1957.

81. De Terra, M.: Beitrage zu einer Odontographie der Menschenrassen. University of Zurich, Inaug Diss, 1905.

82. De Villiers, H.: *The Skull of the South African Negro.* Johannesburg, University Witwtaersrand Press, 1968.

83. Dittrich, R.J.: Lumbosacral spina bifida occulta. *Surg Gynecol Obstet, 53*:378-388, 1931.

84. Dittrich, R.J.: Roentgenologic aspects of spina bifida occulta. *Am J Roentgenol, 39*:937-944, 1938.

85. Dorsey, G.A.: Wormian bones in the artificially deformed Kwakiutl crania. *Am Anthropol, 10*:169-173, 1897.

86. Drennan, M.R.: The torus mandibularis in the Bushman. *J Anat, 72*:66-70, 1937.

87. Dudgeon, J.A.: Maternal rubella and its effect on the fetus. *Arch Dis Child, 42*: 110-125, 1967.

88. Dwight, T.: The size of the articular surfaces of the long bones as characteristic of sex: an anthropological study. *Am J Anat, 4*:19-31, 1904-1905.

89. Dyggve, H.V. and Mikelson, M.: Partial deletion of the short arm of a chromosome of the 4-5 group (Denver). *Arch Dis Child, 40*:82-85, 1965.

90. El-Najjar, M.Y.: *People of Canyon de Chelly, A study of their biology and culture.* Ph. D. dissertation, Arizona State University, Tempe, Arizona, 1974.

91. El-Najjar, M.Y. and Dawson, G.: The effect of artificial cranial deformation on the incidence of wormian bones in the lambdoid suture. *Am J Phys Anthrop, 46(1)*:155-160, 1977.

91a. Elwood, J.H. and Mackenzie, G.: Comparisons of secular and seasonal variations in the incidence of anencephalus in Belfast and four Scottish cities. *Br J Prev Soc Med, 25*:17-25, 1971.

92. Entiknap, J.B.: Albers-Schonberg disease (marble bone), report of a case with a study of the chemical characteristics of the bone. *J Bone Joint Surg, 26B*:123-133, 1954.

93. Epstein, B.S.: *The Spine, Radiological Text and Atlas.* Philadelphia, Lea & Febiger, 1968.

94. Evans, W.A.: Abnormalities of the vertebral body. *Am J Roentgenol, 27*:801-816, 1932.

95. Fairbank, Sir H.A.T.: *An Atlas of General Affections of the Skeleton.* London,

E.S. Livingstone Ltd., 1951.

96. Fairman, D. and Horrax, G.: Classification of craniostenosis. *J Neurosurg, 6:*307-313, 1949.

97. Farkas, A.: Physiological scoliosis. *J Bone Joint Surg, 23:*607-627, 1941.

98. Farkas, A.: Paralytic scoliosis. *J Bone Joint Surg, 25:*581-612, 1943.

99. Feller, A. and Sternberg, H.: Zur Kenntnis der Fehlbildungen der Wirbelsaule. I: Wirbelkorperspalte und ihre formale Genese. *Virchows Arch (Pathol Anat), 272:*613-640, 1929.

100. Finnegan, M. and Faust, M.A.: Bibliography of human and non-human non-metric variation. Report no. 19, Department of Anthropology. Amherst, U Mass, 1974.

101. Fisher, A., Kuhm, G., and Adami, G.: *The Dental Pathology of the Prehistoric Indians of Wisconsin.* Bulletin of the Public Museum of the City of Milwaukee, 1931.

102. Flecker, H.: Roentgenographic observations of the times of appearance of the epiphyses and their fusion with the disphyses. *J Anat, 67:*118-164, 1932/33.

103. French, L.A. and Suechting, R.L.: Familial incidence of craniosynostosis. *Am J Dis Child, 89:*486-488, 1955.

104. Friedlaender, J.S., Sgaramella-Zonta, L.A., Kidd, K., and Lai, L. Bougainville: Anthropometric measurements utilizing tree model and a comparison of these variables with linguistic, geographic and migrational distance. *Am J Hum Genet, 23:*253-270, 1971.

105. Fullenlove, T.M.: Congenital absence of the odontoid process. *Radiology, 63:*72-73, 1954.

106. Fully, G.: Une nouvelle méthode de détermination de la taille. *Ann Med Legale Criminol, 36:*266-273, 1956.

107. Fully, G. and Pineau, H.: Détermination de la stature au moyen de squelette. *Ann Med Legale Criminol, 60:*143, 1960.

108. Furst, C.: Torus mandibularis bie den Eskimos und anderen Rassen. *Anat Anz, 32:*295-296, 1908.

109. Furst, C. and Hansen, C.G.: *Crania Groelandica.* Copenhagen, Host & Son, 1915.

110. Gabriel, A.C.: Genetic types in teeth. In Turner, C.G. II: Three-rooted mandibular first permanent molars and the question of American Indian origin. *Am J Phys Anthropol, 34:*229-241, 1971.

111. Garland, L.H. and Thomas, S.F.: Spondylolisthesis. *Am J Roentgenol, 55:*275-291, 1946.

112. Genovés, S.: Introduction al diganóstico de la edad y del sexo en restos oseos prehistóricos. *Universidad Nacional Autonoma de Mexico Publicaciones del Instituto de Historia, Primera Serie,* Número, 75, México, 1962.

113. Genovés, S.: La proporcionalidad entre los huesos largos y su relación con la estatura en restos mesoamericanos. *Cuadernos del Instituto de Historia, Serie Anthropologica,* Número 19, Universidad de México, México, 1966.

114. Genovés, S.: Proportionality of the long bones and their relation to stature among Mesoamericans. *Am J Phys Anthropol, 26:*67-77, 1967.

115. Giannini, M.J., Borrelli, F.J., and Greenberg, W.H.: Agenesis of the vertebral bodies, a cause of dwarfism. *Am J Roentgenol, 59:*705-711, 1948.

116. Giblin, N. and Alley, A.: A method of measuring bone growth in the skull. *Anat Rec, 83:*381-387, 1942.

117. Gilbert, B.M.: Misapplication to females of the standard for aging the male Os

pubis. *Am J Phys Anthropol, 38:*39-40, 1973.

118. Gilbert, B.M. and McKern, T.W.: A method for aging the female Os pubis. *Am J Phys Anthrpol, 38:*31-38, 1973.

119. Giles, E.: Sex determination by discriminant function analysis of the mandible. *Am J Phys Anthropol, 22:*129-135, 1964.

120. Giles, E.: Discriminant function sexing of the human skeleton. In Stewart, T.D. (Ed.): *Personal Identification in Mass Disasters.* Washington, D.C., U.S. National Museum, 1970a.

121. Giles, E.: Sexing crania by discriminant function analysis: effects of age and number of variables. *Proceedings VIIIth International Congress of Anthropological and Ethnological Sciences, Tokyo, 1:*59-61, 1970b.

122. Giles, E. and Elliot, O.: Race identification from cranial measurements. *J Forensic Sci, 7:*147-157, 1962.

123. Giles, E. and Elliot, O.: Sex determination by discriminant function analysis of crania. *Am J Phys Anthropol, 21:*53-68, 1963.

124. Giles, R.E.: Vertebral anomalies. *Radiology, 17:*1262-1266, 1931.

125. Gill, G.W.: The Glendo skeleton and its meaning in light of post-contact racial dynamics in the Great Plains. *Plains Anthropol, 21:*81-88, 1976.

126. Gillman, E.L.: Congenital absence of the odontoid process of the axis. *J Bone Joint Surg, 41A:*345-348, 1959.

127. Goldstein, M.S.: Congenital absence and impaction of the third molars in the Eskima mandible. *Am J Phys Anthropol, 16:*381-388, 1932.

128. Goldstein, M.S.: Dentition of the Indian crania from Texas. *Am J Phys Anthropol, 6:*63-84, 1948.

129. Gottlieb, B.: Rachitis and enamel hypoplasia. *Dental Cosmos, 62:*1209-1221, 1920.

130. Grahnen, H., Sjolin, S., and Stenstorm, A.: Mineralization defects of primary teeth in children born pre-term. *Scan J Dent Res, 82:*396-400, 1974.

131. Gregory, H.E.: The Navajo Country. U.S. Geographical Survey, Water Supply Paper 380. Washington, D.C., Government Printing Office, 1916.

131a. Greig, D.M.: Congenital kyphosis. *Edinburgh Med J, 16:*93-99, 1916.

132. Greig, D.M.: Oxycephaly. *Edinburgh Med J, 16:*93-99, 1926.

133. Grewal, M.S.: The rate of genetic divergence of sublines in the C57BL strain of mice. *Genet Res, 3:*226-237, 1962.

134. Gruneberg, H.: The genetics of a tooth defect in the mouse. *Proc Roy Soc Land, 138:*437-449, 1951.

135. Gruneberg, H.: Genes and genotypes affecting the teeth of the mouse. *J Embryol Exper Morphol, 14:*137-159, 1965.

136. Gulledge, W.H. and Brav, E.A.: Non-tuberculous thoracic kyphosis with paraplegia. *J Bone Joint Surg, 32A:*900-903, 1950.

137. Haas, S.L.: Experimental production of scoliosis. *J Bone Joint Surg, 21:*963-968, 1939.

138. Hachisuka, M.: Ueber tuberculum Carabelli der Milchzahne. *Nippon Shikai, 17:*949-957, 1937.

139. Hadley, L.A.: Congenital absence of the pedicles from the cervical vertebrae. *Am J Roentgenol, 55:*193-197, 1946.

140. Hadley, L.A.: *The Spine.* Springfield, Thomas, 1956.

141. Hanihara, K.: Sexual diagnosis of Japanese long bones by means of discriminant function. *J Anthropol Soc Nippon, 66:*187-196, 1958.

142. Hanihara, K.: Sex diagnosis of Japanese skulls and scapulae by means of discriminant function. *J Anthropol Soc Nippon, 67:*191-197, 1959.

143. Hanihara, K., Kimura, K., and Minamidates, T.: The sexing of Japanese skeletons by means of discriminant function. *Jap J Legal Med, 18:*107-114, 1964.

144. Hanna, B.L.: The biological relationships among Indian groups of the Southwest. *Am J Phys Anthropol, 20:*499-508, 1962.

145. Hansen, G.: Die Altersbestimmung am proximalen Humerus und Femurende im Rahmen der Identifizierung Menschlicher Skelettreste. *Wiss Z Humboldt-Universitat zu Berlin, Jg, 3,* 1953/54.

146. Hellman, M.: Racial characters in human dentition. *Proc Am Phil Soc, 67:*157-174, 1928.

147. Hellner, H. and Poppe, H.: *Roentgenologische Differentiagnose der Knochencrankungen.* Stuttgart, Thieme, 1956.

148. Hess, L.: Ossicula wormiana. *Hum Biol, 18:*61-80, 1946a.

149. Hess, L.: The metopic suture and the metopic syndrome. *Hum Biol, 17:*107-136, 1946b.

150. Hiernaux, J.: Discussion of T. Bielicki's paper, "some possibilities of estimating interpopulation relationships on the basis of continuous traits." *Curr Anthropol, 3:*3-8, 1962.

151. Holt, J.F. and Hodges, F.J.: Significant skeletal irregularities of the hands. *Radiology, 44:*23-31, 1945 .

152. Hooton, E.A.: On certain Eskimoid characters in Icelandic skulls. *Am J Phys Anthropol, 1:*53-76, 1918.

153. Hooton, E.A.: *The Indians of Pecos Pueblo, A Study of Their Skeletal Remains.* New Haven, Yale Pr, 1930.

154. Hope, J.W., Spitze, E.B., and Slade, H.W.: The early recognition of premature cranial synostosis. *Radiology, 65:*183-193, 1955.

155. Horowitz, S.L. and Shapiro, H.H.: Modification of skull and jaw architecture following removal of the masseter muscle in the rat. *Am J Phys Anthropol, 13:*301-322, 1955.

156. Houghton, P.: The relationship of the pre-auricular groove of the ilium to pregnancy. *Am J Phys Anthropol, 41:*381-389, 1974.

157. Howe, P.R.: Studies on dental disorders following experimental feeding with monkeys. *JAMA, 11:*1149-1169, 1924.

158. Howells, W.W.: Multivariate analysis for the identification of race from crania. In Stewart, T.D. (Ed.): *Personal Identification in Mass Disasters.* National Museum of Natural History, Washington, 1970.

159. Hrdlička, A.: Human dentition and teeth from the evolutionary and racial standpoint. *Dominion Dent J, 23:*403-417, 1911.

160. Hrdlička, A.: Shovel shaped teeth. *Am J Phys Anthropol, 3:*429-465, 1920.

161. Hrdlička, A.: Further studies of tooth morphology. *Am J Phys Anthropol, 4:*141-176, 1921.

162. Hrdlička, A.: Ear exostoses. *Smith Misc Coll,* no. 93, 1935.

163. Hrdlička, A.: Mandibular and maxillary hyperostosis. *Am J Phys Anthropol, 27:*1-68, 1940.

164. Hrdlička, A.: In Stewart, T.D. (Ed.): *Practical Anthropometry,* 3rd ed. Philadelphia, Wistar Institute, 1947.

165. Hurme, V.O.: Time and sequence of tooth eruption. *J Forensic Sci, 2:*377-388, 1957.

166. Insley, J.: Syndrome associated with a deficiency of part of the long arm of chromosome no. 18. *Arch Dis Child, 42:*140-146, 1967.

167. James, J.I.P.: Idiopathic scoliosis: The prognosis and operative indications related to curve patterns and the age at onset. *J Bone Joint Surg, 36*:36-48, 1954.

168. James, J.I.P.: Kyphoscoliosis. *J Bone Joint Surg, 37*:414-426, 1955.

169. Jantz, R.L.: *Change and Variation in Skeletal Population of Arikara Indians.* Ph D. dissertation, University of Kansas, 1970.

170. Jit, I. and Singh, S.: The sexing of the adult clavicles. *Indian J Med Res, 54*:1-121, 1966.

171. Johnson, C.C., Gorlin, R.J., and Anderson, V.E.: Torus mandibularis: a genetic study. *Am J Hum Genet, 17*:433-439, 1965.

172. Karshner, R.G.: Osteopetrosis. *Am J Roentgenol, 16*:405-419, 1926.

173. Kellock, W.L. and Parsons, P.A.: Variation of minor non-metrical cranial variants in Australian Aborigines. *Am J Phys Anthropol, 32*:409-422, 1970.

174. Kellock, W.L. and Parsons, P.A.: A comparison of the incidence of minor non-metrical cranial variants in Australian Aborigines with those of Melanesia and Polynesia. *Am J Phys Anthropol, 33*:235-240, 1970.

175. Kerely, E.R.: The microscopic determination of age in human bones. *Am J Phys Anthropol, 23*:149-163, 1965.

176. Kereley, E.R.: Forensic anthropology. In *Legal Medicine Annual 1973.* New York, Appleton, 1973.

177. Keer, D.A.: Relations between periodontal diseases and systematic diseases. *J Dent Res, 41*:302-304, 1962.

178. Kiszely, I.: On the possibilities and methods of the chemical determination of sex from bones. *OSSA, 1*:51-62, 1973.

179. Klatsky, M.: The incidence of six anomalies of the teeth and jaws. *Hum Biol, 28*:420-428, 1956.

180. Kraus, B.S.: Carabelli's anomaly of the maxillary molar teeth. Observations on Mexican and Papago Indians and an interpretation of the inheritance. *Am J Hum Genet, 3*:348-355, 1951.

181. Krogman, W.M.: *The Human Skeleton in Forensic Medicine.* Springfield, Thomas, 1962.

182. Lasker, G.: Penetrance estimated by frequency of unilateral occurrence and by discordance in monozygotic twins. *Hum Biol, 19*:217-230, 1947.

183. Lasker, G.: Genetic analysis of racial traits of the teeth. *Cold Spring Harbor Symp Quant Biol, 15*:191-203, 1950.

184. Lasker, G. and Lee, M.G.: Racial traits in the human teeth. *J Forensic Sci, 2*:401-419, 1957.

185. Laughlin, W.S.: Eskimos and Aleuts: their origins and evolution. *Science, 142*:633-645, 1963.

186. Laughlin, W.S. and Jørgensen, J.B.: Isolate variation in Greenlandic Eskimo crania. *Acta Genet, 6*:3-12, 1956.

187. Laurence, K.M.: The natural history of hydrocephalus. *Postgrad Med J, 36*:662-667, 1960.

188. LeDouble, A.F.: *Traité des Variations des Os du Crâne de l'homme.* Paris, Vigot, 1903.

189. LeDouble, A.F.: *Traité des Variations des Os de la Face de l'homme.* Paris, Vigot, 1907.

190. Leigh, R.W.: Dental pathology of the Eskimo. *Dental Cosmos, 67*:884-898, 1925.

191. Lester, C.W. and Shapiro, H.L.: Vertebral arch defect in the lumbar vertebrae of

prehistoric American Eskimos. *Am J Phys Anthropol*, *28*:43-48, 1968.

192. Levine, R.S.: Neonatal enamel hypoplasia in association with symmetric neonatal hypocalcemia. *Br Dent J*, *137*:429-433, 1974.

193. Lewis, L.: A case of twin anencephalic pregnancy. *Br Med J*, *5211*:1500-1501, 1960.

194. Limson, M.: Metopism as found in Filipino skulls. *Am J Phys Anthropol*, *7*:317-324, 1924.

195. Livingstone, F.B.: Evolution of quantitative characteristics which are determined by several additive loci. *Am J Phys Anthropol*, *31*:355-361, 1969.

196. Luck, V.J.: *Bone and Joint Disease*. Springfield, Thomas, 1950.

197. Manouvrier, L.: La détermination de la taille d'après les grands os des membres. *Mem Soc Anthropol, Paris*, *4*:347-402, 1892.

198. Marfan, R.: cited in Sear, H.R., and Sydney, M.B., "Some notes on craniostenosis." *Br J Radiol*, *10*:445-487, 1937.

199. Martin, H.P.: Microcephaly and mental retardation. *Am J Dis Child*, *119*:128-131, 1970.

200. Martin, R. and Saller, K.: *Lehrbuch der Anthropologie*. Stuttgart, Gustav Fischer Vorlag, 1959.

201. Maslovskie, V.V.: O Metopizme. *Russkaya Anthropologiska Zhurnal*, *15*:7-12, 1927.

202. Matthews, G.P.: Mandibular and palatine tori and their etiology. *J Dent Res*, *13*: 245, 1933.

203. Matthews, W.: The Inca bone and kindred formations among the ancient Americans. *Am Anthropol*, *2*:237-345, 1889.

204. McKern, T.W. and Stewart, T.D.: *Skeletal Age Changes in Young American Males*. Technical Report EP-45. Natik, Mass, Headquarters Quartermaster Research and Development Command, 1957.

205. McKusick, V.A., Mahloudji, M., Abbot, M.H., Lindenberg, R., and Kepas, D. Seckel's Birdheaded dwarfism, *N Engl J Med*, *277*:279-286, 1967.

206. McWilliams, K.R.: Physical anthropology of Wann and Sam, two Fourche Maline Focus Archaic sites in eastern Oklahoma. *Bulletin of the Oklahoma Anthropological Society*, no. 19, 1970.

207. McWilliams, K.R.: *Gran Quivira Pueblo and Biological Distance in the U.S. Southwest*. Ph. D. dissertation, Arizona State University, Tempe, Arizona, 1974.

207a. Meikel, A.H.: Structural elements of the teeth. In Morrey, L.W. and Nelson, R.J. (Eds.):: *Dental Science Handbook*. Washington, DHEW Publication No. (NIH) 72-336, 1970.

208. Merbs, C.F.: *Blood Group Distribution in the American Southwest*. Unpublished manuscript, 1965.

209. Mertz, H.O. and Smith, L.A.: Spina bifida occulta; its relation to dilatations of the upper urinary infections in childhood. *Radiology*, *12*:193-198, 1929.

210. Meschan, I.: *Analysis of Roentgen Signs in General Radiology*. Philadelphia, Saunders, 1973, Vol. I.

211. Miller, S.C. and Roth, H.: Torus palatinus, a statistical study. *J Am Dent Assoc*, *27*:1950-1957, 1940.

212. Miller, W.: Der Einfluss der Mikroorganismen auf die Caries der menschlichen Zahne. *Arch Exp Pathol Pharmakol*, *16*:291-304, 1883a.

213. Miller, W.: Agency of micro-organisms in decay of human teeth. *Dental Cosmos*, *25*:1-12, 1883b.

214. Mixer, W.J.: In Lewis (Ed.): *Practice of Surgery.* Haggerstown, Md, W.F. Prior, Ci., 1945, Vol. 12.

215. Montagu, M.F.A.: The medio-frontal suture and the problem of metopism in the primates. *J Royal Anthropol Inst, 67*:157-201, 1937.

216. Montagu, M.F.A.: The direction and position of the mental foramen in the great apes and man. *Am J Phys Anthropol, 12*:503-518, 1954.

217. Montagu, M.F.A.: *A Handbook of Anthropometry.* Springfield, Thomas, 1960.

218. Moodie, L.: *Paleopathology, an Introduction to the Study of Ancient Evidences of Diseases.* Urbana, U Illinois Pr, 1923.

219. Moorrees, C.F.A.: *The Aleut Dentition.* Cambridge, Harvard U Pr, 1957.

220. Moorrees, C.F.A., Osborne, R.H., and Wilde, E.: Torus mandibularis: its occurrence in Aleut children and its genetic determinants. *Am J Phys Anthropol, 10*:319-329, 1952.

221. Moreton, R.D.: Spondylolysis. *JAMA, 195*:671-673, 1966.

222. Morley, T.P.: Congenital rotation of spinal cord. *J Neurosurg, 10*:690-692, 1953.

223. Morrey, L.W. and Nelson, R.J.: Dental Science Handbook. DHEW Publication no. (NIH) 72-336, Washington, D.C., 1970.

224. Morse, D.: *Ancient Disease in the Midwest.* Springfield, Illinois State Museum, 1967.

225. Morse, D., Crusoe, D., and Smith, H.G.: Forensic Archeology. *J Forensic Sic, 21*:323-332, 1976.

226. Morselli, M.: Sur la scaphocéphalie. *Bull de la Soc d'Anthropol de Paris, 10*:445, 1875.

227. Moss, M.L.: Experimental alteration of sutural area morphology. *Anat Rec, 127*:569-589, 1957a.

228. Moss, M.L.: Premature synostosis of the frontal suture in the cleft palate skull. *Plast Reconstr Surg, 20*:199-205, 1957b.

229. Moss, M.L.: The pathogenesis of premature cranial synostosis in man. *Acta Anat, 37*:351-370, 1959.

230. Moss, M.L. and Simon, M.R.: Growth of the human mandibular angular process: a functional cranial analysis. *Am J Phys Anthropol, 28*:127-138, 1968.

231. Mourant, A.E.: Discussion of T. Bielicki's paper, "some possibilities for estimating interpopulation relationships on the basis of continuous traits." *Curr Anthropol, 3*:3-8, 1962.

232. Muhlreiter, E.: *Anatomie des Menschlichen Gebisses.* Leipzig, Arthur Felix, Ltd., 1870.

233. Müller, G.: Zur Bestimmung der lange beschadigter Extremitatenknochen. *Antropol Anz, 12*:70-72, 1935.

234. Murphy, D.P.: Ovarian irradiation; its effect on the health of subsequent children. *Surg Gynecol Obstet, 47*:201-215, 1928.

235. Murphy, T.: The pterion in the Australian Aborigines. *Am J Phys Anthropol, 14*:225-244, 1956.

236. Naggan, L. and MacMahon, B.: Ethnic differences in the presence of anencephaly and spina bifida in Boston. *N Engl J Med, 271*:1119-1123, 1967.

237. Nakano, K.K.: Anencephaly: a review. *Dev Med Child Neurol, 15*:383-400, 1973.

238. Nat, B.S.: Estimation of stature from long bones in Indian of the United Provinces. *Indian J Med Res, Calcutta, 18*:1245-1253, 1931.

238a. Nelson, C.T.: The teeth of the Indians of Pecos Pueblo. *Am J Phys Anthrop, 23*:261-293, 1938.

239. Nemeskeri, J.: Die archaologischen und anthropologischen Voraus setzungen palao-demographischer Forschungen. *Praihistorische Aeitschrift, 47:*5-46, 1972.

240. Oakley, K.P., Brooke, W., Akester, R., and Brothwell, D.R.: Contributions on trepanning or trepanation in ancient and modern times. *Man, 59:*93-107, 1959.

241. Oetteking, B.: Craniology of the North Pacific Coast. *Mem Am Mus Nat Hist, Jesup North Pacific Expedition 11:*1-391, 1930.

242. Olivier, G.: *Practical Anthropology.* Springfield, Thomas, 1969.

243. Olivier, G. and Pineau, H.: Biométrie du scapulum. *Arch Anat, 5:*67-88, 1957.

244. Osborne, R.H. and De Gorge, F.V.: *Genetic Basis of Morphological Variability.* Cambridge, Harvard U Pr, 1959.

245. Ossenberg, N.: *Discontinuous Morphological Variation in the Human Cranium.* Ph. D. Dissertation, University of Toronto, 1969.

246. Ossenberg, N.: The influence of artificial cranial deformation on discontinous morphological traits. *Am J Phys Anthropol, 33:*357-372, 1970.

247. Park, E.A. and Powers, G.F.: Acrocephaly and scaphocephaly with symmetrically distributed malformation of the extremities. *Am J Dis Child, 20:*235-315, 1920.

248. Parker, A.S. and Hare, H.F.: Arachnodactyly. *Radiology, 45:*220-226, 1945.

249. Pearson, K.: On the reconstruction of stature of prehistoric races. *Philos Trans Soc, A, 192:*169-244, 1899.

250. Pearson, K.: A study of the long bones of the English skeleton. I. The femur. In Draper's Co.: *Research Memoir.* University of Londan. Biometric Series X. 1917/19.

251. Pedersen, P.O.: *The East Greenland Eskimo Dentition.* Copenhagen, Meddelesser om Grøland, 142, 1-256, 1949.

252. Pendergrass, E.P., Schaeffer, J.P., and Hodes, P.J.: *The Head and Neck in Roentgen Diagnosis.* Springfield, Thomas, 1956.

253. Perna, G.: Sur cranle basilare madiano e sul significato della fossetta faringea dell' osso occipitali. *Anat Anz, 28:*379-394, 1906.

254. Petras, M.L.: Studies of natural populations of Mus IV. Skeletal variations. *Can J Genet Cytol, 4:*575-588, 1967.

255. Phenice, T.W.: A newly developed visual method of sexing os pubis. *Am J Phys Anthropol, 30:*297-302, 1967.

256. Pipper, R.K. and Irving-Jones, E.: Arachnodactylia and its association with congenital heart disease. *Am J Dis Child, 31:*832-839, 1926.

257. Pittard, E. and Baicoyano, M.: Recherches sur le développement de la mâchoire et des dents triturantes en fonction de la capacité crânienne. *Arch Suisses d'Anthropol Gen, 5:*1-23, 1928-29.

258. Rees, J.W.: Morphologic variation in the cranium and mandible of the White-tailed deer. *J Morphol, 128:*95-112, 1969a.

259. Rees, J.W.: Morphologic variation in the mandible of the White-tailed deer. *J Morphol, 128:*113-130, 1969b.

260. Reisman, L.E. and Matheny, L.: Corticosteriods in pregnancy. *Lancet, 1:*592-593, 1968.

261. Rieping, A.: Zur Pathogenese des Turmschadels. *Dtsch Z Chir, 148:*1, 1919.

261. Riesenfeld, A.: Multiple infraorbital, ethmoidal, and mental foramina in the races of man. *Am J Phys Anthropol, 14:*85-100, 1956.

262. Rizzo, A.: Canale cranio faringeo, fossetta faringea, interparietali e pre-interparietali nel cranio umano. *Monitore Zoo Italiano, 12:*241-252, 1901.

263. Robinson, J.T.: Some hominid features of the ape-man dentition. *J Dent Assoc S Africa, 7:*102-113, 1952.

264. Romiti, G.: La fossetta faringea nell'osso occipitale dell'uomo. *Atti della Societa Toscana di Scienze Naturali Residente in Pisa,* Memoria II, Pisa, 1891.

265. Rossi, U.: II canale cranio-faringea e le fossetta faringea. *Monitore Zoo Italiano,* 2:117-122, 1891.

266. Rowe, G. and Roche, T.: The etiology of separate neural arch. *J Bone Joint Surg, 35A:*102-110, 1953.

267. Ruffer, M.A.: Studies in paleopathology. Some recent researches on prehistoric trephining. *J Pathol, 22:*90-104, 1918-19.

268. Russell, F.: Studies in cranial variation. *Am Nat, 34:*737-743, 1900.

269. Russo, I.G. and Bologa, V.: Trephenation in Gebiet des Rumanien. *Sudhoffs Arch Gesch Med, 45:*34, 1961.

270. Sabatier, B.: *Traité Complete d' Anatomie.* Paris, 1777.

271. Salmon, D.D.: Hereditary cleidocaranial dysostosis. *Radiology, 42:*391-395, 1944.

272. Sanghvi, L.D.: Comparison of genetical and morphological methods for a study of biological differences. *Am J Phys Anthropol, 11:*385-394, 1953.

273. Schmorl, G. and Junghanns, H.: *The Human Spine in Health and Disease.* New York, Grune, 1971.

274. Schour, I. and Massler, M.: Studies in tooth development: The growth pattern of human teeth. Part II. *J Am Dent Assoc, 27:*1918-1931, 1940.

275. Schranz, D.: Age determination from the internal structure of the humerus. *Am J Phys Anthropol, 17:*273-277, 1959.

276. Schuller, A.: *Roentgen Diagnosis of Diseases of the Head.* Trans. F.F. Stocking. St. Louis, Mosby, 1918.

277. Schultz, A.H.: The metopic fontanelle, fissure, and suture. *Am J Anat, 44:*475-499, 1929.

278. Schultz, A.H.: Die foramina Infraorbitalia der Primaten. *Z Morphol Anthropol, 46:*404-407, 1954.

279. Scott, J.: Muscle growth and function in relation to skeletal morphology. *Am J Phys Anthropol, 15:*197-234, 1957.

280. Sear, H.R. and Sydney, M.B.: Some notes on craniostenosis. *Br J Radiol, 10:* 445-487, 1937.

281. Searle, A.G.: The incidence of anencephaly in a polytypic population. *Ann Hum Genet, 23:*279-288, 1959.

282. Seigman, E. and Kilby, W.: Osteopetrosis: report of a case and review of recent literature. *Am J Roentgenol, 63:*865-970, 1950.

283. Shank, S.C. and Kerley, P. (Eds.): *A Text of X-ray Diagnosis by British Authors,* 2nd ed. Philadelphia, Saunders, 1950.

284. Shaw, J.H.: The relation of nutrition to periodontal disease. *J Dent Res, 41:*264-271, 1962.

285. Sheppard, P.M.: *Natural Selection in Human Populations.* New York, Har-Row, 1960.

286. Sicard, J.A. and Lermoyez, J.: Formes frustes, evolutive, familiale du syndrome de Klippel-Fiel. *Rev Neurol (Paris), 39:*71-74, 1923.

287. Simmons, D.R. and Peyton, W.T.: Premature closure of the caranial sutures. *J Pediatr, 31:*528-547, 1947.

288. Snyder, R.G., Burdi, A., and Gaul, G.: A rapid technique for preparation of human fetal and adult skeletal material. *J Forensic Sci, 20:*576-580, 1975.

289. Sognnaes, R.F.: Caries-conducive effect of a purified diet when fed to rodents during teeth development. *J Am Dent Assoc, 37:*676-696, 1948a.

290. Sognnaes, R.F.: Analysis of wartime reduction of dental caries in European children with special regards to observations in Norway. *Am J Dis Child, 75:*792-821, 1948b.

291. Sognnaes, R.F.: Histological evidence of developmental lesions teeth originating from Paleolithic, prehistoric and ancient times. *Am J Pathol, 32:*547-577, 1956.

292. South, M.A., Tompkins, W.A.F., Morris, C.R., and Rawls, W.E.: Congenital malformation of the central nervous system associated with genital type (type 2) herpes virus. *J Pediatr, 75:*13-18, 1969.

293. Spielman, R.: Differences among Yanomama Indian villages. Do the patterns of allle frequencies, anthropometry and map location correspond? *Am J Phys Anthropol, 39:*461-480, 1973.

294. Spier, L.: Cultural relations of the Gila River and Lower Colorado River tribes. Yale Univ Pub in Anthropol, no. 3, 1936.

295. Spuhler, J.N.: Some problems in physical anthropology of the American Southwest. *Am Anthropol, 56:*604-625, 1954.

296. Stanislavjevic, S. and St. John, E.G.: Congenital fusion of three lumbar vertebral bodies. *Radiology, 71:*425-427, 1958.

297. Steele, D.G. and McKern, T.M.: A method for assessment of maximum long bone length and living stature from fragmentary long bones. *Am J Phys Anthropol, 31:*215-227, 1969.

298. Steele, D.G.: Estimation of stature from long limb bones. In Stewart, T.D. (Ed.): *Personal Identification in Mass Distasters.* Washington, Nat Mus Nat Hist, 1970.

299. Steinbach, H.L., Boldrey, E.B., and Sooy, F.A.: Congenital absence of the pedicle and superior facet from a cervical vertebra. *Radiology, 59:*838-840, 1952.

300. Stern, C.: *Principles of Human Genetics.* San Francisco, W.H. Freeman & Co., 1960.

301. Stewart, T.D.: Incidence of separate neural arch in the lumbar vertebrae of Eskimos. *Am J Phys Anthropol, 16:*51-62, 1931.

302. Stewart, T.D. (Ed.): *Hrdlička's Practical Anthropometry.* Philadelphia, The Wistar Institute, 1947.

303. Stewart, T.D.: The age incidence of neural arch defects in Alaskan natives considered from the standpoint of etiology. *J Bone Joint Surg, 35A:*937-950, 1953.

304. Stewart, T.D.: Distortion of the pubic symphyseal surface in female and its effect on age determination. *Am J Phys Anthropol, 15:*9-18, 1957.

305. Stewart, T.D.: Stone age skull surgery: a general review with emphasis on the New World. *Smith Instit Rep,* 1957, 1958a.

306. Stewart, T.D.: Identification of scars of parturition in the skeletal remains of females. In Stewart, T.D. (Ed): *Personal Identification in Mass Disasters.* Washington, Natl Mus Nat Hist, 1970.

307. Sublett, A.J.: *Seneca Physical Type and Changes Through Time.* Ph. D. dissertation, SUNNY Buffalo, University Microfilms 66-12, 133, 1970.

308. Sullivan, L.R.: The fossa pharyngea in American Indian crania. *Am Anthropol, 22:*237-243, 1920.

309. Sullivan, L.R.: The frequency and distribution of some anatomical variations in American crania. *Am Mus Nat Hist Pap, 23:*207-258, 1922.

310. Suzuki, M. and Sakai, T.: A familial study of torus palatinus and torus mandibularis. *Am J Phys Anthropol, 18:*263-272, 1960.

311. Taylor, A.E.: Variations in the human tooth-form as met with in isolated teeth. *J Anat Physiol, 33:*268-272, 1899.

312. Telkka, A.: On the prediction of human stature from the long bones. *Acta Anat, 9:*103-117, 1950.

313. Terry, R.J.: On measuring and photographing the cadaver. *Am J Phys Anthropol, 26:*433-447, 1940.

314. Thieme, F.P.: Sex in Negro skeletons. *J Forensic Med, 4:*72-81, 1957.

315. Thoma, K.H.: Torus palatinus. *Int J Orthod Oral Surg, 23:*194-202, 1937.

316. Thoma, R.: Synostosis sutures sagittalis cranii. Ein Beitrag zur Histomechanick des Skeletts und zur Lehre von dem interstitiellen Knochenwchstum. *Virchows Arch, 188:*248-360, 1907.

317. Thompson, S.: Missing teeth with special reference to the population of Tristan da Cunha. *Am J Phys Anthropol, 10:*155-168, 1952.

318. Todd, T.W.: Age changes in the pubic bone. I. The male white pubis. *Am J Phys Anthropol, 3:*285-334, 1920.

319. Torgerson, J.H.: Hereditary factors in the sutural pattern of the skull. *Acta Radiol, 36:*374-382, 1951a.

320. Torgerson, J.H.: The developmental genetics and evolutionary meaning of the metopic suture. *Am J Phys Anthropol, 9:*193-210, 1951b.

321. Trattman, E.K.: Three-rooted lower molars in man and their racial distribution. *Br Dent J, 64:*264-274, 1938.

322. Trattman, E.K.: A comparison of the teeth of people. Indo-European racial stock with the Mongoloid racial stock. In Lasker, G.W. and Angel, J.L. (Eds.): *Yearbook of Physical Anthropolgy.* New York, Wenner Gren Foundation, 1951.

323. Trevor, J.C.: Notes in the human remains of Romano-British from Norton, York. In Whitley, H.: *The Romano Pottery from Norton, East Yorkshire.* (Roman Malton and District Report no. 7). Leeds, 1950b.

324. Trial, R. and Rescanieres, A.: A propos des blocs vertebraux lumbaires. *J Radiol Electrol Med Nucl, 26:*315-317, 1944/45.

325. Trotter, M.: Estimation of stature from intact long bones. In Stewart, T.D. (Ed.): *Personal Identification in Mass Disasters.* Washington, Nat Museum Nat Hist, 1970.

326. Trotter, M. and Gleser, G.C.: The effect of aging on stature. *Am J Phys Anthropol, 9:*311-324, 1951.

327. Trotter, M. and Gleser, G.C.: Estimation of stature from long bones of American Whites and Negroes. *Am J Phys Anthropol, 10:*463-514, 1952.

328. Trotter, M. and Gleser, G.C.: A re-evaluation of estimation of stature taken during life and of long bones after death. *Am J Phys Anthropol, 16:*79-123, 1958.

329. Turner, C.G., II and Laughlin, W.S.: Postnatal development of the Sadlermiut Eskimo temporal bone. *Am J Phys Anthropol, 21:*406, 1963.

330. Turner, C.G., II: Microevolutionary interpretation from the dentition. *Am J Phys Anthropol, 30:*421-426, 1969.

331. Turner, C.G., II: Three-rooted mandibular first permanent molars and the question of American Indian origin. *Am J Phys Anthropol, 34:*229-241, 1971.

332. Turner, W.: On exostoses in the external auditory meatus. *J Anat Physiol, 13:*2-13, 1879.

333. Ulrich, H.: Estimation of fertility by means of pregnancy and childbirth alternations at the pubis, thilium, and the sacrum. *OSSA, 2:*23-39, 1975.

334. Urison, M.I.: Metopism U Chelovska. *Sovetskaya Antropologiva, 3:*3-19, 1959.

335. Van Arsdell, P.: Maternal hyperparathyroidism as a cause of neonatal tetany. *J Clin Endocrinol Metab, 15:*680-684, 1955.

336. Virchow,: Uber der Cretinismus namentlich in Franken und über Pathologische Schadel-formen, verhandl Physik Med. *Gesellschaft Wurzburg, 2:230,* 1851.

337. Von Carabelli, G.: *Systematisches Handbuch der Zahnheilkunde,* vol. II. *Anatomie de Mundes.* Vienna, Braumuller und Seidel, 1842.

338. Wacholz, L.: Uber die Altersbestimmung an Leichen auf Grund des ossifications Prozesses im oberen Humerusende. *Freidreichs Blatter Gerichtl Med, 45:*210, 1894.

339. Washburn, S.L.: The relation of the temporal muscle to the form of the skull. *Anat Rec, 99:*239-248, 1947.

340. Watson, A.W., Massler, M., and Perlstein, M.A.: Tooth ring analysis in cerebral palsy. *Am J Dis Child, 107:*370-382, 1964.

341. Weidenreich, F.: The dentition of Sinanthropus pekinensis. *Paleontol Sinica,* Whole Series 01, new series D-1, 1937.

342. Weidenreich, F.: *Apes, Giants and Men.* Chicago, U Chicago Pr, 1946.

343. Weiss, K.M.: On the systematic bias on skeletal sexing. *Am J Phys Anthropol,* 37:*239-249, 1972.

344. Wheeler, R.C.: *A Textbook of Dental Anatomy and Physiology.* Philadelphia, Saunders, 1968.

345. Whitney, E.A.: Microcephaly. *Med J Rec, 135:*166-168, 1932.

346. Wiltse, L.L.: The etiology of spondylolisthesis. *J Bone Joint Surg, 44A:*539-560, 1962.

347. Woo, J.: Racial and sexual differences in the frontal curvature and its relation to metopism. *Am J Phys Anthropol, 7:*215-226, 1949a.

348. Woo, J.: Direction and type of the transverse palatine suture and its relation to the form of the hard palate. *Am J Phys Anthropol, 7:*385-400, 1949b.

349. Woo, J.: Torus palatinus. *Am J Phys Anthropol, 8:*81-100, 1950.

350. Wood-Jones, F.: The non-metric morphological characters of the skull as criteria for racial diagnosis. I, II, III. *J Anat, 65:*179-195, 368-378, 438-445, 1931.

351. Wood-Jones, F.: The non-metric morphological characters of the skull as criteria for racial diagnosis. IV, V. *J Anat, 68:*96-108, 323-330, 1934.

351a.Workman, P.L. and Niswander, J.D.: Population studies of Southwestern Indian Tribes, II, local genetic differences in the Papago. *Am J Hum Genet., 22:*24-29, 1970.

352. Yamaguchi, B.: A comparative ecological study of the Australian Aborigines. *Australian Inst,* Aborig Stud, Occ Papers, Hum Biol, Series 2, *10:*000, 1967.

353. Young, F.W.: Acrocephaly. *Arch Pediatr, 39:*629-000, 1922.

354. Zappert, J.: Fetal microcephalia due to roentgen therapy. *Arch F. Kinderh, 80:* 34, 1926.

# INDEX

## A

Accessory lesser palatine foramen, 145, 146, fig. 36
Acetabulum, 34
Achondroplasia, 161
Acromial process, 30
Age estimation, 55
adolescence, 60
infancy/early childhood, 56-57
late childhood, 57-60
neonate, 56
old adult, 69-72
young adult, 60, 65-69
Alveolar process, 20, 21, 43, 85, 107
Anatomical directions, 114
Anencephaly, 159
Anomalies, 153
Anterior palatine alveolar foramen, 133, 145, fig. 32
Anthropometry, 106
Anthroposcopy, 106
Antiformin, 7, 8
Apical foramen, 44
Arachnodactyly (Marfan's Syndrome), 159, 160
Asterion, 106
Asterionic bone, 126
Attrition, 53-54
Auditory exostoses, 124, 138, 139, fig. 25
Auricular process, 25

## B

Basilar suture
Bone(s), *see also* specific names
alveolar, 16, 141
asterionic, 124, 126
bregma, 16
capitate, 33
carpal, 33
cuboid, 35
ear, 21
epipteric, 16, 123, 124
ethmoid, 19
facial, 19
frontal, 15, 16, 18, 84, 122
hamate, 33
hyoid, 21

Inca, 127-129
lacrimal, 19
lambdoid, 127, 128
lunate, 33
maxillary, 16, 21
metacarpal, 33
multangular, 33
nasal, 16, 17, 19
navicular, 33, 35
occipital, 16-19
parietal, 16, 18
pisiform, 33
sesamoid, 34
sphenoid, 16, 18, 136
temporal, 16, 17
wormian, 116, 123, 124, 129-131

## C

Calcaneus, 35
Calva, 106
Calvarium, 106
Canines, 41, 42
Capitulum of humerus, 32
Carabelli's trait, 42, 47-49, fig. 11
Caucasians, 7
Cementum, 41, 44
Chin, 85
Cingulum, 44
Clavicle, 27, 29, 30, fig. 6e, 6f
sex estimation from, 86
Cleidocranial dysotosis, 163, 164
Coccyx, 26
Condylar process, 21
Condyle, 37, 38
Condyloid foramen, 19
Congenital, 153
Congenital absence of pedicles, 162, 163
Coronal suture, 15, 16, 18
Coronoid fossa, 32
Coronoid process, 20, 28, 31, 151
Cranial indices, 110-111
Cranial landmarks, 106-108
Cranial measurements, 108-110
Craniometry, 106
Craniostenosis, 153-156
Cranium, 106